The Costs of
Educational Media

Guidelines for
Planning and Evaluation

PEOPLE AND COMMUNICATION

Series Editors: F. GERALD KLINE *Department of Journalism*
PETER CLARKE *University of Michigan*

Volumes in this series:

Volume 1: How Children Learn to Buy: The Development of Consumer Information-Processing Skills
SCOTT WARD, DANIEL B. WACKMAN, ELLEN WARTELLA

Volume 2: Big Media, Little Media: Tools and Technologies for Instruction
WILBUR SCHRAMM

Volume 3: The Costs of Educational Media: Guidelines for Planning
and Evaluation
DEAN JAMISON, STEVEN J. KLEES, STUART J. WELLS

The Costs of
Educational
Media

Guidelines for
Planning and Evaluation

Dean T. Jamison
Steven J. Klees
Stuart J. Wells

Foreword by Wilbur Schramm

SAGE Publications
Beverly Hills   London

For information address:

SAGE PUBLICATIONS, INC.
275 South Beverly Drive
Beverly Hills, California 90212

SAGE PUBLICATIONS LTD
28 Banner Street
London EC1Y 8QE, England

Printed in the United States of America

Library of Congress Cataloging in Publication Data

Jamison, Dean.
   The costs of educational media.

   (People and communication; v. 3)

   1. Educational technology. 2. Media programs.
3. Education—Costs. I. Klees, Steven J., joint
author. II. Wells, Stuart J., joint author.
III. Title.
LB1028.3.J35   371.3'078   77-17782
ISBN 0-8039-0747-8
ISBN 0-8039-0748-6 pbk.

FIRST PRINTING

CONTENTS

LIST OF TABLES

LIST OF FIGURES

ACKNOWLEDGMENTS

The U.S. Agency for International Development (through Contract 931-11-999-987-73) and the U.S. National Science Foundation (through Grant EPP74-23504) provided financial support to the Educational Testing Service (ETS), Princeton, New Jersey, to conduct the research reported here. Dean T. Jamison, while on the staff of ETS, was Principal Investigator on these efforts; Steven J. Klees and Stuart J. Wells served as consultants to ETS. Jamison is now with the Development Economics Department of the World Bank; Klees is a private consultant; and Wells is with the School of Business, San Jose State University.

UNESCO's International Institute for Educational Planning made their facilities available to the authors during the writing of the manuscript, and the authors benefited from related ongoing studies of UNESCO's Division of Educational Materials, Methods, and Techniques. The conclusions and opinions expressed herein do not necessarily reflect the official views of any of the sources of support.

The authors have received valuable comments from a number of individuals on outlines and an earlier draft of this manuscript and wish to acknowledge the following with thanks: Eduardo Arena (Presidencia of Mexico), John E. Austin (Harvard University), Clifford Block (U.S. Agency for International Development), Clifton Chadwick (Organization of American States), William Charleson (U.S. Agency for International Development), Russell Davis (Harvard University, Douglas E. Hall (New ERA, Concord, N.H.), Wallace II. Hannum (Florida State University), Robert Hornik (Stanford University), Marshall V. Jamison, Yoon Tai Kim (Korean Educational Development Institute), Yeap Lay Leng (Institute of Education, Singapore), John Mayo (Florida State University), François Orivel (University of Dijon), Barbara Searle (Stanford University), David Sprague (U.S. Agency for International Development), Claude Tibi (International Institute for Educational Planning), and Kan-Hua Young.

The authors especially wish to thank Stella M. Evans of Trenton State College for her excellent assistance in all phases of the preparation of this manuscript; her effort and expertise improved this work considerably and is greatly appreciated.

FOREWORD

There have been at least four major sources of intellectual input into educational policy beyond the basic ones from the power structure and the culture. For many centuries these inputs were chiefly religious and philosophical. With public education and the looming possibility of general education, political and administrative science became important. Then psychologists brought in theories of learning and teaching, and experiments to evaluate materials and method. And now, finally, economists have become interested in analyzing the costs of education against its outputs. Their contribution, as this book indicates, promises to be a major one.

About twenty years ago a few economists began to work on some of the macro-economic problems of education—for example, trying to untangle education's effect from other effects on income, wealth, productivity, development, and other large social goals. The approach represented by this book is, however, more micro than macro. It is suggested by the sentence with which these three authors begin their volume: "Budgets constrain choices." Educational managers have always had to make budgets and allocate resources, and therefore, to make use of cost-accounting and need forecasting. Educational psychologists have contributed to this activity sophisticated methods for measuring the cognitive effects of different resource allocations and system use. Drs. Jamison, Klees and Wells enter at the other side of the cost-effectiveness equation and bring the sophisticated analytical skills of the economist to bear on the study of system *costs*.

They are modest about what they have done. "Use of the term "cost-effectiveness analysis" to describe the activities involved in modeling input-output relations in education is misleading to the extent that it implies the task to be one for economists," they write (p. 21). "Experts in educational psychology, media research, statistics, and organizational theory play a more central role." This undervalues what the economist can contribute. Whereas those of us who have tried to study educational projects have had some qualms about our measures of cognitive and behavioral effects, we have had little, if any, confidence in the measures of cost available to us. Future costs have almost invariably been underestimated. Past costs have been hard to compare from project to project and have often been challenged for ignoring hidden costs or understating open ones. Improvement and standardizing of the methods of cost analysis in educational projects, therefore, is something devoutly to be wished and gratefully to be received.

This is especially true now that technology is bulking so large in educational operations. Each generation of new communication media, from the film to the computer, has given birth to new educational technology. The larger and more expensive these systems, the more they challenge administrators and planners to face up to questions of cost effectiveness: What is the cost differential between television and radio? What kind and amount of use justifies a school system in spending a million dollars on an open-circuit television installation? What is likely to be the total cost of computerized instruction, and at what level of cost will it justify its presence in the school budget? What has been the true cost of an ongoing project, and what has that expenditure brought? What can a developing country expect to have to invest in a satellite, and what can it expect in return? Questions like these are important for good planning and management anywhere; for systems that are financially hard-pressed, and for developing countries that are not blessed with oil wells, such questions are crucial.

The authors of this volume provide in clear and simple prose, well-explained tables, and no more mathematics than necessary, a solid basis for dealing with the cost analyses involved in questions like those. Two chapters on the methodology and problems of educational cost analysis in general, and two chapters on the special considerations of making cost-analyses of instructional radio and television projects are followed by cost analyses of seven instructional technology projects, two using radio and five television. These are presented with admirable clarity and dispassion, so that they not only provide a model for this kind of analysis but also suggest certain general conclusions it is possible to draw from the experiences described. For example, although instructional radio and television used in (not out of) school are necessarily an add-on to the cost of other instruction, they may in some cases facilitate the reduction of other costs to such an extent that overall unit costs might actually be lowered. This is what the authors calculate could happen in El Salvador, if the planned expansion of the system and the policies with references to the class size and teaching hours are maintained. The Mexican Telesecundaria, they say quite correctly, is "one of the most interesting ITV systems in operation in the world today" since it appears to be one of the few shown to be cost-effective vis-à-vis the traditional direct teaching system (p. 273). The Telesecundaria makes secondary school study possible in towns where there is no secondary school. Jamison, Klees and Wells calculate that it would cost about sixty-five percent more to extend the present secondary school system to do what Telesecundaria is doing, but nevertheless, students in the Telesecundaria seem to perform as well on achievement tests as students in the same grades in Mexico City. Most school systems, however, do not reduce unit costs by introducing instructional radio or television, and the decision in that case must rest upon a comparison, the difficulty of which is fully acknowledged by these authors: the value placed on the additional learning, if any, versus the additional cost. But even in such a case as that of the Telesecundaria, Jamison, Klees and Wells point out that several other questions must be asked before all the evidence is out in the open and an informed decision can be made. Among them is the question of whether the diploma from the Telesecundaria will be as marketable as that of the regular high schools. And again, will putting the Telesecundaria in small towns encourage its graduates to seek their livelihood in the big cities? If so, trouble lies ahead, for these cities are already overcrowded, and employment is at a premium.

A good example for reporting costs fully and frankly is what Jamison, Klees and Wells say about the cost of cost analysis itself. "The total cost of the research and writing of this book was, we would estimate, on the order of $125,000, plus or minus 30%," they say. "A comprehensive cost analysis of a complete range of technological options for educational reform in a country or region would cost $50,000 to $150,000, though much valuable information could be produced by a $5,000 to $10,000 consulting effort properly done. For planning purposes a small effort should almost always precede a large one in order to lay out options in broad terms for the appropriate decision makers," (p. 20).

This refreshing approach to a difficult and often ponderous topic characterizes the book, and will be appreciated both by educational researchers and practitioners.

—*Wilbur Schramm*

PREFACE

Budgets constrain choices. They are not the only constraints; law, custom, tradition, political alignments, and inertia all serve to limit further a decision maker's options. Nevertheless, budgets remain a central constraint. With his budget a Minister of Education, say, can buy teachers, books, schoolhouses, radio sets, and the other inputs he needs to run his school system. The amount of each input that he can feasibly buy depends on the costs of the inputs and the level of his budget; his feasible *alternatives* constitute the set of all possible combinations of inputs whose total cost falls within the budget. In order to know which potential alternatives are feasible and which are not, the Minister must assemble information on input costs. Our purpose in this book is to present a methodology for the cost evaluation of ongoing educational projects and for the planning of future ones. Part One of the book develops this methodology in general terms; Part Two illustrates its application by examining the cost structure of instructional radio and television projects, with particular attention to those located in developing countries. Part Three contains nine cost case studies; these cases provide much of the empirical information upon which Part Two is based. Most of these cases combine evaluation of a project's heretofore incurred costs with projection and planning for future ones.

Obtaining costs in order to determine the set of economically feasible alternatives is the first step in educational planning, but it is only a first step. The Minister of Education must also obtain available information concerning the linkage between educational inputs and educational outputs and the linkage between educational outputs and economic and social outcomes.

Cost-effectiveness analysis uses knowledge concerning the first linkage, between educational inputs and outputs, to help ascertain which of the feasible alternatives will result in the "maximum" educational output. (As educational output is multidimensional, for example, number of graduates of each level per year, the term "maximum" output is used here to mean an output that can be increased on no one dimension without either being decreased on another or violating the budget constraint.) Cost-effectiveness analysis, then, deals with the problem of how to get the most in terms of educational output from the funds available to the educational system.[1] It constitutes the second step in educational planning.

The third step in educational planning deals with the relationship between the outputs of the educational system and various economic and social goals. Are educated individuals more economically productive, less inclined to crime, better citizens? If so, which types of education constributed most to these goals? Answers to these questions would assist the Minister of Education and the Central Planning Agency in ascertaining how much should be spent on education altogether and how that amount should be distributed across various types of education. In the terms of the preceding paragraph these answers would help enable the Minister to decide which of the maximum levels of output is most desirable for any given budget and to decide on an appropriate budget level. Cost-benefit analysis is the term economists use to describe this third step of educational planning, and economic research in education has focused on measurements of benefits for improving cost-benefit analyses.

Our purposes in this book—development of a cost evaluation methodology and provision of improved information concerning the costs of instructional television and radio—can be viewed as an attempt to improve cost-effectiveness and cost-benefit analyses in education. This is the role of cost analysis. We wish to make explicit, however, that our present effort in no way attempts to provide a cost-effectiveness or cost-benefit analysis of the extent to which these new media should be used. Such analyses need be done in the context of a particular country's price system, nonbudgetary constraints, overall economic situation, and development objectives.

Just as cost analysts begin increasingly to scrutinize educational projects, it is worthwhile to examine the costs (and benefits) of undertaking evaluations and, in particular, cost evaluations. This book fails to address this issue in any substantive way, but it may be worthwhile for us to record our observations on the matter here. The total cost of the research and writing of this book was, we would estimate, on the order of $125,000, plus or minus 30%. A comprehensive cost analysis of a complete range of technological options for educational reform in a country or region could cost $50,000 to $150,000, though much valuable information could be produced by a $5,000 to $10,000 consulting effort properly done. For planning purposes a small effort should almost always precede a large one in order to lay out options in broad terms for the appropriate decision makers; this might be followed by a more comprehensive and focused cost planning study.

The *potential* benefits of cost analysis are several. First, a properly done cost analysis will cost a range of options helping to force generation of options and comparisons among them. Second, cost evaluations help pinpoint the sources of major cost items and can help thereby to provide information useful in reducing costs. Third, a good cost analysis will force a decision maker to recognize that costs will almost inevitably be higher than he and his advisors may be tempted to think (see Chapter II, Section 3); this may help lead to the abandonment of unduly costly projects.

The potential benefits can only be realized if the relevant decision maker(s) use and interact with the cost analysts. We hope in this book to provide a methodological and empirical base that will help facilitate that interaction.

NOTE

1. Jamison (1972), Wells (1976), and Klees and Wells (1977a) discuss methodologies for cost-effectiveness analysis of schooling in developing countries and provide references to the literature. Jamison (1977b) has undertaken a cost-effectiveness analysis of the Nicaraguan Radio Mathematics Project that implements some of these methodologies. Use of the term "cost-effectiveness analysis" to describe the activities involved in modeling input-out relations in education is misleading to the extent that it implies the task to be one for economists. Experts in educational psychology, media research, statistics, and organizational theory play a more central role.

PART ONE

COST ANALYSIS FOR EDUCATIONAL

PLANNING AND EVALUATION

Chapter I

COST ANALYSIS: METHODOLOGY

Our aim in this chapter is to set forth the methodologies appropriate to the cost analysis of educational systems for planning and evaluation purposes, paying specific attention to their application to instructional technology systems. There is by now a reasonably extensive literature concerning educational costs,[1] but the methodologies of the literature are generally inadequate for dealing with capital investments in education. The reason appears to be that with the exception of building costs, concerning which a decision maker usually has little choice, most educational costs are recurrent. Decisions to utilize a technology, on the other hand, entail acceptance of a commitment to pay now and reap the benefits later; for this reason an adequate analysis of the cost of instructional radio and television (and indeed of any system requiring substantial capital investment) must grapple directly with the problem of the temporal structure of cost and utilization.

In this chapter we describe the methodology we use to handle this problem of cost and utilization occurring at different points in time. Costs are considered as a function of the *inputs*[2] to the educational process. Our methods draw on the standard economic theory of inter-temporal choice, but, as often occurs when applying economic theory, minor modifications are required to deal with the problem at hand. In what follows, Section 1 will briefly discuss some of the more important aspects of the collection and organization of cost data; Section 2 describes cost functions and their properties; Section 3 then describes methods of annualizing capital costs; Section 4 points out that using annualized capital costs can misstate the true costs of a project and introduces a method for incorporating the time structure of utilization into the analysis; Section 5 examines a slightly different notion of cost, opportunity cost, and discusses how, given a limited set of alternatives, the costs of a decision may fruitfully be thought of in terms of the real trade-offs that can occur; and finally, Section 6 sums up and concludes the discussion.

1. COLLECTION AND ORGANIZATION OF COST DATA

The primary emphasis of this report is the development of the appropriate methodological approaches to the analysis of system cost information. However, the cost analysis depends greatly upon the initial collection and organization of the relevant cost data and in this section we will briefly comment on some of the more important aspects of this procedure.

In order to understand the salient features of the initial cost collection procedure it is helpful to have an overview of the cost analysis process. The analysis may be thought of as proceeding in three stages, although work on the different stages often proceeds simultaneously: first, historical cost information on the system is collected; second, the historical relationship between these costs and the system variables that influence them is specified; and third, future system costs are projected based on hypotheses concerning the future configuration of cost-influencing system variables. Although it is the first stage that is concerned directly with the collection of historical cost data, it is necessary to remember that the historical data are required to feed into the second and third stages of the analysis. In particular, the cost analyst needs to gather not only historical system cost information, but also information on the amount of physical resources purchased in each category and the period associated with the expenditure, as well as the level of the key structural variables of the system that influence these resource needs. For example, in the case of an instructional television system, not only does the analyst need to know how much was spent on television receivers in a given year, but he also requires information such as the number of receivers purchased and the number of students the system serves.

In order to begin data collection activities, the analyst should previously have enumerated a rather exhaustive and detailed list of the resource categories relevant to the particular system under study. This initial step is quite important as components that are excluded from this conceptual phase of the analysis may never be costed. The analyst can usually draw on his or her experience with similar projects in making such a list, but it is much better to have a close familiarity with the particular project under study, either through firsthand experience or secondary sources, since each system usually has its own peculiarities that can too easily be missed. (For example, in the Ivory Coast the theft of television receivers is sometimes a problem and may represent a significant cost item that could easily be overlooked.)

Once the list of resource categories is drawn up, cost collection activities may proceed in two general ways. First, cost information for each resource category may be found in the analysis of budget and expense documents. Unfortunately, budgetary and expense information is often collected for purposes quite separate from economic evaluation and it is usually a difficult task to translate such data into a form useable for the cost analysis. Further, many system resources may not be reflected in project budget or expense documents, but may be contributed by foreign donors, other government agencies, or the private sector. Such cost data need to be sought from the appropriate sources. One of the most difficult categories to cost are those physical or human resources that are donated to the project, without an explicit monetary charge. Nonetheless, if such resources have a value to the economy in alternative uses they represent a real societal cost that must be estimated (see Chapter II, Section 1 for a further discussion).

Sometimes budgetary and expense information is so poor for cost evaluation purposes (or, for some projects, may not even exist), that it is necessary to estimate costs by cataloguing the resources needed or used in each resource category and then finding the appropriate prices for these resources. For example, in Mexico, no cost information was available for the production equipment used in the production of ITV programs. One of the authors had to go through the production facilities, note all the equipment used, and go to manufacturers for estimates of the prices of such equipment. More commonly this procedure may be followed to estimate system expenditures for items such as television receivers, where information could be gathered on student enrollment, on the average ratio of students to receivers, and on the price of a receiver.

Care must, then, be taken in the organization and collection of cost data (see Chapter II, Section 3). The collection of these data will generate an historical cost table, which lists the costs incurred under each resource category for each year of the project's operation. The data in this cost table, along with the historical information on physical resources used and the historical level of the relevant system variables, will form the basis for the projection of the year by year cost table into the future as well as for the estimation of the relevant cost functions. Although in what follows we emphasize the methodology necessary to proper cost analysis, it should be remembered that the analysis can be no better than data that are put into it, and experience and careful judgment in the collection of cost data are vital to a meaningful evaluation.

2. COST FUNCTIONS AND THEIR PROPERTIES

We begin this section by defining the concepts of total cost, average (or unit) cost and marginal cost; we then examine the special case in which it is appropriate to separate costs into fixed costs and variable costs. We conclude by discussing the situation in which there are multiple inputs to the cost function.

TOTAL, AVERAGE AND MARGINAL COST

It is useful to think of costs as functions rather than as numbers: a total cost function for an input gives the total cost required to finance an input as a function of the amount of the input required. To take an example, let

$$\text{Total Cost} = TC = TC(N),$$

where $TC(N)$ is the total cost required to provide an input of instructional television to N students.[3]

The *average cost function* (or, equivalently, the *unit cost function*) is defined to equal the total cost divided by the number of units of the input provided:

$$\text{Average Cost} = AC(N) = TC(N)/N.$$

Just as the total cost depends on N, so may the average cost.

The *marginal cost function* gives the additional cost of providing one more unit of input (i.e., in this example, of providing instructional television to one more student) as a function of the number of units already provided. Stated slightly more precisely, the marginal cost function is the derivative of the total cost function:[4]

$$\text{Marginal Cost} = MC(N) = dTC(N)/dN.$$

Again, it is important to keep in mind that the marginal cost will in general be a function of N.

To illustrate the concepts above let us construct a simple arithmetic example. In Table I.1, the first column indicates the number of students served by a particular educational program, while the second column indicates the total costs of serving that number of students. We see that the example has been constructed to indicate that total costs are some function of the number of students; that is, total costs increase as the number of students increases. From the information presented in the first and second columns we can derive the average and marginal cost information presented in the third and fourth columns. The average cost is simply the total cost divided by the number of students, while the marginal cost is the addition to total costs caused by the addition of one more student to the system. The average cost measure is most useful as an historical summary of the system's efficiency

TABLE I.1

Total, Average, and Marginal Cost Example

Unit (students)	Total Cost	Average Cost	Marginal Cost
0	$ 0	$ 0	
1	30	30	$30
2	70	35	40
3	105	35	35
4	120	30	15
5	130	26	10

in doing its task, while the marginal cost measure is more useful for examining the cost consequences of expanding or contracting the system, in terms of the number of students served.

This example also illustrates the relationship between average costs and marginal costs. For the average cost to rise as the system expands the marginal cost of adding another student must be greater than the average cost. For example, in expanding from serving one student to serving two students the marginal cost is $40, which is greater than the $30 average cost of serving one student—therefore, when the system expands to two students the average cost rises (from $30 to $35 in this case). Similarly, if the marginal cost is below the average cost, the average cost will fall as the system expands; this is illustrated in our example as the system expands to serve more than three students. When average and marginal costs are equal, expansion will yield the same average cost. This is illustrated in the table in the increase from two students to three students where the marginal cost of the increase is $35, which is the same as the average cost for two students, thus yielding an average cost of $35 for three students.

FIXED AND VARIABLE COSTS

It is often possible to separate costs into fixed costs and variable costs. For example in the simple and convenient linear form,

(I.1) $$TC(N) = F + VN,$$

F would be the *fixed cost* because the value of cost contributed by the first term on the right hand side is independent of N; V is the *variable cost* per unit of input because the value of total cost contributed by the second term on the right hand side varies directly with N. When the total cost function is linear, as in equation I.1, the average cost is simply equal to the fixed cost divided by N plus the variable cost $(AC(N) = F/N + V)$; the marginal cost is equal to V. Thus the average cost declines as N increases (by spreading the fixed cost over more units) until, when N is very large, the average cost is close to the marginal cost.

Equation I.1 is a reasonably good rough approximation to the cost behavior of instructional technology systems.[5] Program preparation and transmission tend to be fixed independently of the number of students using the system. Reception costs, on the other hand, tend to vary directly with the number of students.

MULTIPLE INPUTS TO THE COST FUNCTION

In the preceding subsections we have assumed that the total cost of providing instructional radio or television depended on only a single variable, the number of students reached. This is a reasonable approach in circumstances where one can assume other potentially relevant variables to be fixed. Often, however, particularly in planning situations, it is important to consider explicitly the other variables. The input one wishes to cost is not just instructional television for N students; it is instead instructional television for h hours per year for N students spread over a geographical region of x square miles. More variables could be added.[6]

Aside from potential practical complications, then, there is small conceptual difficulty in going from consideration of a single determinant to multiple determinants of cost. In the analysis of the cost of ongoing projects presented in Chapter III and in the case studies presented in Part Three, we will rely heavily on a cost function model that assumes total costs to be a linear function of the annual number of students in the system, N, and the annual number of programming hours broadcast, h, as follows:[7]

(I.2) $$TC(N,h) = F + V_N N + V_h h,$$

where   F   = the fixed costs of the system in the sense that they are independent of N and h,

V_N = the variable cost per student,

and V_h = the variable cost per hour of programming broadcast.

In order to let the number of students and programming in hours in the system be the sole determining cost variables, as in equation I.2, it is necessary to let the values of F, V_N and V_h depend on aspects of the system that are assumed to remain unchanged. F will depend, among other things, on the number of grade levels the students to be reached are in, as well as the geographical area over which they are spread. V_h will depend on the quality of programming, while V_N will depend on class size. To the extent that the situation warrants assuming these other variables will change little, the use of a simplified cost function such as that presented in equation I.2 is warranted. In Chapter IV, more detailed cost function will be utilized, reflecting the utility of considering multiple determinants of costs in the planning process.

3. TREATMENT OF TIME:
ANNUALIZATION OF CAPITAL COSTS

A *capital cost* is one that is incurred to acquire goods or service that will have a useful lifetime that extends beyond the time of purchase. *Recurrent costs,* on the other hand, are incurred for goods or services that are used up as they are bought. The principal cost of schools is the recurrent cost of teachers' time; since teachers are paid while they provide their service, the useful lifetime of what is actually purchased simply coincides with the pay period. (In this example we neglect the human capital forming aspect of teacher training colleges.) The cost of a pencil would seem to be a capital cost since, depending on one's penchant for writing, it could last for several months. In fact, pencils are treated as recurrent costs for the reason that their expected lifetime is less than the accounting period (usually one year) of school systems. The line between capital and recurrent costs is, then, usually drawn at one year; if the lifetime of a piece of equipment is greater than that, its cost is usually treated as a capital cost. Coombs and Hallak (1972, Chapter 9) point out that school systems often adhere only loosely to this one year convention, and they provide a valuable practical discussion of how to examine school building and facilities costs.

An occasional source of confusion is between fixed costs and capital costs. There can be fixed costs that are recurrent; an example is the electric power required to operate a television transmitter. Likewise there can be capital costs that are variable; an example is the receiver component of reception costs. Thus the concepts of fixed costs and capital costs are distinct, though it is often true that major capital expenditures are associated with substantial fixed costs.

How does one construct the cost functions discussed in the preceding subsection if capital costs are present? Let us say that a school system buys a radio transmitter and 6000 receivers in year one for a total cost of $220,000. It would clearly be inappropriate to include the entire $220,000 as a year one cost in attempting to determine the unit cost of the use of radio in year one; likewise it would be inappropriate, in computing year three costs, to consider the use of transmitter and receivers as free. In order to construct a useful cost function it is necessary to *annualize* the expenditure on capital equipment.

Two variables are important in annualizing expenditures on capital equipment. The first of these is the *lifetime* of the equipment; if the equipment lasts n years, a fraction, on the average equal to 1/n, of its cost should be charged to each year. This is a *depreciation* cost.

The second variable that is important in annualizing capital expenditures is the social discount rate. The social discount rate reflects a value judgment concerning the cost to society of withdrawing resources from consumption now in order to have more consumption later. It is represented as an interest rate because in an important sense the "cost" of capital is the interest charge that must be paid for its use. One way of obtaining an approximation for an appropriate value for the social discount rate is to examine the private cost of capital. If a country has invested $220,000 in radio facilities, the capital thereby committed cannot be used elsewhere. For example, it cannot be used to construct a bicycle factory or fertilizer plant. To see the importance of this let us assume that the lifetime, n, of the $220,000 worth of radio equipment is ten years and that the country could, if it chose, rent the equipment for $22,000 per year instead of buying it. Whether the country rents or buys then, over the ten-year period it will spend $220,000 on equipment. But it is obvious that the country would be foolish to buy under these circumstances for the simple reason that if it rented the radio equipment it could put the $220,000 in a savings bank in Switzerland (or in a fertilizer plant) and collect interest (or profits from the sale of fertilizer). Of course, for most of the time the country would collect interest on only a part of the $220,000 if it were paying the rent out of this account: nevertheless, if it were receiving 7.5% interest, there would be $132,560 in the bank at the end of the ten years.

As this example has indicated, there is a cost (interest charge) involved in having capital tied up in a project, and this cost is measured, to some extent, by the potential rate of return to capital elsewhere in the economy.[8] The total amount of this cost depends, of course, on the amount of capital that is tied up; if the value of the capital in a project is depreciating, as it must be as its lifetime draws to a close, then the amount of capital tied up decreases from year to year. It is thus *inappropriate* in annualizing capital costs to depreciate the value of initial capital by 1/n and add a capital charge equal to the social rate of discount times the initial value of the capital.[9] One must take into account the changing value of the capital over the project life.

If we take this changing value into account and are given an initial cost, C, for an item of capital equipment, its lifetime, n, and the social rate of discount, r, the annualized cost of capital is given by a(r, n) multiplied by C, where the annualization factor, a(r, n), is given by equation I.3:

(I.3) $$a(r, n) = [r(1 + r)^n] / [(1 + r)^n - 1].$$

Table I.2 shows a(r, n) for a number of values of r and n. When r is equal to zero, equation I.3 can be shown to be mathematically equal to 1/n. The

TABLE I.2
Values of the Annualization Factor a(r, n)

n	0	r = 7.5%	15%
1	1.000	1.000	1.000
2	.500	.557	.615
3	.333	.385	.438
4	.250	.299	.350
5	.200	.247	.298
6	.167	.213	.264
7	.143	.189	.240
8	.125	.171	.223
9	.111	.157	.210
10	.100	.146	.199
11	.091	.137	.191
12	.083	.129	.184
13	.077	.123	.179
14	.071	.118	.175
15	.067	.113	.171
20	.050	.098	.160
25	.040	.090	.155
50	.020	.077	.150

derivation of equation I.3 would lead us astray from our main purposes; we refer the interested reader to the complete account in Kemeny et al. (1962, Chapter VI). In our television example we assumed a value of C equal to $220,000 and a lifetime of ten years; if we assume a social discount rate of 7.5% we have the following:

$$\text{annualized cost} = [0.075(1.075)^{10}] / [(1.075)^{10} - 1] \times 220{,}000.$$

This is equal to $32,051 per year.

It is important to realize that the use of an appropriate social rate of discount, r, is not just a theoretical nicety, but makes a significant practical difference in terms of assessing the real costs of an instructional technology project. Not to do so, that is, to use a zero interest rate, implies that the project planner is indifferent, for example, to spending a million dollars now rather than doing so ten years from now; such treatment can seriously understate the costs of an instructional technology project, and thus make it look more favorable in a cost comparison with a traditional system, since the former usually involves greater capital expenditures than the latter.

To illustrate the extent to which inclusion of an appropriate interest rate makes a practical difference in costing projects, Table I.3 presents the average cost per student for the projects discussed in Chapter III (based on the annualized cost function, evaluated for the specific year stated for each case) and

TABLE I.3

The Extent of Cost Underestimation Due to Not Utilizing
the Appropriate Interest Rate in Analyzing Ongoing
Instructional Technology Projects[a]

	Average Cost per Student (in 1972 U.S. dollars) at r =			Cost Underestimate (in percent) if r = 0 is used and true r =	
	0%	7.5%	15%	7.5%	15%
Instructional Technology Project					
Radio-based					
Nicaragua	3.65	3.86	4.07	5.4	10.3
Radioprimaria	12.63	13.12	13.72	3.8	8.0
Tarahumara	35.94	42.20	49.34	14.8	27.2
Thailand	.29	.35	.41	17.1	29.3
Television-based					
El Salvador	19.72	24.35	29.37	19.0	32.9
Stanford ITV	146.60	159.20	175.10	7.9	16.3
Hagerstown	51.54	54.23	57.78	5.0	10.8
Korea	2.76	3.22	3.74	14.3	26.2
Telesecundaria	23.02	24.27	25.74	5.2	10.6

a. Cost data are based on the average cost per student reported in Chapter III; the year
for which the data are relevant is that given in Chapter III. The El Salvador estimates
refer to costing the total project.

depicts the degree to which such costs are underestimated if no discount
rate is used (that is, r = 0) when the appropriate time preference for resources
should be expressed by an interest rate of 7.5% or 15%. We see that the percentage underestimation will vary from project to project; on the average,
if no interest rate is utilized and r should equal 7.5%, project costs estimates
for these cases are underestimated by 10.3%, while if the true interest rate is
15%, costs would be underestimated by 19.1%. Although the difference in
dollar amounts may not appear to be great at first glance, it should be remembered that total project costs will be underestimated by the same percentage,
and thus a small dollar difference may reflect an underestimate of true system costs that may be hundreds of thousands or even millions of dollars,
depending on the extent of student utilization.

If all capital costs are annualized in the way suggested here it becomes
possible to compute the annualized values of F, V_N, and V_h for the total
cost function of equation I.2 (or to compute the parameters of a more complicated cost function). If assessment of the parameters is all that is desired—
and that, indeed, is much of what one needs to know—no further theoretical

work is necessary. But if one wishes to compute, say, an average cost, one needs in addition a value for N, the number of students using the system (and of h, the number of programming hours). Not only does the incidence of cost vary with time but so does N; more specifically, in contrast to cost, N tends to be low at the outset and large later. Our purpose in the next section is to examine the effects on unit costs of considering explicitly the time structure of utilization.

4. TREATMENT OF TIME: STUDENT UTILIZATION OVER TIME

This section develops a method for displaying the unit costs of an educational investment that takes explicit account of the time structure of utilization, as well as of costs, and that allows examination of costs from a number of time perspectives. The question of time perspective is important. Before undertaking a project, a policy maker faces the substantial investment costs required to buy equipment, develop programs, and start up the operations. Three or four years later these costs will have been incurred to a substantial extent, and the cost picture facing the Minister is very different indeed. His initial capital costs are sunk, and except for the potential (slight) resale value of his equipment, there is nothing to be recovered from abandoning the project.[10] What is desirable, then, is a method for displaying costs from the perspective of a decision maker prior to commitment to a project, one year into the project, two years into the project, etc.

It is also desirable to consider various time horizons for the decision maker. What will the average costs have been if the project is abandoned after three years? Allowed to run for fifteen years? This suggests the value of looking at average costs[11] as seen from year i of the project with a horizon through year j. We will denote the "average cost from i to j" by the symbol AC_{ij} and define it to mean total expenditures on the project between years i and j divided by total usage of the project (number of students), with both costs and usage discounted back to year i by the social rate of discount, r.[12] Let C_i be equal to the total amount spent on the project in year i, including fixed and variable costs, and capital and recurrent costs. Let N_i be the total number of students served by the project in year i. Then AC_{ij} is given by:[13]

$$(I.4) \qquad AC_{ij} = \frac{\displaystyle\sum_{k=i}^{j} C_k/(1+r)^{k-i}}{\displaystyle\sum_{k=i}^{j} N_k/(1+r)^{k-i}}$$

A decision maker at the beginning of i can in no way influence expenditures of student usage before time i so that costs and benefits incurred up to that time are for his decision irrelevant and are not incorporated into AC_{ij}. What AC_{ij} tells him is the cost per student of continuing the project through year j, under the assumption that year j will be the final year of the project. By examining how AC_{ij} behaves as j varies the decision maker can obtain a feel for how long the project must continue for unit costs to fall to the point of making the continuation worthwhile. When the decision maker is considering whether the project should be undertaken at all, he should let i = 1; i.e., he should compute AC_{1j} for various values of j. In these considerations ideally the decision maker should base decisions on the value of AC_{ij} calculated for the j corresponding to the end of the project, for his discounting of the future is already taken into account by equation I.4. In the real world, however, there is a possibility that the project will be terminated prior to its planned end, and it is thus of value to the decision maker to see how many years it takes AC_{1j} to drop to a reasonable value and how many years more before it stabilizes to an asymptotic level. Clearly projections such as these rest on *planned* costs and utilization rates.

At this point it may be of value to include a brief example to illustrate the concepts; in Chapter III and in the case studies we will apply this method of analysis to cost data from a number of actual instructional technology projects. In our example we assume a project life of six years. In year one a $1,000 investment is made and no students use the system. In years two through six costs of $250 per year are incurred and fifty students per year use the system. Table I.4 shows C_i and N_i for each of the six years of the project and Table I.5 shows AC_{ij} under the assumption that the social rate of discount is 7.5%.

We should make a few comments about the values of AC_{ij} in Table I.5. First, there are no entries in the lower left; this is natural because the horizon (j) must be at least as far into the future as the time from which it is viewed (i). Second, for values of i greater than or equal to 2, AC_{ij} is uniformly $5.00 (= $250/50). This is because the only capital cost is incurred in period one

TABLE I.4
Example Cost and Student Usage

Year i	C_i (in $)	N_i
1	1000	0
2	250	50
3	250	50
4	250	50
5	250	50
6	250	50

TABLE I.5
Example Values of AC_{ij}

Year i	Horizon Year j					
	1	2	3	4	5	6
1	–	26.46	16.14	12.69	10.97	9.95
2		5.00	5.00	5.00	5.00	5.00
3			5.00	5.00	5.00	5.00
4				5.00	5.00	5.00
5					5.00	5.00
6						5.00

and from period two on, future costs and utilization are discounted to the present in the same proportion. (It is natural, once the capital cost is incurred, that the decision maker view the unit cost as $5.00 from that time on.) Third, AC_{11} is indefinite: because costs have been incurred and no students have used the system, the unit cost becomes indefinitely large. Fourth, in this example the interesting numbers occur in row one. As the time recedes further into the future, the unit costs are spread over more students reducing AC_{1j}: if the project had a long enough life, AC_{1j} would become closer and closer to $5.00 as j got larger. AC_{1j} shows how the average cost behavior of the project looks prior to its initiation, and the value of AC_{1j} (for j near the project lifetime value) should be important in determining whether to proceed.

The AC_{ij} estimate, like that of the average cost per student based on an annualized cost function, is also quite sensitive to the social rate of discount chosen. In fact, not taking account of social time preference (that is, utilizing a zero discount rate) usually understates the AC_{ij} measure by an even greater amount than that indicated for the annualized specific year, average cost measure which we discussed.

It is the authors' opinion that the AC_{ij} cost concept is a much more meaningful summary cost measure than that provided by calculating the average cost per student from an annualized cost function, based on student utilization in one particular year. The latter figure merely gives a snapshot picture of project efficiency (in a cost sense) at one point in time, while the AC_{ij} measure captures both the history and projected plans for the particular project under consideration. In effect, an average cost per student figure is a very rough cost-effectiveness ratio that tells an analyst the resource costs of giving an individual a year's education (of given quality); it would seem to make good sense to evaluate this particular aspect of the cost-effectiveness of a project over the project lifetime and not for any particular year. Nevertheless, since most previous analysis uses an average cost figure, based on an annualized cost function, we will also present such calculations for selected years for the case studies presented in Chapter III and Part Three of this report; wherever sufficient cost data are available, we will also present estimates of the AC_{ij}'s.

It should be noted that in the absence of perfect markets there is no necessary reason to choose the same interest rate for discounting both costs and students, as was done in equation I.4. It is entirely possible that the rate of time preference relating to students receiving an education and that associated with resource investments may be different, although in the absence of a specific notion of what this discount rate difference may be, the same rate will be applied to both resources and students in the analysis of instruction of technology costs in Chapter III and the case studies. It is interesting to observe that in an entirely separate effort, Levin (1974) also suggests the use of a cost concept which takes into account system utilization over time and which additionally would discount this utilization stream by an appropriate discount rate; in essence, his suggestion amounts to a general description of the type of AC_{ij} concept we have developed and presented above.

5. COST TRADEOFFS

A slightly different, but related, notion of cost than that used above is that of *opportunity cost*. The opportunity cost of a choice from among a limited set of alternatives is the value to the decision maker (or to the society) of what he or she turned down in order to be able to choose what he or she did. In a competitive market economy the price of goods and services is one measure of the opportunity cost, as the price of that item both reflects what the user of the item gives up, since the money allocated to that item could have been spent elsewhere, and reflects the cost to the economy of utilizing its resources to produce that item, resources that could have been productive in other endeavors (see Section 1 of the following chapter for a discussion of some circumstances in which this latter connection may not hold, that is, when the price of a goods or service may not reflect its opportunity cost to the economy). However, it is often useful, within a constrained choice situation, to examine the opportunity cost of an activity in nonprice terms, as measured by the activity, or physical resources, that are given up through following a particular choice. If, for example, the superintendent tells a principal that he can have either two new teachers or a science laboratory and the principal chooses the teachers, the opportunity cost to him of the teachers was a science laboratory. This section briefly discusses the means for examing such relationships, within the context of instructional technology system choices.

If a school system's per student expenditure is constrained by a fixed budget, then having more of any one thing implies there must be less of something else. For this reason, it may be useful to a decision maker to see explicitly what these opportunity costs are for certain important categories of alternatives.[14] Since the largest expenditure category for schools is presently teacher salaries, we will examine the opportunity cost of introducing something new (for example, instructional television or radio) under the assumption that its opportunity cost is less teacher input. Let S be the student to teacher ratio (this is not necessarily the same as class size; it also depends on the relative amount of time students and teachers spend in school) before the technology is introduced, and let W be the teacher's annual wage. Let A equal the average annual cost of the technology and let I be the increase in class size required to make the posttechnology per student instructional cost equal to R times the pretechnology instructional cost of W/S. Neglecting the minor influence of changes in S on A, the posttechnology instructional cost equals $[W + A (S + I)]/(S + I)$ and the following must hold:

$$W/S = R[W + A (S + I)]/(S + I).$$

To find the increase in student to teacher ratio required to pay for the introduction of the technology, the above equation is solved for I giving:

(I.5) $I = [SW(1 - R) + AS^2 R] / [W - ASR]$.

I represents, then, the opportunity cost of introducing a technology in terms of increased student to teacher ratio. Under the assumption that per student costs remain unchanged, i.e., $R = 1$, Table I.6 shows values of I for several values of A and W, and for values of S equal to 25 and 40. If, for example, $S = 25$, $W = \$1,500$, $A = \$9.00$, and $R = 1$ Table I.6 shows that $I = 4.41$; that is, the student to teacher ratio after technology is introduced equals 29.41. While the formula of equation I.5 was developed for expressing the opportunity cost of introducing a technology in terms of student to teacher ratio, similar formulas could be developed between other pairs of inputs. All such formulas would essentially represent ways of analytically evaluating the tradeoffs within a fixed budget constraint.

6. SUMMARY

We began this chapter by presenting a brief overview of the cost analysis process and discussing some of the more important aspects of the collection and organization of cost data. Again we would like to stress the necessity for a great deal of care to be exercised in this initial stage of the cost analysis procedure for without carefully acquired data even the best methodological analysis is of quite limited value.

We began the discussion of cost analysis methodology in Section 2 by defining a total cost function and the related concepts of average cost function

TABLE I.6

Increase in Student to Teacher Ratio Required to Finance Technology[a]

A	W = Teacher Annual Wage			
	$750	$1500	$2250	$3000
$S^b = 25$				
$ 1.80	1.60	0.77	0.51	0.38
$ 4.50	4.41	2.03	1.32	0.97
$ 9.00	10.71	4.41	2.78	2.03
$18.00	37.50	10.71	6.25	4.41
$S^b = 40$				
$ 1.80	4.25	2.02	1.32	.98
$ 4.50	12.63	5.45	3.48	2.55
$ 9.00	36.92	12.63	7.62	5.45
$18.00		36.92	15.24	12.63

a. This table shows the increase in average student to teacher ratio that is required if per student instructional costs (teacher cost plus technology cost) is to remain unchanged after a technology costing A dollars per student per year is introduced into the system. The values of A chosen reflect costs per student per day of $.01, $.025, $.05, and $.10 if the school year is 180 days.
b. S is the value of the student to teacher ratio before the technology is introduced.

and marginal cost function. We then examined the special case when costs can be separated into fixed and variable. To apply these concepts to real world data, it is necessary to annualize capital costs in a way that appropriately accounts for depreciation and the social rate of discount. Section 3 described the method for doing this and observed that most prior treatments of educational technology costs failed to annualize capital costs properly. The annualized capital costs, plus values for recurrent costs, give the parameters F (fixed), V_N (variable with the number of students, N), and V_h (variable with the number of programming hours broadcast, h), in the simplified total cost function $TC(N,h) = F + V_N N + V_h h$. To obtain average or unit costs per student, one also needs a value of N (and h). In any one year, say year j, the appropriate average cost per student for that year is $(F + V_h h_j)/N_j + V_N$ where N_j is the number of students using the system and h_j is the number of programming hours broadcast in year j. Since N is typically zero or very low for the first few years of the project, and then rises, the use of a (high) value of N from late in the project to compute average costs is misleading. It will tend to understate the average costs that have actually been incurred over the life of the project, even though the estimated values of F, V_N and V_h might give an adequate picture of the cost function.

To avoid this difficulty, we suggested a method in Section 4 for displaying the "average cost from i to j," that is, the total present value of costs incurred from time i through time j divided by total present value of system usage in that time interval. We used the symbol AC_{ij} to denote the average cost from i to j when costs and usage are properly discounted. Use of AC_{ij} gives a more accurate picture of average costs than does simply inserting a value of N from late in the life of the project into the average cost equation. The AC_{ij}'s also enable a decision maker to see clearly the structure of his future unit costs after he has committed himself to capital acquisitions; this annualized costs are unable to do. The additional usefulness of the AC_{ij}'s comes with a price, namely, much more information is required to obtain them. One needs a detailed time pattern of expenditure and utilization (either actual or projected) to compute values of AC_{ij}.

To this point we considered the costs of resources in terms of their monetary value. In Section 5 we introduced the notion of *opportunity cost* and presented an example of how this concept allows examination of the implications of a decision, from among a set of limited alternatives, in terms of the very real tradeoffs that that decision may imply. In particular, we looked at how the "cost" of introducing an educational innovation might be considered in terms of the increased class size that would be required to maintain expenditures at the same level (or some multiple or fraction of that level) as before the innovation. In many instances such analysis of the concrete tradeoffs involved in a decision may be more useful to some decision makers than an examination of the monetary costs of the decision. The opportunity cost analysis could easily be extended to include more than tradeoffs between class size and technology costs; tradeoffs among other variables can also be examined.

In conclusion, this chapter presents the essential concepts and methods necessary to a proper cost analysis for educational planning and evaluation. In the following chapter we will treat some special problems of which the cost analyst must be cognizant when undertaking a study of educational costs.

NOTES

1. Perhaps the most valuable discussion of educational costs is a recent book of Coombs and Hallak (1972); this is one in a series of studies, sponsored by UNESCO's International Institute for Educational Planning, that also includes Vaizey and Chesswas (1967) and Hallak (1969). Other general discussions of educational costs include Bowman (1966), Davis (1966), Edding (1966), Thomas (1971, Chapter 3), Haller (1974), and Levin (1974). Vaizey et al. (1972, Part Six) treat teacher costs in some detail, and Schultz (1971, Chapters 6 and 7) discusses the important and occasionally overlooked cost of students' time. Previous discussions of educational technology costs appear in Schramm et al. (1967b, Chapter 4 and the accompanying volumes of case studies), General Learning Corporation (1968), and Hayman and Levin (1973), Carnoy (1975),

and Carnoy and Levin (1975). Some recent case studies of instructional television system costs were undertaken by the Educational Policy Research Center (1976). However, perhaps most relevant to the discussion of our topic is the recently published parallel effort undertaken by UNESCO (1977), applying cost analysis to educational media evaluation. Fisher (1971) provides an excellent discussion of cost analysis with specific reference to national defense systems.

2. Most discussion of cost in economics centers around how the cost of *output* varies with its quantity, under the assumption that the producer of the output is economically efficient; see, for example, Henderson and Quandt (1958, pp. 55, 62). The concepts of total, average, and marginal cost that are usually used to describe output cost can also be used to describe input costs. Usually, however, the cost of an input is simply assumed to equal the quantity utilized, multiplied by its unit price. This simple model of input costs is inadequate for our purposes. Walsh (1970, Chapter 22) engagingly synopsizes the history of economists' usage of the term "cost," and provides a clear statement of modern views.

3. For those readers unfamiliar with functional rotation, TC(N) stands for some mathematical function that depicts total costs as dependent on N. The specific form of the function is not stated; other variables in the parentheses would indicate other factors on which total cost depends.

4. For those readers unfamiliar with the concept of derivative, perhaps a more useful formula for illustrating the marginal cost concept would be:

$$\text{Marginal Cost} = MC(N) = TC(N+1) - TC(N).$$

That is, the marginal cost at any given level of student utilization, N, is equal to the total cost for N+1 students minus the total cost for N students. This is an accurate representation of marginal cost and is utilized in the textual example that follows; however, this formulation has the disadvantage that it must be recomputed for each level of N, while the derivative formulation yields a *function* that allows the calculation of marginal cost for any level of N.

5. It should be emphasized that this linear formulation of the total cost function is in many cases only a rough approximation. For example, as the system expands to cover students from more heterogeneous cultures, more geographically distant locations, of less densely populated areas both the variable cost per student and the marginal cost per student may not remain constant (and will not necessarily be equal either), but may increase. See Chapter IV for a more extensive discussion of this point.

6. While treatment of multiple inputs involves some additional complication, the basic concepts introduced so far change but little. Total cost is now a function of several variables; in our new example,

$$TC = TC(N,h,x).$$

The marginal costs become the amount total cost changes for a unit change in *each* of the determining variables: in this three-variable example, we have three marginal costs defined mathematically by partial derivatives as follows:

$$MC_N = \frac{\partial TC}{\partial N} \; : \; MC_h = \frac{\partial TC}{\partial h} \; : \; \text{and } MC_x = \frac{\partial TC}{\partial x} \; .$$

Each of these marginal costs may well depend on N, h, and x.

Similar to the discussion in footnote 4 for any given value of N, h, or x, the marginal cost with respect to N, h, or x, can also be represented by the increase in total cost caused by adding one student, one hour of programming, or one square mile of coverage, respectively. This formulation would yield an accurate estimate of marginal cost only for a specified level of N, h, and x, from which we want to examine an incremental expansion of one of the variables, holding the other two constant. The derivative formulation again has the advantage that it yields a *functional* representation of the marginal cost with respect to N, h, or x that allows one to calculate the marginal costs of expansion of N, h, or x, at any level of the three variables without having to calculate the total costs in each instance.

7. It should be noted that a more detailed formulation of the total cost function would have several different types of "h" variables: production costs depend most closely on the number of programming hours *produced* each year; transmission costs depend on the number of programming hours *broadcast* annually; and reception costs will vary somewhat (due to the costs of supplying power to the television or radio recievers) with the number of programming hours the average television or radio set *receives* annually. The second definition is the one used in the case studies and in Chapter III (unless specified differently for a particular project); given certain assumptions as to program lifetime and receiver utilization, the three definitions may be linearly related.

8. The issues involved in determining a value for the social rate of discount are actually rather complex and involve consideration of reinvestment of returns as opposed to consumption of them. The productivity of capital in an economy is a measure of what must be given up to finance a project; there remains the problem of comparing net costs and benefits that occur at different points in time. DasGupta et al. (1972, Chapters 13 and 14) review these issues and argue forcibly that a discount rate to make net returns at different points in time comparable reflects a social value judgment. They argue, therefore, that the policy analyst should use a number of social discount rates in order to exhibit clearly the sensitivity of the results to the values chosen. This we do, using annual discount rates of zero, 7.5%, and 15%.

9. Unfortunately this is the procedure used by the economists involved in the IIEP (1967) case studies of the *New Educational Media in Action* (Schramm, Coombs, Kahnert, and Lyle, 1967). Their approach overstates the cost of the media, though such a low discount rate is used (about 3%) that the mistake is partially counterbalanced. The studies of satellite and other technologies for ITV distribution undertaken by the Educational Policy Research Center (1976) also chose to use no discount rate. Speagle (1972, p. 228), in his assessment of the cost of instructional television in El Salvador, concluded that "the inclusion of interest charges would not have made much practical difference for the usefulness of this study as a policy instrument while opening a Pandora's Box of theoretical arguments, imputations, and adjustments." We feel that inclusion of interest charges does have practical relevance for understanding the El Salvador experience, and we indicate its magnitude in Chapter III and Chapter VII. The neglect of a discount rate is clearly a mistake if there are alternative investment possibilities with different structure of capital investment. For persuasive and practical arguments to this effect see the report on the subject made by the U.S. Subcommittee on Economy in Government (1968).

10. It may nonetheless be wise to abandon the project—if, to be specific, still to be incurred costs exceed the benefits of continuing.

11. One could also look at total and marginal costs; in our treatment here we focus on average costs because we feel them to be useful in aiding the decision maker's intuition, prior to project commitment. Expansion decisions should, of course, rely on marginal costs. The concept AC_{ij} being developed here is implicitly based on the concept of a vector valued total cost function, where the dependent variable is a vector giving total

cost in each time period. The independent variables, too, become vectors potentially assuming different values at different times.

12. It may aid in understanding equation I.4 to explain the concept of the present value of a cost. Assume that a cost of $4,000 is to be incurred eight years from now. The *present value* of that cost is the amount that would have to be put aside now, at interest, to be able to pay the $4,000 in eight years. If the interest rate is 6% and we put aside an amount z now, in eight years we will have $z (1.06)^8 = \$4,000$, or $z = \$4,000/1.06^8$; z is the present value of $4,000 eight years from now when the interest rate is 6%; its numerical value is $2,509.65. The numerator of equation I.4 is the present value (viewed from the perspective of year i as the "present") of all costs incurred between years i and j. The denominator is the present value of student utilization.

13. It should be noted that the potential for the use of the AC_{ij} concept is much greater than would be indicated by the restricted definition given here, focussing on average cost per student. For example, for instructional technology project evaluation it may be as, or more, useful to think of utilization in student hour terms and the denominator could be redefined as such. More generally, the denominator could be defined in terms of any input or output of any production process, and need not only be applied to educational evaluation.

14. This discussion of cost tradeoffs is drawn from Jamison, Fletcher, Suppes, and Atkinson (1976, pp. 236-238), which contains a somewhat more extended discussion.

Chapter II

COST ANALYSIS: SPECIAL PROBLEMS

Although the basic methodology for the analysis of educational system costs has been presented in the previous chapter, it is important to realize that a cost analysis is not necessarily a straightforward, programmable task. In many ways such an analysis is an art, not a science, that requires ingenuity, as well as expertise and careful thought. In this chapter we examine some special problems related to cost analysis that should give the reader an idea of why this is so and of what some of the more important judgmental aspects are. Section 1 looks at the question of shadow prices for certain inputs, explaining why prices may be an inadequate estimate of true economic costs in some instances; Section 2 briefly examines the relationship of the project planner and the project manager with regard to cost analysis; Section 3 discusses some of the more serious problems related to errors in cost estimation; Section 4 raises some of the problems of system finance that relate to an analysis of costs; and finally, Section 5 summarizes and concludes.

1. TREATMENT OF SHADOW PRICES

When analyzing the costs of project resources, it is most common to use the prices of these various resources as a measure of their value. Prices, however, do not always reflect the true economic value of a resource. In a sense, we have already seen this in the case of expenditures on capital resources. If a piece of capital equipment with a lifetime of ten years is purchased for a project for $1000, the real economic cost in annual terms is *not* $100 a year, but is a somewhat higher figure that reflects the opportunities lost for utilizing that initial $1000 over a ten-year period. In economics the true cost of a resource is sometimes termed its *shadow price*. Economists consider the true cost of a resource to society (its shadow price) to be the opportunity cost of that resource, that is, the value that resource would have in its best alternative use. This shadow price may or may not the equal to the market price of the resource.[1] In the previous chapter we have, in effect, estimated the shadow price of capital equipment investment through utilization of an appropriate social rate of discount.

In most circumstances it is difficult to determine whether the market price of any given resource represents its true economic value to the society. One means economists use to obtain shadow price estimates is the development of optimization models of the whole economy, or certain sectors of it, usually through the use of linear programming techniques. Generating solutions for these often complex models will yield shadow price estimates for the resources specified in the model; these shadow prices can be compared with the appropriate market prices to see the extent to which the latter reflect the true economic value of any particular resource. (See Goreux and Manne, 1973, for a discussion and application to the Mexican economy, and Bowles, 1969, for a specific application to educational planning in Nigeria.) Unfortunately, the extent to which we can adequately model the complex interactions of a country's economy is still quite limited. Nonetheless, it is possible to make rather simple observations that could give a planner a reasonable idea of the relationship between a resource's market price and shadow price; this could have substantial practical implications for the initiation of an instructional technology project. Below we will examine these implications in terms of two resources that can significantly affect the evaluation of an instructional technology project: teachers and foreign exchange.

TEACHER PRICES

In a market-based economy, the price the market sets on a resource will equal the shadow price of that resource only if the market is in equilibrium. If there is a surplus of a particular resource, say teachers, then the price charged in the market, in this case the teacher's salary, is an overestimate of the true cost to the economy of employing an individual as a teacher.[2] Given this situation, if one used the market price of teachers in comparing the cost of an instructional technology system to that of a traditional direct teaching system, where the latter is more labor-intensive (utilizing more or better paid teachers), one would be showing the instructional technology project in a more favorable light than is actually the case; that is, actually, the true economic cost to society of using the direct teaching system is less than calculated, given a teacher surplus situation.

The reverse would be true if there were a teacher shortage. The salaries paid to teachers would underestimate their true economic value, and therefore the same project comparison would make the instructional technology system less favorable than the situation warranted. In some respects, educational planners may take this into account in an intuitive way when, for example, they reason that given a teacher surplus, they should make more extensive use of the traditional system, as opposed to initiating an instructional technology project, or when they reason conversely in the case of a teacher shortage. It is interesting to note that since many developing countries face teacher surpluses in urban areas and teacher shortages in rural areas, instructional technology projects are less attractive in the urban regions and even more attractive in the rural ones than a cost comparison based on market prices would indicate.

It is important to point out that the analysis above has significant equity implications. Despite the fact that the market price may not reflect true economic costs to the society of a particular resource, the market price is what is paid for the resource. This means that in the case of a surplus, teachers are being paid more than their economic value to society, and given a fixed economic pie at any given point in time, this implies that other individuals are receiving less than they deserve. The converse is true in a teacher shortage situation; in this case teachers are paid less than their economic value to society. In both instances serious questions of fairness are raised.

The use of shadow prices as opposed to market prices is not without distributional consequences as well, despite its being the best figure for economic efficiency considerations. For example, given a teacher surplus situation which would reflect an artificially inflated teacher wage rate, perhaps due to union pressure or government fiat, one might reasonably decide to expand the direct teaching system, as opposed to utilizing an equally effective, equally costly (in market price terms), instructional technology system. This would be the proper move in terms of economic efficiency, since if the technology system was equally, or even slightly more, costly in terms of market price than the direct teaching system, the latter would have a lower true economic cost than the former, since the teachers' market price is greater than their shadow price in a surplus situation. However, this would mean expanding the number of teachers hired, which in turn means paying even more individuals than previously a wage rate greater than their true economic value to society and consequently, given a fixed economic pie, paying others in the system less than they merit.

FOREIGN CURRENCY PRICES

Similar problems are encountered in examining another "resource," quite significant in instructional technology projects, namely, foreign currency. Many such projects are capital intensive, and moreover, the capital products utilized may not be produced within the nation developing the project, but must be purchased on the world market. Thus instructional projects are often more foreign exchange intensive than traditional direct teaching systems. The question then arises as to what is the true cost to the country's economy of purchasing goods on the international market.

Again, normally the view taken in costing projects is that the "price" of foreign currency, reflected in the market exchange rate, is the appropriate means for translating imported resources into value terms. However, the market for foreign currency, like that for any other resource (for example, teachers, as discussed above) may not be in equilibrium. In such cases the market price of foreign currency will not be equal to its shadow price, which is its true cost to the economy.

Suppose a country's currency is overvalued on the world market; an indication that this may be so is the existence of a "black market" for currency, as in India, where one can obtain a higher exchange rate than the official rate for foreign currency. In such a case there is a shortage of foreign currency in the country, usually accompanied by government rationing of it. The official exchange rate is thus lower than it should be to represent the true economic value of foreign currency to the economy. In such a case, a relatively foreign exchange intensive instructional technology project will appear less expensive than it really is to the economy, if one simply uses the official exchange rate to cost imported resources. The reverse would be true if the official exchange rate were pegged too high.

Again, it must be recognized that fixing an exchange rate at a different level than the market would warrant has income distribution consequences in addition to the economic efficiency considerations discussed above. When the exchange rate is pegged too low, the government is, in effect, subsidizing those importers to whom it allocates the right to purchase foreign exchange. (See Balassa, 1974, for a more technical discussion of the shadow price of foreign exchange in project evaluation.)

RESOURCE TAXES

Taxes should also be mentioned in this section since they, like deviation of actual from shadow prices, also cause the apparent price of a resource to differ from its actual price to the economy. This occurs when the country in which a project is based places a tax—be it an import tax, a consumption tax or any other type—on the resource we are concerned with. The true economic cost of that resource to the nation is the price before taxes, assuming the market for the resource is approximately in equilibrium, and therefore the shadow price problems discussed earlier do not apply. The tax amounts to a redistribution of resources within the country, from the person or agency paying the tax to those who receive it. This has great significance for most instructional technology projects, which often utilize heavily taxed capital goods, especially imported ones, though a Ministry of Education may well have to pay the tax out of its budget to utilize a taxed resource. Nonetheless, the true economic costs that should be used in the project evaluation are those based on resource prices *before* taxes.

DISCUSSION

In the analysis of the costs of ongoing technology projects and project planning that follows this chapter, we unfortunately do not incorporate most of the points raised in this section. This should not be construed as indicating that these points are merely esoteric considerations that have no practical value in project planning. Usually information available to project evaluators, especially those from another country, is insufficiently detailed to allow any precise estimate of the extent to which shadow prices of resources may differ from market prices. However, to the project planner in a country, such estimates are possible, even if only on an intuitive level, and need to be taken into account in a comparative evaluation of alternative instructional strategies. It is probably beyond the power of most of these individuals to act to make the market price more truly reflect economic value for example, by changing the wage offered to teachers or by influencing decisions on foreign currency exchange rates, but they still may make relative project evaluations based on true economic costs, making judgments as to the extent of disequilibrium in the market for any particular resource. Squire and van der Tak (1975) provide a valuable general discussion of how to incorporate shadow prices into project appraisals and, in particular, they discuss the use of shadow prices to assess the income distributional consequences of projects.

2. COST ANALYSIS FOR THE HIGHER LEVEL VERSUS LOWER LEVEL DECISION MAKER

The perspective of an individual working at a level high enough that he or she evaluates projects in their entirety differs from that of the project manager working in an operational setting, who manages the project in terms of budget, cash flow and internal resource allocation considerations.

One problem is obvious from the definitional distinction made between these two types of individuals—evaluations of alternative instructional strategies made by the manager will not necessarily be the optimal ones in terms of the society as a whole. Examples of this problem are probably familiar to most observers of instructional technology projects (or any other large system, for that matter). For instance, in the Ivory Coast, which is instituting an extensive instructional television system at the primary school level, many areas are without electricity and thus rely on a rather expensive battery system to power the television receivers. There has been a number of reports that localities with available mainline current still utilize the much more expensive battery power source, simply because batteries are supplied at no cost to the schools by the project's central administration, while electricity charges for the use of mainline current come out of the school's budget.

There appear to be two primary strategies for resolving this type of difficulty. The first would be to take all such evaluational decisions out of the hands of the manager, and leave them to the higher level decision maker. This approach is totally impractical in that it requires too much work for the planning office, and often leads to frustration on the part of the project manager who wants to have a responsible, decision-making position. Further, the project manager usually has a much greater awareness of the specifics of any particular situation than does the planner, and thus may have a better knowledge base on which to make a decision.

The second, and probably more sensible, strategy to handle this problem is for the higher level decision maker to attempt to structure the budgetary incentives in such a way that the project manager is induced to make optimal decisions. To do this is obviously somewhat complicated. Nevertheless, from the Ivory Coast example given above we see that it is not simply a two-level dilemma but that the high and low distinction is a relative one—at each level the decision maker must properly structure the incentives for those to whom he or she delegates decision-making power.[3] This type of solution has worked to some extent in many private sector businesses; in fact, there is some literature in the operations research, systems analysis, and business management areas dealing with how to structure such incentives in a variety of situations.

It should be stressed that although it may be quite difficult to structure the constraints on lower level decision makers so that they always choose optimally, much can be accomplished by education and open communications between higher and lower level decision makers. Sometimes individuals make poor choices because they are unaware of the proper considerations in project evaluation decisions. Sometimes too, individuals make a poor choice knowing that their choice is a poor one from a higher level perspective, but they make it anyway because they see that the success criteria for their positions are structured to make that poor choice accord with their own personal interests. In the latter case it may well be that individuals would go to higher level management and explain why they think the incentives should be structured differently in order for them to make better decisions, if they believed that those above them would be responsibe to their suggestions. In the former case, the education of lower level management concerning the best way to conceive of costs, effects, and benefits, might aid substantially in generating better decisions.

This report is chiefly concerned with cost analysis from the perspective of a high level decision maker; the primary consideration in this chapter, and in those that follow, is the determination of the true economic costs of the project. Nonetheless, as implied by the preceding discussion, the actual decision-making structure of any particular project deserves careful attention. It is insufficient for the project planner to choose to implement the best alternative instructional strategy if, once that project is initiated, the decision-making environment in which the project manager operates consistently encourages him or her to make suboptimal decisions.

3. ERRORS IN COST ESTIMATION

In undertaking a cost analysis one must be aware not only of the correct methodological approach but also of sources of errors—and their potential magnitude—in cost estimation. In this section we take a brief look at the types of errors that commonly pose problems to a cost analysis of an instructional technology system and at what can be done to minimize them.

At the outset, it is useful to distinguish between two types of cost analyses: *historical* cost analyses, which examine the past, already incurred, costs of a system, and *projected* cost analyses, which develop estimates of future system costs. Most cost studies involve both types of analysis, following a succession of steps: first, the historical costs of a system are studied; second, the historical relationship between these costs and the system variables that influence them is specified; and third, future system costs are projected based on hypotheses concerning the future configuration of cost-influencing system variables. The potential sources for error may be different at each step in the cost analysis.

A potentially major source of error is initially encountered in attempting to put together existing cost data that will give an accurate historical portrait of system costs. In all likelihood it is not that the cost data available are incorrect, although this is possible, but that the available cost information is, in a sense, disguised. Levin (1974), in an excellent article on cost-effectiveness evaluation as applied to education in general, points out that the collection of cost data relevant to evaluation is rarely built into a project. Cost information systems, if they even exist, are usually designed for accounting and managerial control purposes, and the expense categories utilized are often quite different from the functional classification needed for system evaluation. Many significant costs of the total system may not even be included in the project's budget; in the case of an instructional technology system, relevant system costs may be borne by foreign governments or international aid agencies, by other ministries within the country (such as those responsible for radio and television communications), by other departments within the education ministry (especially some of the central administration costs), or by other sectors of the economy or private individuals (as in the case of "donated" transmission time, facilities, or the efforts of individuals). Furthermore, even when good cost information systems exist, they are frequently subject to change over time, may not be comparable with other cost data collection systems that contain cost information relevant to the project evaluation, and always need to be corrected for inflation induced changes in real costs. Even the most expert cost analyst will find that he or she has to spend a great deal of time in making adjustments to the cost data available to correct for the data deficiencies mentioned above. As Fisher (1971, p. 143) suggests in a very thorough discussion of cost analysis applied to national defense systems, "what is required is ingenuity, persistence, and just plain hard work."[4]

A problem related to those already discussed enters in the second step of the cost analysis in which the analyst develops the relationship between the historical costs of the system and those characteristics of the system that affected the magnitude of the costs incurred. In an instructional technology system such variables would include the number of students served by the system, the number of hours of programming produced annually, the number of hours broadcast annually, the lifetime of instructional programs, the geographical area covered, the power source used for television receivers, etc. (see Chapter IV for a fuller discussion of these variables and their relationship to system costs). Fisher (1971, p. 131) points out the data collection problem aspect of this endeavor, in that

> the analyst must not only collect historical *cost* data in the right format. He must also obtain information on quantities, physical and performance characteristics, activity rates, and other types of cost-generating variables—all of which must be matched specifically to the cost data points.
>
> Sometimes this is difficult because information on the cost-generating variables must be extracted from different sets of records than those containing the cost data. And differing sets of records are often compiled on different principles.

Further, even with an accurate matching of historical costs to the relevant cost-generating system characteristics, the estimated relationship between the two is necessarily an approximation and is, thus, subject to error.

The final step of the cost analysis process will not only reflect (and perhaps magnify) the errors associated with the prior stages of the analysis but may also introduce new, and probably greater, errors into the study. The essential problem faced is the obvious one—future projections of any sort are fraught with uncertainty. The first part of this third step involves projecting the levels of those cost-influencing system variables that will be required for the system to function according to the present plans for the future shape of the system. To the extent that these plans for the future are modified, or are subject to error, the projections of future costs will be inaccurate. Further, many aspects of these plans depend on future environmental factors that may not be subject to control by the project, such as the birth rate, the propensity of individuals to take schooling, or the availability of instructional and technical personnel.

Once the required future levels of the cost-influencing variables are determined, it is necessary to relate these to future system costs. The cost-estimating relationships derived in the second step of the cost analysis process usually form the basis for such projections, but again there are problems that can lead to erroneous projections. First, there is always a danger in extrapolating beyond the range of the historical experience; that is, the relationships between system resource requirements (and therefore costs) and the key structural characteristics of the system that were observed in the past may not be identical in the future. The average relationships that hold in the past are usually easier to observe than the marginal ones. Yet the marginal relationships are most relevant to future projections in that, for example, one needs to know how system resource requirements, the need for teachers and types of programs, will change in the future as students are added to the system. This problem is not usually as great for educational systems as it is for manufacturing systems, since the configuration of the latter as it expands or contracts may be changed to maximize productivity, while in educational systems we (perhaps unfortunately) usually determine resource configurations by convention or fiat; nonetheless this problem should not be neglected.

Second, given that one has projected the future levels of cost-influencing system variables and has translated these to the physical resources required by the system, it is then necessary to convert these resource needs to costs. Here enters one of the more serious and difficult to deal with sources of error, the estimation of the future prices, in real terms (corrected for inflation), of the resources needed for system operation. The costs of technologies are quite difficult to project due to innovations and changes in both supply and demand conditions. A somewhat more tractable, but nonetheless difficult task, is to estimate accurately the salaries (again, in real terms) of personnel, such as teachers. Historical trends, though far from infallible, may serve as a guide.[5]

We have seen that there appears to be significant potential for errors at all stages in the cost analysis. A final point that should be made relevant to sources of error concerns a usually overlooked, but valid, criticism levied by Carnoy and Levin (1975) in an article that specifically focuses on instructional technology system evaluation. They refer to the "first law" which James Q. Wilson (1973, p. 138) set out as applicable to all cases of social science evaluation of public policy, namely that "[a]ll policy interventions in social problems produce the intended effect—*if* the research is carried out by those implementing the policy of their friends."[6] Carnoy and Levin translate this to the evaluation of instructional technology systems by pointing out that a good many of the authors of such evaluations have close contacts with the funding agencies supporting such projects, and "often their evaluations have been sponsored directly by the agencies and personnel who have planned, funded, and implemented the particular educational technology that is being reviewed." They go on to say that this sort of activity often represents the "dominant professional concern" of the evaluator, and although Carnoy and Levin do not equate expertise with bias (and do explicitly recognize the advantages inherent in expertise and close associations with a project), they suggest that many such evaluators tend to give the "benefit of the doubt" to the technology project; it is not that such evaluators are "overtly partisan," but that in their examination of system costs (and effectiveness), they tend to have an implicitly favorable attitude towards technology that causes them to deal· with the previously discussed potential sources for error in a way which understates the true costs of the technology system.[7]

Despite the knowledge available or the potential sources for error in cost analysis, as has been discussed, it is difficult to assess the general magnitude of the errors involved, and the relative importance of the various possible sources of error. This is not too surprising considering that resources are usually devoted to only one cost analysis of any particular system and detailed cost analyses are a relatively recent addition to instructional technology system evaluation. Consequently, different cost studies of the same system are not available to compare nor has sufficient time elapsed to examine the accuracy of recently made cost projections for the few projects for which they are available. Nonetheless, costing experience in other areas, such as defense systems, which have been more closely studied, provides some approximate guides.

Fisher (1971) compares the costs of defense systems made during the conceptual phase of development with those made of the same system at a much later stage of the program. He reports that even after adjusting for price level changes, the latter cost estimates are 2 or 3 times the former, with the ratios for hardware requirements in the later evaluations reported by one study ranging from .7 to 7 times the estimates made by earlier studies. Jamison (1972) reports that other analyses of capital intensive public sector projects in the United States indicate cost overruns of initial estimates by factors of 3 or 4. Fisher suggests that as far as'the sources of these errors is concerned, the misestimation of future system resource requirements is 5 to 10 times more important than misspecification of the cost estimating relationships. Although Fisher does not believe that bias is an important source of error, the consistent *underestimation* of system costs lends some credence to Carnoy (1975) and Carnoy and Levin (1975); both provide examples of cost underestimates in instructional technology evaluations that they feel reflect the "benefit of the doubt" type bias.[8]

The sources of potential error are many and the potential extent of inaccuracy may be significant. Unfortunately, there is not much detailed advice that can be given to the cost analyst, other than to be aware of the possible problems and as Fisher (1971, p. 157) exhorts: "Be careful—use good judgment!" Suggestions to improve cost information collection systems are worthy of serious attention (see, for example, Coleman and Karweit, 1968), and more care needs to be given to tying these systems to evaluation needs. One very useful suggestion, often ignored, is to collect and retain cost information on as disaggregated a basis as possible. Nonetheless the substantial expense of a new information system must be evaluated itself in terms of whether the additional benefits accruing from it are worth the additional costs.

It is probably a good idea for the cost analyst of an instructional technology system to be conservative, that is, to err on the side of overestimation, in costing a new technology system. This is especially true given the likelihood of cost underestimation we have seen and the probability that the costs of the new technology system will be compared to those of a traditional system on which more reliable historical cost data exist. The analyst is well advised to engage in and report sensitivity analyses of his or her cost estimates, that is, the sensitivity of cost estimates to small changes in the various assumptions he or she must necessarily make in the analysis. Further, it must be realized that cost analyses are perhaps most useful as management tools, and as such, should be tied directly to the decision-making process, as well as be continually modified and revised in the light of new information.

Finally, we should emphasize that cost analysis is much more subject to error, and even irrelevance, if it is considered to be a separate component of a project evaluation. Fisher (1971, p. 304) clearly points out the dangers of such an approach:

> To be effective, the cost analyst must function as an integral part of the systems analysis interdisciplinary study team. He must be on hand from the start to help in the difficult task of structuring the problem to be analyzed, and to assist in the formulation of questions and hypotheses to be examined. Only then will his input to the total analytical process be relevant. Cost estimates can be relevant only when they reflect the consequences of an appropriately defined decision or choice.

It may be surprising to many that such care needs to be taken in what is often considered one of the most straightforward aspects of a project's evaluation and management. However, it should be evident from this discussion that in many respects cost analysis is more an art than a science and needs to be undertaken in this light.

4. PROBLEMS OF FINANCE

An issue which is conceptually separate from that of the aggregate level of, and uses for, a project's resources, which are reflected in cost functions, is that of who bears the costs. This is the problem of project finance. For major education projects the following broad categories include most potential sources of finance:

> multilateral and bilateral international donor agencies,
> central governments,
> local governments and communities, and
> students and their families.

Understanding the sources of finance of ongoing projects and planning finances carefully for future projects are important for at least three reasons. First, projects must cover their costs: the question of which project configurations are, and which are not, financially feasible is an important one. Second, the structure of the financing will affect project development and utilization through its incentive effects. If, for example, an international donor agency will finance only capital equipment, local project managers may have a strong incentive to design a more capital-intensive project than prevailing prices would indicate to be optimal. Or, to take a second example, if a central government requires that local communities or students bear a large fraction of the costs (in money or in kind), they can expect that utilization will be lower than if the central government provided more subsidy. This may be desirable or undesirable; the point is simply that these incentive effects are apt to be there and, perhaps, to be strong. Finally, the financing structure will have important implications for the income distributional effects of a project. The overall distributional impact of the project will be determined by the answers to the two questions: Who benefits? Who pays? Study of system finance can provide an answer to the second of these distributional questions.

Evaluations of the funding sources, motivational impact and distributional impact of major educational projects have, to the authors' knowledge, rarely been undertaken. We feel that further research along these lines has high priority in light of the increased concern on the part of a number of governments and lending organizations—for example, the World Bank and the Agency for International Development—for distributional questions. We offer, however, a number of tentative observations on the matter of finance.

1. The typical terms of repayment for loans from an international donor agency entail a substantial grant component. By grant component we mean the difference between the value of the loan received and the value of the repayment stream required to pay back the loan.[9]

In order to calculate the grant value of a loan, one must calculate the value of the repayment stream. This requires knowledge of the precise terms of the loan and of an annual discounting factor to convert future repayments into their "present" value so they can be compared to the loan. This annual discounting factor is the sum of two components—the rate of inflation of the currency in which the loan must be repaid and the social discount rate of the recipient country.[10] The rate of inflation of the repayment currency is clearly important; the more rapidly the currency inflates, the lower will be the *real* value of future repayments. This is exactly analogous to a homeowner's repayment of a mortgage; his or her payments are fixed in, say, dollar terms and if the dollar is inflating then the real value of the payments decreases and hence he or she benefits. The social discount rate for a country is a planning concept that allows comparison of (inflation-adjusted) resources at the present with resources in the future. Most individuals (and countries) have positive social discount rates; that is, they prefer resources now rather than in the future. A country with a social discount rate of 10% would be indifferent between $1,000,000 now and $1,100,000 one year from now, assuming no inflation. For the purpose of computing the grant component of a loan, a discounting factor of at least 9% should be used to reflect a minimal inflation rate for hard currencies; typical values of social discount rates could take the discounting factor to a level of 15% or more.

In Table II.1 we show how the grant component of a loan varies with the annual discounting factor for loans with repayment terms customarily used by the U.S. Agency for International Development. Footnote 'a' of the table states these terms. At a minimal discounting factor of 7.5% (reflecting only inflation, and probably a low estimate for that), Table II.1 shows that the grant component of an AID loan is 57%; if the discounting factor is 15%, the grant component is 82%. Another way of putting this is that if the discounting factor is 15%, the recipient country would be indifferent between receiving a loan on the AID terms and receiving an outright grant whose value was 82% of the value of the loan.

The grant component of these AID and other, similar, international development loans is thus quite high; exactly how high is determined by the (uncertain) inflation rate of the repayment currency and the recipient country's social rate of discount.

2. A second observation on finance is that existing patterns of finance for major educational projects can often impart a capital-intensive bias to them. If international loans or grants are tied to equipment purchase or major construction activities then, from the viewpoint of the local planner, these items have little scarcity value. He will tend to treat them as relatively costless in contrast to, for example, studio personnel whose salaries must be paid out of a local budget. Though this might be rational from the local perspective, it can lead to major misallocations of resources. The authors are aware of one example where new studio facilities were constructed with

TABLE II.1

Calculated Grant Component of AID
Hard Currency Loans[a]

Annual Discounting Factor[b]	A Present Value of Interest Payments[c]	B Present Value of Loan Repayments[d]	C(=A+B) Present Value of All Payments	Percent Grant[e]
5%	$156	$480	$636	36%
7.5	139	291	430	57
10	125	184	309	69
12.5	112	121	233	77
15	102	82	184	82
17.5	93	57	150	85
20	85	41	126	87

a. The entries in the columns labelled A, B, and C are the present values of future repayments of a loan of value $1000 to a recipient country. The standard AID repayment schedule is as follows: (i) For the first ten years after receipt of the loan the recipient country repays the U.S. accumulated interest semiannually; the rate of interest is 2% per annum. (ii) Loan repayment begins after ten years and the interest rate charged increases to 3%; the repayment schedule calls for equal semiannual payments over a period of thirty years.
b. To compute the grant component of a loan it is necessary to have a discounting factor for future repayments. This discounting factor is the sum of two items—the expected rate of inflation of the dollar and the real social discount rate of the recipient country. For simplicity of computation and because of lack of alternative information, we assume a constant discounting factor.
c. The entries in this column are the present values of the interest payment during the ten-year period prior to commencing repayment of the loan, assuming the initial value of the loan to be $1000.
d. The entries in this column are the present values of the 30-year loan repayment stream, which begins ten years after granting the loan, assuming the initial value of the loan to be $1000.
e. This column indicates the percentage of a loan that is actually a grant; it equals 1000 minus the value of column C, divided by 1000, expressed as a percentage. The grant component increases to a high fraction of the loan as future repayments become more heavily discounted.

international funds even though perfectly adequate studios already existed. They are aware of numerous examples of studios more elaborately equipped than appears to be necessary for instructional television production. We expect that some of the overemphasis on TV in comparison to radio results from donor agency willingness to fund capital costs.

In the terminology of the previous chapter, most international finance of instructional technology is restricted to capital costs, particularly fixed capital costs. (Some financing goes for variable capital costs, such as receivers.) Mechanisms should be sought to allow international finance to cover more in the way of recurrent and variable costs;[11] once these mechanisms are available, lending agencies should consider explicitly the question of whether and how best to control utilization of grant and loan funds.

3. A third point concerning the financial aspects of instructional technology projects is that they are often claimed to have important favorable redistributional effects. The bases for this claim are, first, that for a given level of expenditure the technologies can provide relatively better instruction in rural areas (and in the poorer parts of urban areas), and second, that the incidence of cost of technological approaches to instruction is more progressive than for traditional approaches. We believe that these claims are probably correct for most, but not all, existing projects and that with proper design the redistributive potential of investment in instructional technologies could be enhanced. We stress, however, that almost no data exist on this increasingly important matter.[12]

The preceding three points on the nature and impact of financing mechanisms for instructional technology systems point clearly to the need for more research. Though it would be desirable to know more about the pedagogical impact and cost of instructional technology systems, much valuable data are available and have been analyzed. Not so for finance. We have almost no empirical information on the distributional impact of existing instructional technology systems, on the extent to which differential subsidization of system components distorts incentives, on how varying financial structures do (could) affect demand and utilization. Even limited research efforts should provide valuable information.

5. SUMMARY

In Chapter I we assumed that the information utilized in a cost analysis would be the market prices paid for the particular resources employed in the project. In Section 1 of this chapter we examined why this may not be so. In some situations market prices fail to reflect the true economic value of a resource (that is, its shadow price) and consequently, suboptimal decisions could be made when evaluating alternative instructional strategies, if market prices of resources are utilized unquestioningly. In particular, the wages of teachers may *overstate* their economic value in urban areas (where teacher surpluses are common) and *understate* their value in rural areas (where teachers shortages are common), and the market price of foreign exchange may often *understate* its economic value.

Section 2 discussed why the methodological considerations developed in the previous sections are insufficient to insure adequate project evaluation and decision-making. Care must be taken to see that those individuals invested with decision-making responsibility have adequate knowledge and incentives to make the correct choices.

In Section 3 we looked at the possible errors in cost estimation and their likely sources. Cost assessment and cost projection are, in some senses, arts rather than sciences and require ingenuity as well as careful judgment by the analyst. Historical experience in education and other sectors suggests that costs are *almost always* underestimated in a project's planning and early implementation stages. Thus, it is reasonable to estimate the costs of an instructional technology project conservatively, that is, to attempt to err on the side of overestimation. It is also worthwhile to examine explicitly the sensitivity of estimated project costs to alternative assumptions about project resource requirements.

Finally, in Section 4 we discussed problems of evaluating and planning for the financing of education projects. There is reason to believe that instructional technology potentially redistributes social resources more equitably than does traditional instruction; little is known empirically, however, about the actual incidence of costs or benefits from existing projects. Methodologies for evaluation and planning must, in addition to examining the distributional impact of a project and its financing, also examine the effects of financing on the motivations of local decision makers.

In what follows, we will apply the concepts and methodology developed here to the evaluation of costs for instructional radio and television projects. Part 2 will discuss results from cost evaluations of ongoing projects and applications to the planning of new projects. Part 3 contains seven cost case studies upon which much of the material of Part 2 is based.

NOTES

1. The shadow price concept is closely related to the opportunity cost concept developed in the previous chapter, considering opportunity cost in the sense of the true cost of a resource to the economy as a whole (not in terms of costs in a narrower context, for example, the opportunity costs to a particular decision maker, as considered in Chapter I). Although in the discussion above we are considering opportunity costs to the economy (i.e., shadow prices) for resources that do have a market price, the concept is also important for resources that do *not* have an explicit price. For example, although the costs of student time in an educational system are usually not priced, they do represent an opportunity cost both to the individual student and to the society in terms of the income the student foregoes by participating in the educational program and the consequent employment productivity of that student that the society foregoes. Likewise, resources which are contributed to an educational program (for example, facilities, people's time) represent a real cost to the economy to the extent that they have alternative uses which are valued. In any comparison of alternative courses of action these costs should be explicitly estimated, as well as possible, and included in the examination of the differences in costs between the options being considered. In the cost analyses presented in Chapter III and the case studies, this dimension of costs will be considered only to the extent that it contributes to the production, distribution, and reception costs of the particular instructional radio or television system (for example, in the Mexican *Telesecundaria* case study, donated reception and transmission facilities are

costed). It should be noted that consideration of the opportunity costs of student time can often make an instructional technology system more attractive (especially a distance learning system) if it uses less student time than does a traditional system, and if the student's time has alternative productive value.

2. One way of seeing why this is so is to realize that the existence of a teacher surplus generally implies that the alternative employment opportunities for prospective teachers are at lower wages than those offered to teachers; if not, teachers would take other positions and a surplus would no longer exist. Thus, the opportunity cost to the economy, which is the real definition of a shadow price, of employing an individual as a teacher is necessarily lower than the teacher's wage. It should be noted that the reasoning above implies two assumptions: first, that wages reflect marginal productivity, for if such were not the case, it would not make sense to talk of someone's alternative wage as the opportunity cost to the economy; and second, that individuals are by and large income maximizers, for if this were the case there might, for example, be a surplus of teachers even if their alternative wage was higher than that offered to teachers—if these assumptions do not hold, the existence of a surplus (or shortage) does not give us any information on the relationship of market price to shadow price since it would be possible to have a teacher surplus with a market price lower than the shadow price.

3. The project planner versus manager distinction is applicable to the discussion of shadow price in the previous section in the sense that a person in the planning ministry would want to encourage an educational project manager to use the true economic costs (shadow price) of resources in comparing and evaluating competing alternatives, even though it is the actual market price for the particular resource that would usually be paid from the manager's budget. Similarly, the distinction is relevant to some aspects of the finance discussion in the following section; many instructional technology projects in developing nations are subsidized to some extent by foreign governments or foreign aid agencies and these external agents should ideally structure incentives to encourage the project manager to consider alternatives from the perspective of total world costs, that is, not just from the perspective of costs incurred by the nation in which the project is being developed.

4. Fisher (1971, p. 142) estimates that even under the best circumstances cost analysts must "spend at least half their time struggling with the data problem."

5. It should be noted that in comparing the costs of a relatively capital intensive instructional technology system with those of a relative more labor-intensive traditional educational system, the consideration of future real price changes, corrected for inflation can be quite important. Historically, we have seen the real prices of many technologies fall over recent years, while the real wages of teachers have increased; if this trend were to continue, as we expect it to, the use of present prices to project future costs may seriously *overstate* the costs of the technology system and *understate* the costs of the traditional system.

6. Carnoy and Levin point out the ramifications of the "law" for the analysis of instructional technology system effectiveness, as well as costs, although the former aspect will not be discussed here. We should also mention that Carnoy and Levin do explicitly acknowledge the relevance of Wilson's (1973, p. 138) "second law" to their own evaluation, namely that "[n] o policy intervention in social problems produce the intended effect—*if* the research is carried out by independent third parties, especially those skeptical of the policy."

7. Carnoy and Levin's criticism is closely related to a problem that is unfortunately too common in cost analyses. It is often politically desirable, for example, for factions within a Ministry of Education who desire to initiate a particular project, to under-

estimate the project's costs. This problem is also related to the planner-manager discussion in the preceding section, and its resolution probably requires some restructuring of incentives as discussed previously.

8. Although evidence for the extent of error in the cost analysis of instructional technology projects is scarce some information exists. Carnoy and Levin (1975) point out that Speagle's (1972) estimates of the costs of the El Salvador project are almost 50% lower than those generated in this study (see Chapters III and XII), while recent, not yet published, evidence suggests that a detailed cost study done in the planning stages of the Ivory Coast ITV project underestimated costs by almost 70%.

9. We neglect in this discussion the loss in purchasing power that may result from a loan's being tied to purchases in the lending country.

10. This discussion is oriented toward predicting the grant component. Due to the difficulty in predicting exchange rates and based upon an assumption that changes in exchange rates solely reflect relative changes in inflation rates it is appropriate to utilize the inflation rate of the repayment currency. However, if one is calculating the grant component of a loan that has been repaid, it would be appropriate to use the inflation rate of the recipient country and the rate of change of exchange rates between the recipient and donor country currencies.

11. An AID loan to the elementary/middle school project of the Korean Educational Development Institute (Chapter VII) is an example of one such mechanism. The Koreans wished to put the loan in a bank and use the interest payments to finance recurrent expenses. AID consented, though apparently with some questioning on the part of their auditors.

12. Klees (1975, Chapter VI) discusses the impact on achievement inequality of the Mexican *Telesecundaria* from several perspectives. His most important conclusion from the point of view of policy was that, because of its presently lower cost than traditional instruction, *Telesecundaria* could be more inequality reducing. However, it should also be noted, that the financing of the *Telesecundaria*, as discussed in Klees (1975) and in Chapter XI of this report, appears to be less egalitarian than the financing of the traditional Mexican educational system.

PART TWO

COST ANALYSIS OF INSTRUCTIONAL

TECHNOLOGY PROJECTS

Once heard claims that various instructional technologies would quickly and dramatically influence educational practice now seem far off the mark; there have, nonetheless, been increasing numbers of educational authorities actively exploring the operational use of technology in education. One important rationale for the increased use of instructional technologies is that a large number of research studies conducted over the past several decades, as well as recent experience on an operational level in many countries, have demonstrated the pedagogical effectiveness of many of these technologies. Although, as indicated previously, our primary concern here is to examine the cost side of the picture, we will briefly review the literature on the effectiveness of instructional radio and television.

Both instructional radio (IR) and instructional television (ITV) have been utilized and tested in a wide variety of situations, although adequate evaluations of IR have been less common than those of ITV. Most comparative effectiveness studies come from the developed nations, in spite of the fact that perhaps the most widespread utilization of IR and ITV occurs in less developed countries.

The relative effectiveness of IR has been surveyed several times in recent years. Jamison, Suppes, and Wells (1974, pp. 30-31) review two recent surveys (see also Schramm, 1977), and report:

Two surveys review information relevant to the effectiveness of IR. One is Section VI of Chu and Schramm's (1967) comprehensive review of learning by television. The second is a position paper by Forsythe (1970) that, in an earlier form, was prepared for the President's Commission on Instructional Technology. Sources of further information on IR may be found in a 432-entry indexed bibliography compiled by

R. Madden (1968), and an early review of research undertaken primarily in the late 1930s and early 1940s may be found in Woelfel and Tyler (1945).

Chu and Schramm (1967) numbered the principal conclusions of their extensive survey. The ones most relevant to IR follow.

1953. Given favorable conditions, pupils can learn from any instructional media that are now available.

1958. The use of visual images will improve learning of manual tasks as well as other learning where visual images can facilitate the association process. Otherwise, visual images may cause distraction and interfere with learning.

1960. Student response is effectively controlled by programmed methods, regardless of the instructional medium.

Their general conclusion is that radio, particularly when appropriately supplemented by visual material, can teach effectively and, for many purposes, as well as other media.

Forsythe (1970) reached a similar conclusion. In summarizing studies of radio's effectiveness he concluded:

Research clearly indicates that radio is effective in instruction. Experimental studies comparing radio teaching with other means or media have found radio as effective as the so-called "conventional methods." Even though radio has been criticized for being only an audio medium, studies have shown that visual elements in learning are not uniformly important. In many educational situations visuals may be more harmful than helpful. Also, the efficiency of combined audio and visual media has been challenged by studies which show that multi-channel communications may not be inherently more effective than single channel presentations.

To support his conclusions, Forsythe listed, among others, studies of Carpenter (1934), Cook and Nemzek (1939), Harrison (1932), Heron and Ziebarth (1946), Lumley (1933), Miles (1940), and Wiles (1940). He also mentioned two experiments by NHK in Japan (NHK 1955, 1956) that favored radio. Forsythe, along with Chu and Schramm, concluded 'that IR compares well with TI (Traditional Instruction). It should be kept in mind, though, that most of these studies are old, and that in many of them the statistical controls were imperfect, the amount of instruction carried by IR was small, or the classroom teacher did participate in the program. Nonetheless, we believe that the overall conclusions of Chu and Schramm and of Forsythe are consistent with the available evidence. We also feel that there is substantial value, particularly for developing countries, in obtaining much more extensive evidence on the effectiveness of IR; of particular importance would be experiments using IR to carry the bulk of instruction in one or more subject matters for periods of at least one academic year.

Jamison, Suppes, and Wells (1974, pp. 34-36) also provide us with a review of three surveys of comparative effectiveness studies of ITV. They report as follows:

Chu and Schramm surveyed 421 comparisons of ITV with TI [Traditional Instruction] that are reported in 207 separate studies. . . . Their survey indicates that students at all grade levels learn well from ITV, though this seems somewhat less true for older students than for younger ones . . . [and] . . . that the effectiveness of ITV cuts across virtually every subject matter.

Dubin and Hedley (1969) provided a more detailed survey of the effectiveness of ITV at the college level. They reported on 191 comparisons of which 102 favored ITV and 89 favored TI, although most of the differences were insignificant at standard levels of statistical significance.

An unusually stringent criterion for interpretability of results was utilized by Stickell (1963) in comparing ITV to TI, and it is worth commenting on his survey here. After examining 250 comparisons of ITV to TI Stickell found 10 studies that fully met his requirements for adequate controls and statistical method (interpretability) and 23 that partially met his requirements. Schramm (1973) provides clear tabular summaries of these studies. None of the fully interpretable studies and 3 of the partially interpretable ones showed statistically significant cases favored the ITV group. It should perhaps be noted that when highly stringent controls are imposed on a study, the nature of the controls tends to force the methods of presentation into such similar formats that one can only expect the 'no significant differences' that are in fact found. When ITV is used in a way that takes advantage of the potential the medium offers—as, perhaps, with Sesame Street— we would expect more cases of significant differences between the experimental group and the 'alternative treatment' (for it would not be a 'control' in Stickell's sense) group.

Careful evaluations of the effectiveness of operational instructional technology projects are much rarer than the experimental and quasi-experimental comparisons reported above. Schramm (1977) provides a review and discussion of the results that have been obtained and generally supports the conclusions reached by Jamison, Suppes, and Wells—that is, that radio and television can be used as quite effective vehicles to teach cognitive knowledge. It should be remembered, however, that the transmission of cognitive knowledge is by no means the only purpose of an educational system, and little research has been done to evaluate the other effects that an instructional technology system may have. (Mayo, Hornik and McAnany's [1976] evalua-tion of educational television in El Salvador is an exception; they examine the effects of television and educational reform on student attitudes and aspirations as well as achievements.)

Nonetheless, the demonstrated ability of instructional radio and television (as well as other technologies—see Jamison, Suppes, and Wells, 1974, and Schramm, 1977, for a review) to effectively transmit cognitive skills leads educational decision makers to focus on other criteria, especially system cost considerations, in order to evaluate the reasonability and feasibility of initi-ating an instructional technology system. Historical experience over the last two decades has shown rapidly rising educational system costs for both de-veloping and developed nations. One reason for the observed increasing ex-penditures on education has been large enrollment expansion, especially in developing countries. However, also of great importance, is that, over time, it is becoming more expensive to educate each child in the system.

The increasing costs of educating a student do not appear to be the result of increases in the quality of education offered. On the contrary, it is prob-able that the quality of educational output is at best remaining constant or perhaps even declining (see Woodhall and Blaug, 1968). The most plausible explanation of the increasing costs per student was formalized by Baumol (1967) and stated simply by Coombs (1968, p. 7): "Education's technology, by and large, has made surprisingly little progress beyond the handicraft stage." Essentially, the point is that although the educational process had made little, if any, gains in productivity, most other sectors of the economy have. Relatively progressive industries, using the more advanced technologies, partially determine the salary levels that the less progressive industries will have to attract competent people. Therefore, in general, educational systems have had to pay more over time for the same quality teacher. It has been the hope that innovations in instructional technology can aid the education sector in increasing its productivity along with the more progressive sectors of the economy. Relatively little of the potential of such technologies has yet been realized. However, it is likely that the near future will bring in-creased traditional educational system costs (through rising real costs) relative to instructional technology system costs (through reduction in or mainte-nance of the real costs of various technological alternatives), and thus the pressures to introduce these latter, more capital-intensive, techniques will be increased.

An initial and important step in determining whether or not to introduce an instructional technology system is therefore the determination of its cost. In Part One of this book we developed a methodology with which to ap-proach the cost analysis of educational systems. In Part Two, we now apply this methodology to the examination of the cost structure of instructional radio and television projects, with particular attention to those located in developing countries.[1] Chapter III will look at the costs of a number of on-going projects, most of which we discuss in much more detail in the case studies included in Part Three, while Chapter IV will analyze the costs of instructional technology systems from the perspective of planning new radio or television based educational projects.

NOTE

1. The case studies in this volume are of uses of instructional technology primarily within a school setting. Radio, television, and correspondence have a long history of use for providing formal education outside a traditional school environment through what the British call "distance learning" systems. Jamison (1977a) discusses this use for technology further and provides information on the costs of several systems in low-income countries.

Chapter III

COST EXPERIENCE WITH INSTRUCTIONAL
RADIO AND TELEVISION SYSTEMS

In this chapter we apply the methodology developed in the preceding chapter to analysis of the cost experience of nine specific projects. Four of these are instructional radio projects, in Nicaragua, Mexico (two projects) and Thailand; five of them are instructional television projects, in El Salvador, the United States (two projects), Korea, and Mexico. All but one of these projects utilize the medium within a school setting for elementary and secondary education. The exception is the Stanford Instructional Television which deals with university level education.[1] All of them have been underway long enough to provide ongoing cost information. In all cases, the analysis is based on data subject to substantial error, and our divisions of costs into various categories is sometimes based on incomplete information and hence may be somewhat arbitrary. The reader should view our conclusions as approximations.

To put the costs into a form that permits the projects to be compared with one another, we have done four things. First, we converted all costs into 1972 U.S. dollars by converting from the foreign currency to U.S. currency at the exchange rate prevailing at the time the information was gathered, then used the U.S. GNP deflator to convert to 1972 dollars (see Appendix A for the exchange rates and deflators used). Due to differing relative prices in different countries and exchange rate rigidities, there may be distortions introduced by this procedure (see Vaizey et al., 1972, Chapters 15 and 16). Second, we use the same interest rates (social rate of discount) to evaluate each project. To allow examination of the sensitivity of the conclusions to the rates chosen, we use three values for the interest rate—zero, 7.5% and 15% per year.[2] Third, we have attempted to include and exclude the same items in each cost analysis. We include central administration costs, program production costs, transmission costs, and reception costs. We exclude the costs of teacher retraining and printed material. Fourth, we have assumed common capital lifetimes for all projects—twenty years for buildings and start up costs, ten years for transmission and studio equipment and five years for receivers.

For each project examined we present a brief description and then derive an annualized cost function of the linear form presented in equation 1.2 in Chapter I; that is, we assume there to be a fixed cost, F, a variable cost per student, V_N, and a variable cost per programming hour, V_h, so that total cost, $TC(N, h) = F + V_N N + V_h h$, where N is the number of students using the system and h is the number of programming hours provided in any particular year.[3] This simplified formulation takes *as given* the other cost determining system variables particular to each system, such as the number of grade levels served, the geographical area covered, the fraction of receivers located in electrified areas, the quality of program production, and the average class size. To the extent that we would want to know the sensitivity of a project's costs to changes in the present configuration of these types of variables, more complex cost functions would have had to be estimated, such as those that will be described in Chapter IV for project planning uses.

To obtain the values for F, V_N, and V_h, we allocated each cost into one of six categories: fixed, capital; fixed, current; variable by student, capital; variable by student, recurrent; variable by hour, capital; and variable by hour, recurrent. Capital costs were then annualized using equation I.3 of Chapter I, and the cost function was constructed by letting F equal the sum of all fixed cost components, V_N equal the sum of all variable by student cost components, and V_h equal the sum of all variable by hour cost components.

It should be noted that in some of the cost analyses that follow, the value F is quite low or even zero, as most instructional television and instructional radio system costs are assumed to vary with N and h. More specifically, most production and transmission costs are assumed to vary with h while most reception costs are assumed to vary with N. It is usually only central administration and start up costs (when an estimate of these is available) that are assumed fixed, and sometimes even these may vary with N and h. This assumption is ,somewhat simplistic, but nevertheless, probably reflects the long run picture reasonably accurately; in the short run, for marginal expansion decisions, there may be sufficient excess capacity to increase N or h without increasing all related component costs. However, as the system expands, the excess capacity falls to zero, and all relevant system components need to be increased to allow further expansion (of N or h, for example). Thus the linear function that will be estimated is probably an approximation to what more realistically can be expected to be a step function, which increases in discrete increments as N and h expand to fill the excess system capacity at successive points in time.

In addition to the cost function estimation, three other pieces of cost information will be presented when possible. First, the average cost per student (AC_N) for a particular year of the project will be derived from the cost function. Second, this figure will be compared to the variable cost per student, V_N, to form a ratio, AC_N/V_N. This ratio is presented to give the reader a rough idea of the extent to which the system discussed has achieved the economies of scale available in most instructional television and instructional radio systems in their operations for the particular year in question. AC_N/V_N approaches unity as the system expands to include more students, other things being equal. When AC_N/V_N is large, it indicates that if the system were to increase the number of students enrolled, average costs per student could be decreased substantially by enrollment expansion. Since there is no theoretical upper bound on the ratio AC_N/V_N, it is somewhat difficult to evaluate what it means for a given ratio to be "large," but an idea can be gained from examining this figure for different projects. Third, we also present average cost per student hour of each project, which is probably one of the better measures for comparison between systems, since it takes account of both N and h.[4]

Finally, when sufficient information is available, namely, the time structure of expenditures and student usage, we present selected estimates of the average costs per student from year i to year j (AC_{ij}), a concept that was developed in Section 4 of Chapter I. As discussed in Chapter I, we believe the AC_{ij}'s are a much better summary measure of project costs than that derived from the cost function estimations.

In this chapter, Section 1 will examine each of the four instructional radio projects; Section 2 will examine each of five instructional television projects, and Section 3 will summarize and conclude. A large amount of additional information on all but two of the projects (the Tarahumara radio project in Mexico and the one in Thailand are examined only in this chapter) can be found in the case studies presented in Part Three of this report.

1. INSTRUCTIONAL RADIO PROJECTS

THE NICARAGUAN RADIO MATHEMATICS PROJECT

In early 1975 a group of AID sponsored researchers and mathematics curriculum specialists began working with Nicaraguan counterparts in Masaya, Nicaragua on radio programs to teach elementary school mathematics. The Radio Mathematics Project (RMP) is now near the end of its first year and is reaching approximately 600 first grade students on an experimental basis. During 1976 programming will be extended through the second grade, and a carefully controlled evaluation of a large-scale implementation of the first grade curriculum will be undertaken. Present plans call for continued expansion of curriculum coverage to higher grade levels and for implementation of the radio curriculum throughout Nicaragua.

A paper by Searle, Friend, and Suppes (1975) describes the present status of the project in detail, and of particular importance to other project developers, it emphasizes the psychological principles underlying the project's use of extremely frequent student response as a pedagogical technique. Two other salient features of the RMP that Searle, Friend, and Suppes describe are its heavy use of formative evaluation in curriculum preparation and its concern from the outset with problems of cost and operational implementation of the project results.

In this section overviewing the Radio Mathematics Projects, the authors draw heavily on the introductory material from the case study in this report (see Chapter V) for a description of the project and its research objectives. Results from a cost analysis of the project, reported in Jamison (1974), are then summarized.[5]

The Project. The Radio Mathematics Project assumes responsibility for all of the mathematics instruction children receive. A daily lesson consists of a thirty-minute radio presentation, followed by approximately thirty minutes of teacher directed activities, for which instructions are contained in a teacher's guide developed in the project. No textbooks are used and printed material is limited to a one page worksheet for each child each day. For reasons of cost, the RMP may reduce or eliminate the use of printed worksheets from this original level. All instruction, including the radio lesson, is given in Spanish.

Before the broadcast portion of the lesson the teacher gives each child a worksheet on which the child writes his name and student number, a task that most first graders can learn to do adequately. Then the broadcast lesson is turned on. During each lesson two main characters join with one or two subordinate characters to sing, play and talk mathematics, usually inviting the children to join in. The children are asked to respond orally, physically and in writing, and they do so forty to fifty times during each thirty-minute lesson. Initially the RMP used stories to engage the children and embedded mathematical work in a story context to maintain interest. Early tests of lessons with stories, using kindergarten and first grade children in California and first grade children in Nicaragua, convinced the curriculum developers "that the mathematical activities are intrinsically interesting to the children and do not need story support, as long as the children are asked to respond frequently" (Searle, Friend, and Suppes, 1975, p. 13).

Sometimes children handle concrete materials during the broadcasts—for example, counting or grouping small objects. Dialogue between radio characters introduces new mathematical material and children are asked to respond orally. In later lessons, the same exercises are repeated and the children respond individually on their worksheets.

After the radio transmission, the teacher continues the lesson, following the directions given in the teacher's guide. Usually children continue working on the worksheet during this portion of the lesson. During the experimental phase of the project, worksheets are collected and returned to the project office for analysis.

Research objectives. The research aims of the project can be broadly characterized as falling in three realms: (1) radio and educational achievement, (2) the economics of radio as a technology of instruction and (3) the generalizability of the results to other settings. Among the educational questions of concern are: Can mathematics be taught effectively using radio as the primary source of instruction? How are achievement gains related to student characteristics? How does achievement of students' learning by radio compare with learning in the conventional classroom? How does the instructional program affect student and teacher attitudes towards mathematics, towards school, towards learning by radio? Do attendance and dropout patterns change when radio instruction is introduced in the classroom? Does the failure rate attributable to mathematics change? Does performance in other school subjects change? The bulk of the project's substantial research budget is devoted to seeking at least partial answers to these questions.

The economic aspects of the instructional system are the second major research concern. What are the development costs of the program? What are the operational costs? Can the cost of implementing the system in a different setting be estimated? What are the economic consequences of using radio in the classroom? Is the rate of flow of students through the school system, and hence the per pupil cost of education, affected? What is the cost of each of the components of the system and how is that cost related to its effectiveness? How much teacher training is necessary to maintain an effective level of instruction? How much supplementary material must be prepared for students? How much supervision will teachers need in order to use the radio in the classroom?

The third research area, that of generalizability, is less well defined than the preceding two but is, perhaps, more critical to the ultimate success of the RMP. Even if it turns out that the RMP is a major pedagogical success and that its costs are low, if it is difficult to disseminate its results, the project will have been of limited value. Project developers are thus experimenting with alternative approaches to diffusing the project within Nicaragua, and the Agency for International Development is considering experimenting with its implementation elsewhere.

Cost function for the Radio Mathematics Project. As with the other instructional technology projects to be discussed, the cost function for the RMP will be constructed to give annualized total cost, TC, as a linear function of two independent variables—the number of hours of lessons presented per year, h, and the number of students enrolled in a course, N. Each enrolled student would take seventy-five hours (150 lessons) in a single year's course. The cost function we are assuming has, then, the following form:

$$TC = F + V_N N + V_h h$$

where F, V_N, and V_h are cost parameters, data concerning which are presented in detail in Chapter V.

The first parameter, F, consists of all cost components invariant with respect to hours of programming or student usage, that is, it consists of central project costs:

> F = annualized starting costs + project administration costs
> + (research costs).

Research costs are in parentheses because it is dubious that these general research costs should be included in the Nicaragua cost function. As most of the research covered by these costs has results directed outside Nicaragua, they will be excluded from our total cost equation. On the other hand, we *do* include the cost of formative evaluation research as being directly related to program production. The value of F when capital costs are annualized at 7.5% is $73,400 per year.

The next parameter, V_h, depends on transmission costs and program production costs; it equals the annualized cost of a lesson plus the cost of transmitting it once. The annualized cost of a sesson is $128 at a 7.5% discount rate; the cost of transmission is $13.[6] Thus we have a cost of $141 per lesson per year, or, since each lesson lasts thirty minutes, V_h = $282 per hour of programming per year.

The final cost parameter, V_N, depends only on the cost per enrolled student per year; as estimated, V_N = $3.06/year.

Our final cost equation is, then given by (in dollars per year)

$$TC(N, h) = 73,400 + 282h + 3.06N.$$

Even with between 10,000 and 50,000 users, it can be computed from the above cost function that the average costs per student remain substantially above the marginal cost of $3.06 per student per year. And, because of both high marginal costs per student and high programming costs, the costs of the RMP are substantially higher than for most other radio projects.

Three basic points emerge from the analysis just presented of the costs of the RMP in Nicaragua:

1. The intensive efforts put into program preparation suggest that, unless careful effort is undertaken to make these programs available to many users, the cost per student of program production will be extremely high. The costs can be spread among users by insuring a long life (ten plus years) for the programs, by implementing the RMP through all of most of Nicaragua and by attempting to use the same programs with only slight revision for Spanish-speaking students in Latin America and the U.S.

2. The presently planned levels of classroom supervision, teacher training and student workbook usage result in per student reception costs of $3.06 per year, or assuming 150 thirty-minute lessons in a year, costs of 4.2¢ per student hour. These costs are high, suggesting the value of continued, careful experimentation with lower levels of supervision, less frequent and less intensive teacher training and more limited workbook use.

3. It appears possible to reduce substantially the reception site costs and to spread programming costs over a large audience. Even if this were to be done, the project is apt to remain expensive by the standards of instructional radio projects. For this reason, principal emphasis in evaluation of the Radio Mathematics Project must be placed on its capacity to improve the effectiveness of instruction, as indicated by its effects on mathematics achievement test scores and student repetition rates.[7]

THE MEXICAN RADIOPRIMARIA

Mexico's Radioprimaria is an experimental program, instituted in the State of San Luis Potosi in 1970, and aimed at utilizing instructional radio to help provide fourth, fifth and sixth grade education to those rural and semi-rural communities that had incomplete primary schools. In theory, fourth, fifth and sixth grade students were to be combined in one classroom with one teacher, with radio lessons used to aid and supplement the teacher's instruction. In practice, some schools participating in the Radioprimaria system combine only two of the three grades, while others have a teacher for each grade but still utilize the instructional radio lessons.

Spain (1973) describes and evaluates the system in detail; cost information was gathered by one of the authors and is discussed fully in Chapter VI. In 1972 the system broadcast about 280 hours, with approximately 80% of the lessons aimed at the combined three-grade audience, while the remaining 20% consisted of lessons aimed at a specific grade. Thus each student received about 242 hours of instructional radio lessons during the year. There were 2,800 students enrolled in the system in 1972. The cost function is as follows:

	Total Cost Equation	AC_N	AC_N/V_N	Cost per Student Hour
$r = 0\%$	TC = .13 N + 125.09 h	12.63	84.33	.052
$r = 7.5\%$	TC = .15 N + 129.64 h	13.12	77.24	.054
$r = 15\%$	TC = .17 N + 135.51 h	13.72	72.32	.057

It should be noted that average costs, and consequently total costs, are quite sensitive to the interest rate chosen. Not discounting the future can understate costs by almost 10%. The relatively high average cost per student and per student hour reflects the experimental nature and consequent low utilization of the system; the high ratio of average cost per student to variable cost per student indicates that costs could be decreased substantially by expanding student enrollments.

Radioprimaria is a quite interesting and unique project that offers the potential for a vast saving of resources for primary education, since the additional costs of the instructional radio components of the system are far more than offset by the reduced teacher and facility costs resulting from combining three grades in one classroom. Whether such a system is as pedagogically effective as a traditional direct teaching system needs further research, as is discussed in Chapter VI.

THE TARAHUMARA RADIO SCHOOLS

The Sierra Tarahumara is a mountainous, 15,000 square mile region in the state of Chihuahua in Northwest Mexico. In 1960 the total population of this area was 125,000, of which 50,000 were Tarahumara Indians. The Tarahumara remain relatively isolated from Mexican society, forming a distinct indigenous subculture, with its own language and customs. The Catholic Church has had a Jesuit mission in the region since 1900 and the Jesuits have run boarding schools for the Tarahumara since the early 1900s. The Radio Schools were begun in 1955, with the intent of extending the educational work of the Jesuits to a larger proportion of the native population. Although initially much of the education had a religious focus, since about 1960 the Jesuits have cooperated with the Mexican Secretariat of Public Education, which has few public schools in the region, to provide a secular education through the radio schools, following the official government curriculum and using the official textbooks, for the first four grades of primary school. The aim has been to provide an education sufficient to allow graduates of the radio schools to continue their studies in the public schools if they so desire. The information presented here is based on an evaluation of the system conducted in 1971 by Sylvia Schmelkes de Sotelo of the Center for Educational Studies in Mexico City (reported in Schmelkes de Sotelo, 1972, 1973). The interested reader is referred to either report for many more details.

Instructional radio lessons are broadcast from the Jesuit mission head-quarters in Sisoguichi. All lessons are prepared by two teachers from a near-by primary teacher training school. In 1971 there were 46 radio schools, serving 1,081 students spread out over the region. Each school had one or two "auxiliary" teachers, individuals who had no more than a primary educa-tion themselves, to organize and supervise the classes and to guide and correct the students' work. The teachers' education is supplemented by summer training at the Jesuit mission. In about 75% of the schools students from all grades are combined into a single classroom, while the remaining schools divide the students into two classrooms, the average class size being about 19 students. The fifteen-minute instructional radio lessons are grade-specific, and broadcast continuously throughout the school day. During the forty-five minutes of each hour when they are not receiving broadcasts directed to their grade level, students engage in individual exercises.

A rough approximation of the costs of the system is given in the Schmelkes de Sotelo (1973) study and was utilized to derive the cost function and average cost information for the instructional radio components of the radio school system as follows:[8]

	Total Cost Equation	AC_N	AC_N/V_N	Cost per Student Hour
$r = 0\%$	$TC = 26{,}714 + .35\,N + 18.38\,h$	35.94	102.7	.225
$r = 7.5\%$	$TC = 33{,}424 + .40\,N + 18.38\,h$	42.20	105.5	.264
$r = 15\%$	$TC = 41{,}077 + .46\,N + 18.38\,h$	49.34	107.3	.308

The average cost information above is based on the 1971 enrollment of 1,081 students and the broadcast of 160 hours of instructional radio lessons annual-ly to each grade. We see that the average cost per student is relatively high compared to other projects, primarily because of the very low enrollments. If the system could be expanded to serve more students, average costs could fall substantially. Further, we note that not discounting the future may cause one to understate costs by more than 25% (that is $35.94 versus $49.34). It should also be pointed out that, although no attempt has been made to com-pare the total costs of the radio schools with that of traditional primary school instruction in Mexico, the radio schools would probably be signifi-cantly less expensive, despite their relatively high costs of radio instruction, since the salaries paid to auxiliary teachers are about half those of qualified primary school teachers.

Most of Schmelkes de Sotelo's study is devoted to an evaluation of the radio school outcomes. In terms of imparting cognitive knowledge, the sam-ple of fourth grade radio school students scored slightly better than their traditional student counterparts in arithmetic, geometry and Spanish. However, this is perhaps the best that can be said of the radio schools and the results may not even be due to the utilization of the radio lessons. Out of the twenty-four radio schools visited during the study, only seven schools had a radio in operation. Further, dropout rates and nonattendance were very significant problems. Of those students who continue to the fourth grade, few, if any, are Tarahumara (non-Tarahumara Mexicans make up the majority of enrolled students, despite the initial mission to educate the Tarahumara). Schmelkes de Sotelo (1973) was not able to find any relevance between the school curriculum, which was transferred intact from the traditional, urban oriented, primary school one, and local employment opportunities. She finds that, at best, the schools encourage the student to leave the community, "and thus the community loses its better human resources" (p. 33) and in general contributes to "an education that serves the white population of the Sierra and keeps the Tarahumara in a marginal position" (p. 8).

We have seen these criticisms elsewhere in the literature (for example, see Spain, 1973, or Mayo, McAnany, and Klees, 1975)—it is not that instructional technology is incapable of meeting rural development needs but that much more concern must be given to examining those needs prior to the introduction of an educational system. The Radio Schools of the Tarahumara are currently engaged in a complete reevaluation of their efforts (the radio lessons have been temporarily discontinued since the 1973-1974 school year, pending this reevaluation), perhaps in large part due to the evaluation and recommendations made by Schmelkes de Sotelo, and attention is being focused specifically on how to reorient the schools more directly towards the needs of the Tarahumara community.

THAILAND'S INSTRUCTIONAL RADIO PROJECT

Substantially less experience based information exists on the cost of instructional radio than for instructional television. Perhaps the best available information is from the Thai radio education project that began in May, 1958. This project broadcasts relatively small amounts of instruction in music, social studies and English to about 800,000 elementary and beginning secondary level students; in addition, a thirty-minute children's lunch hour program provides education and entertainment during the noon break. Schram et al. (1967) describes the Thai project and provides the basic cost data that we use for our analysis.

We divide the cost information that Schramm provides into fixed and variable and capital and recurrent in ways that seem natural, then apply our annualization methods to obtain total cost functions.[9] These follow:

	Total Cost Equation	AC_N	AC_N/V_N	Cost per Student Hour
$r = 0$	$TC(N) = 89,340 + .182N$	.294	1.61	.012
$r = 7.5\%$	$TC(N) = 100,400 + .221N$	.347	1.57	.014
$r = 15\%$	$TC(N) = 114,700 + .263N$	.406	1.55	.016

The per student hour cost obtained are very close to those of Schramm, but this results from two counterbalancing factors. Our estimated average cost 35¢ (at $r = 7.5\%$) is over double Schramm's estimate of 15¢. This is due in part to a higher interest charge than he uses, but mostly to our using a five- instead of ten-year lifetime for the expensive (132, 1972 dollars each) radio receivers. We assumed that with a five-year lifetime, replacement would take the place of maintenance. This assumption of a five-year lifetime is perhaps over conservative since part of the reason for higher receiver cost was that rugged, long life receivers were purchased.

Counterbalancing our higher estimate of per student annual costs is our somewhat higher estimate of student usage. To obtain a per student hour cost of 1¢ (1.32, 1972 ¢), Schramm assumes that h has the very low value of fifteen hours per student per year; we use twenty-five. Music is broadcast for one-sixth hour per week per grade level offered, English for one-third and social studies for one-half; the lunch hour program is broadcast two and a half hours per week. The school year lasts thirty weeks, so that if a student took the median lengthened English course and listened to the noon hour program once a week he or she would listen for twenty-five hours per year; this is the basis of our computation of costs per student hour. What is important is not the actual number but the observation that costs per student hour respond sensitively indeed to the level of per student utilization.

It is valuable to note that radio can reach student hour costs of 1.5¢ even with highly costly receivers and a low utilization rate.

2. INSTRUCTIONAL TELEVISION PROJECTS

THE EL SALVADOR INSTRUCTIONAL TELEVISION SYSTEM

The El Salvador instructional television system began broadcasting in 1969 to secondary school students. Recently there have been plans to extend the system to cover elementary school, and broadcasts to the fourth grade started on a pilot basis in 1973. Our analysis will only consider the costs of the system without elementary school coverage. Because a substantial amount of the funding for the project came from foreign grants and loans, we will examine costs both from the point of view of total project costs, including the grant and loan money, and from the viewpoint of costs to the Government of

El Salvador (GOES) only. The GOES costs are, of course, substantially less than total project costs.

Consequently we examine two alternatives: (1) total costs for the secondary school ITV system. Cost timetables for each of these alternatives are given in Chapter VII, along with more information on the system. The cost data is based on Speagle (1972) except where footnotes to these tables indicate otherwise. To proceed from the cost timetables to annualized cost figures additional assumptions had to be made and these are explained for each alternative below.

(a) In estimating the total system costs alternative for secondary school coverage, start up costs were treated as an initial capital investment in the system and were annualized over the assumed twenty-five-year lifetime of the system. The 1972 student enrollment estimate of 48,000 was used along with the assumption of an average of 170 hours of programming per grade per year.

The total cost equation for the secondary system is as follows:[10]

	Total Cost Equation	AC_N	AC_N/V_N	Cost per Student Hour
$r = 0\%$	TC(N) = 904,000 + 0.89N	19.72	22.16	0.116
$r = 7.5\%$	TC(N) = 1,116,000 + 1.10N	24.35	22.14	0.143
$r = 15\%$	TC(N) = 1,346,000 + 1.33N	29.37	22.08	0.173

(b) In looking at the costs to El Salvador of secondary school coverage it is necessary to reduce the total expenditures given above by an annualized equivalent of the grants and loans.[11] To find this equivalent the present value of the thirty-year loan repayment series was calculated and this was subtracted from the total amount of the foreign grants and loans (the total amount was assumed to occur in the year 1970). The resulting figure was annualized over the twenty-five years assumed lifetime of the project and subtracted from the fixed costs. The unusual behavior of the fixed costs— they decrease as the discount rate increases—is explained by observing that the loan and grants are worth more in annualized equivalents as r increases. The GOES cost equation for the secondary school ITV system is as follows:

	Total Cost Equation	AC_N	AC_N/V_N	Cost per Student Hour
$r = 0\%$	TC(N) = 806,000 + 0.89N	17.68	19.87	0.104
$r = 7.5\%$	TC(N) = 799,000 + 1.10N	17.75	16.13	0.104
$r = 15\%$	TC(N) = 771,000 + 1.33N	17.39	13.08	0.102

THE STANFORD INSTRUCTIONAL TELEVISION SYSTEM

The Stanford Instructional Television system provides higher education courses to students at their places of employment. The major purpose of the system was to extend education to individuals with full time positions for whom commuting to campus would be difficult. Two organizations use the system. The first administers the broadcasting of regularly scheduled Stanford engineering courses. The second organization, the Association for Continuing Education, administers a wide variety of courses including the entire Master of Business Administration curriculum of Golden Gate University and courses of special interest to participating companies.

The system was first instituted in 1968, with four classrooms and one auditorium equipped with broadcast capabilities and approximately thirty companies within a twenty-five-mile radius of Stanford equipped with reception capabilities and talkback facilities to permit active student participation from off-campus locations. The system operates on four separate channels in the ITFS band. Special equipment is required to convert this signal to the lower frequencies normally transmitted to standard television monitors.

The total initial investment in the system was $1,187,300 for all production, transmission and reception equipment and the production facility. By 1974 a total of 4,942 off-campus students was participating in all programs of the Stanford ITV system, and 6,290 hours of programming were broadcast (approximately 50% of the total time available, at hours convenient to the students at their companies).

Cost functions were calculated using annualized values of capital equipment investment from 1968 through 1974, recurrent expenses for 1974 and utilization for 1974. The costs are in 1972 U.S. dollars and interest rates of zero, 7.5%, and 15% were used to calculate annualized values (more details may be found in the case study reported in Chapter VIII).

	Total Cost Equation	AC_N	AC_N/V_N	Cost per Student Hour
$r = 0\%$	$TC = 169,400 + 5.60N + 83.90h$	146.60	26.18	5.70
$r = 7.5\%$	$TC = 196,900 + 9.20N + 86.60h$	159.20	17.30	6.20
$4 = 15\%$	$TC = 232,100 + 13.50N + 90.10h$	175.10	12.97	6.80

The above calculations include teacher costs and all students. The Stanford engineering courses include auditors who do not receive credit. As regular classes are being broadcast, teacher costs may be excluded, as discussed in Chapter VIII. For the two different data assumptions and for the Stanford engineering courses separately and the entire syste, the following results were obtained for the average cost of the project over an assumed twenty-year lifetime, $AC_{1,20}$:

	Stanford Courses	All Courses
Auditors included:		
Teacher Costs excluded	$155	$ 73
Teacher Costs included	$309	$165
Auditors excluded:		
Teacher Costs excluded	$287	$ 88
Teacher Costs included	$571	$201

While the Stanford system may appear expensive, one should remember that these are the costs for the entire educational system serving the off campus students. If one assumes as a rough rule-of-thumb that tuition covers half the cost of on-campus education, the average cost per on-campus student for a three unit course is $540.

THE HAGERSTOWN INSTRUCTIONAL TELEVISION SYSTEM

The Hagerstown Instructional Television project in Washington County, Maryland has been broadcasting instruction to schools since 1956 and is probably the longest continuously running ITV project in the world. The system has been servicing all students in Washington County since 1959. In 1972, 22,000 students were enrolled in all twelve grades in the school system and 1,440 hours of programming were scheduled. The average student received approximately 117 hours of instruction via television (or 9.3% of total instructional time assuming a 35-hour week and 36 weeks per year).

The central facility, with five studios, is connected with receivers in the schools by a six channel coaxial cable which is leased from the local telephone company which originally installed the cable. With the six channels available, there is a potential for scheduling 7,580 hours of programming during the regular school year.

The original investment in 1955 of $1,049,700 (in 1972 dollars) included the cost of equipping and constructing five studios and the purchase of 342 receivers. The cable costs for transmission are not included as the phone company has an annual charge to the school system for use of the cable. The annual charge is based upon the length of cable and is not related to utilization. The charge for the cable usage remained roughly constant in current dollars and was $164,000 in 1972.

The major expense in recent years has been for personnel salaries. In 1972-1973 there were thirty-one TV teachers, twenty-three persons employed on a full time basis in engineering and production, 32 junior college and other production personnel employed on a part time basis (equivalent to 5.1 full time personnel, and 9.3 full time equivalent personnel from support services, such as cinematography, graphics, audio visual, and instructional materials).

Using utilization and recurrent cost data for 1972 and annualized values of capital expenses from 1955-1972, the following cost functions and average costs were calculated (see Chapter IX for more details):

	Total Cost Equation	AC_N	AC_N/V_N	Cost per Student Hour
$r = 0\%$	$TC = 234{,}500 + .50N + 617h$	51.54	103.80	.44
$r = 7.5\%$	$TC = 234{,}500 + .90N + 652h$	54.23	60.25	.46
$r = 15\%$	$TC = 234{,}500 + 1.50N + 697h$	57.78	38.52	.49

The long experience of Hagerstown in the use of ITV has demonstrated two important aspects of technology projects: the decline in relative prices of equipment and the value of maintenance to increased equipment life. The price of television sets to Hagerstown has been approximately $150 in current dollars throughout the life of the project. However, when an adjustment is made for inflation between 1955 and 1972, the price of the 342 sets purchased in 1955 becomes $286 in 1972 dollars. Television receivers are usually assumed to have a five-year life. In Hagerstown only 200 sets have been removed from operation. If all of these sets were among those originally purchased in 1955, then at least 142 sets are still operating after twenty years.

THE KOREAN ELEMENTARY/MIDDLE SCHOOL PROJECT

In the period 1970-1971 the Republic of Korea undertook a major systems analysis of its educational section. The purpose of the analysis was to ascertain the feasibility of improving the internal efficiency of the educational system and of making the system more responsive to Korea's economic and social needs. Two important conclusions of the analysis were that a single entity within Korea should take responsibility for educational reform activities, and that an important initial target for reform would be the elementary (grades one through six) and middle (grades seven through nine) schools.[12] In August 1972, the Government of Korea responded to these recommendations by establishing the Korean Educational Development Institute (KEDI) under the direction of Dr. Yung Dug Lee. One of the first major tasks facing KEDI was development of a reform project at the elementary and middle school levels (KEDI, 1974). The elementary/middle (E/M) project is now in the course of development, and final plans for implementation remain to be decided on. The E/M project will, however, use instructional television and radio to provide instruction. Present plans call for students in grades two through eight to receive about six twenty-minute television lessons per week by the time the operational phase of the project begins in 1978; more intensive use of ITV will be considered if funds become available. Plans call for students in grades one through nine to receive about ten twenty-minute radio lessons per week. In addition to use of ITV and IR, the E/M project will involve reform of curriculum and textbooks and may involve use of differentiated staffing, use of individual instruction and increasing the student to teacher ratio through double shifting.

At the time of this writing (September, 1975) the E/M project is at a critical juncture. The first phase of its activities—initial planning for and tryouts of the new instructional approaches—is nearing completion. Its transmission facilities and new studios are scheduled to become operational within a few months, thereby allowing the second major phase of the project, comprehensive demonstrations in forty-five schools, to begin. This demonstration phase will continue through February, 1978. A third phase, that of nationwide implementation, will begin in the course of the demonstration, and in parallel with it. Implementation is planned for the period 1976-1980.

The KEDI E/M project is ambitious in the comprehensiveness of the reform it. plans to implement and in the extent to which, like Nicaragua's Radio Mathematics Project (see Chapter V), it will attempt to utilize research results from educational psychology in its instructional design. The project is, in addition, incorporating the most recent technical advance in transmission systems, the tethered aerostat, for signal distribution. KEDI's use of an aerostat will be the first use made of this technology for television broadcasting.[13] For all these reasons, then, the E/M project will be closely observed and its costs will be important to ascertain. The cost information presented below is based in part on costs that have been incurred, and in part on present KEDI plans. The results are thus tentative.

The bulk of E/M project costs are for television, and we feel our estimates of the television costs are less subject to error than those for radio. Thus costs for only the instructional television aspect of the project are presented here. Chapter X discusses radio and print costs as well. The basic cost equations are shown below, with average costs based on the assumption of seventy hours per year broadcast to each of eight grade levels and 1,000,000 students using the system. (Though this utilization figure is high, KEDI plans call for eventual coverage of all 7,000,000 students of this age group.)

	Total Cost Equation	AC_N	AC_N/V_N	Cost per Student Hour
$r = 0\%$	$TC = 109{,}000 + 1.62N + 1848h$	2.76	1.7	.039
$r = 7.5\%$	$TC = 214{,}000 + 1.81N + 2128h$	3.22	1.8	.045
$r = 15\%$	$TC = 348{,}000 + 2.02N + 2467h$	3.74	1.9	.054

THE MEXICAN TELESECUNDARIA

Mexico's Telesecundaria is an experimental program designed to extend secondary school educational opportunities to youth in rural regions, where few secondary schools previously existed. Television lessons carry the primary instructional burden of the system in that programs are produced and broadcast in all subject matters and each grade usually receives one twenty-minute program every hour of the school day. In the classrooms, former primary school teachers are used as classroom coordinators, instead of a teacher trained to instruct at the secondary school level.

Detailed evaluations of the system are presented in Klees (1975) and Mayo, McAnany, and Klees (1975), while an analysis of much of the relevant evidence on Telesecundaria is reported in Chapter XI. In 1972 the system broadcast about 360 hours of instructional lessons to 29,000 students in an eight state region around Mexico City. The summary cost function and average cost information for 1972 is as follows:

	Total Cost Equation	AC_N	AC_N/V_N	Cost per Student Hour
$r = 0\%$	$TC = 3.65N + 520h$	23.02	6.31	.064
$r = 7.5\%$	$TC = 4.23N + 538h$	24.27	5.74	.067
$r = 15\%$	$TC = 4.85N + 561h$	25.74	5.31	.072

It should be noted that not discounting the future may cause one to understate system costs by almost 12% (that is, $23.02 versus $25.74). The relatively low value of the ratio of average cost per student to variable cost per student indicates that some economies of scale have already been achieved, although costs per student could be still lower if enrollments expand.

Given the relatively low utilization of Telesecundaria, it is a surprisingly inexpensive system. Telesecundaria is less costly than many of the other instructional television systems. It is perhaps closest in form to that in El Salvador, whose average cost per student was similar for 1972, even though the El Salvador system was serving 65% more students than Telesecundaria. Further, costs per student hour were considerably lower for Telesecundaria, $.067 versus $.143 (at a 7.5% interest rate) for El Salvador. The cost comparison between the two systems would favor Telesecundaria even more if it was operating in urban areas with an average class size of forty-five, as does the El Salvador system, as opposed to rural areas with an average class size for only twenty-three students.

One of the primary reasons for the low overall cost of Telesecundaria is its low production cost. As discussed in Chapter XI, even utilizing a 15% discount rate, production costs per hour of programming are only $513. Schramm (1973) reports typical production cost estimates for similar instructional television projects (see also Chapter IV below) in other countries range from $1,200 to $2,000 per hour, and indicates that Mexico's Telesecundaria is one of the least expensive systems of its kind in the world.

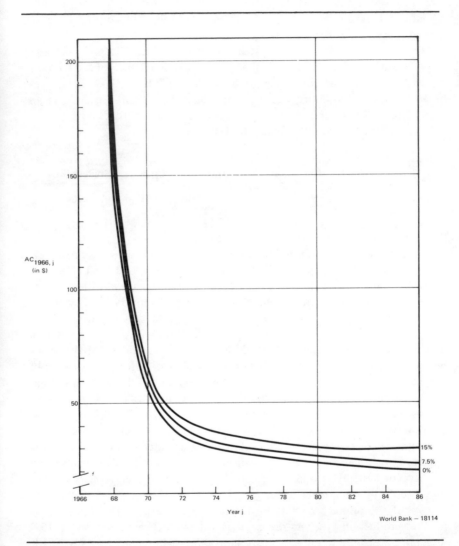

World Bank — 18114

Figure III.1: AVERAGE COST FROM PROJECT INITIATION IN 1966 TO YEAR j
AT INTEREST RATES OF 0%, 7.5%, AND 15% (in 1972 U.S. dollars)

Sufficient data were available for the Telesecundaria project to allow the construction of a year by year cost table (see Table XI.2) and the consequent calculation of AC_{ij}'s. Figure III.1 presents the average costs from project initiation in 1966, assuming different project lifetimes (that is, $AC_{1966, j}$ as $j = 1967$ to 1986) at social rates of discount of zero, 7.5% and 15.0%. This figure serves to indicate several points. First, costs decrease quite rapidly as we project Telesecundaria to continue for more than a few years. For example, if Telesecundaria were to be discontinued next year, the average cost per student over the lifetime of the project ($AC_{1966, 1976}$) would be $30 (at a 7.5% interest rate). Assuming a twenty-year lifetime, the average costs ($AC_{1966, 1986}$) would be considerably less, $23.

Second, we observe that the choice of a discount rate is quite important. As the opportunity costs of resources become greater, so do the real costs of the project. Neglecting the discount rate (that is, choosing a zero discount rate), as many cost studies unfortunately do, serves to understate project cost substantially, even more so than the average cost figure derived in the tableau above for 1972, since utilization was not discounted in this latter figure. For example, if we look at the average costs per student from 1966 to 1986 (assuming a twenty-year lifetime for Telesecundaria), not taking the value of resources over time into account (that is, using a zero discount rate) can result in understating costs by almost 30%, if the appropriate rate is 15% (that is, $20 per student versus $28 per student).

Telesecundaria is an especially interesting instructional technology project in that research has shown it to be more cost effective than the traditional direct teaching system that is used in most secondary schools in Mexico. The interested reader is referred to Chapter XI for a detailed discussion of this point, as well as an analysis of system expansion alternatives, financing, and more extensive cost information.

3. SUMMARY

This chapter, in effect, has summarized the cost information to be presented in the case studies of Part Three of this book and that of a few other projects, based on secondary sources. Rather than review these results twice, we refer the reader to our concluding Chapter XII for a tabular summary of these results. In the following chapter we pursue our cost analysis of IR and ITV systems by looking at how costs may be examined as a function of a number of educational policy decision variables that need to be carefully considered in planning and initiating an instructional technology system.

NOTES

1. Cost information on other uses for the media, including several teacher training and adult education projects, may be found in the Schramm et al. (1967) case studies. Wagner (1972), Laidlaw and Layard (1974), and Lumsden (1975) provide cost information on the Open University in the United Kingdom; Dordick (unpublished) provides cost information on the Bavarian Telekolleg in Germany; Baldwin et al. (1972) and Wagner (1975) provide detailed cost information on a program of Colorado State University to distribute graduate engineering instruction by videotape; and Krival (1970) provides cost information on use of radio and correspondence for teacher training in Kenya. Dodds (1972) reviews some of these and additional uses of media for nonformal education, and provides cost information in some cases. The cost data reported in these papers on nonformal education are amenable to the same methods of analysis used in this paper. For a discussion of the costs, and cost projections, of the school television program in Niger see Lefranc (1967). We have not included it because of the small number of students involved.

2. We have included an interest rate of zero *only* to show the significant difference in estimated costs due to not discounting the future; using $r = 0$ is *not* a sensible alternative to evaluating project costs.

3. To be more precise, some costs may vary with the number of programming hours produced in any year, other costs may vary with the number of hours broadcast, while still others may vary with the number of hours of instructional lessons a class receives (see the discussion in Chapter IV); the cost analysis of ongoing projects presented here is not this detailed and thus h will usually refer to the second definition, the number of hours broadcast. This yields a slightly inaccurate cost representation, but it should be recognized that each definition of h is probably roughly in proportion to the other two, and thus the estimated costs are reasonably accurate.

4. The average cost per student hour can be calculated from the average cost per student AC_N, by dividing AC_N by the number of hours of programming a student can be expected to view annually; this latter figure is *not* the value for h since h is the number of hours broadcast to all the grades in the system, but is the number of hours broadcast annually *per grade,* that is, h divided by the number of grade levels the system serves.

5. Wells and Klees (1978) conducted a further analysis of costs of the Nicaragua project to investigate several decision questions including expansion of radio programs to grade levels other than the first, and appropriate power sources for radio receivers, and construction of a transmission system for education purposes.

6. This assumes that each lesson is broadcast only once per year. The relatively small cost of transmission suggests, if there were either pedagogical advantages for repeat broadcasting or advantages in shifting, the resulting increases in transmission cost would be relatively slight.

7. Searle, Matthews, Suppes, and Friend (1977) reported that students using the radio scored 65 percent correct on a mathematics achievement test whereas students in a control group (no radio) scored only 40 percent correct.

8. To convert the cost information given in the Schmelkes de Sotelo study to this format it is assumed that her estimates for the costs of the land, building and transmitter were based on straight line depreciation over a ten-year life and that the cost of furniture, truck, and plane were depreciated similarly over a five-year life. Further, we assume that the above costs and administrative salaries are fixed costs; that the cost of radio teachers, equipment maintenance, travel, utilities, and miscellaneous items are variable

with the number of hours broadcast; and that the cost of a radio is $20, with 10 percent of this purchase price added annually to cover maintenance and power costs. Costs of training the auxiliary teachers during the summer are not included.

9. The cost function for this project was estimated as a function of the number of students only; variable costs per hour were not calculated and therefore some costs that are variable with the number of hours broadcast are included in the fixed cost estimate.

10. The cost function for this project was estimated as a function of the number of students only. Variable costs per hour were not calculated and therefore some costs that are variable with the number of hours broadcast are included in the fixed cost estimate.

11. Because of the grants and soft loans, total costs exceed GOES costs. Table VII.1 in Chapter VII shows the extent of this in the rows labeled "total costs," "foreign aid and debt repayment," and "total cost to GOES." In the first years of the project, "total cost to GOES" is obtained by subtracting foreign aid (in parentheses) from "total cost." In later years "total cost to GOES" is obtained by adding debt repayment to "total cost."

12. A detailed reporting of much of the analysis for reform of the Korean system is contained in Morgan and Chadwick (1971).

13. The experiences of the Koreans in the implementation of the aerostat system would lead one to conclude that the system is apparently not a viable transmission alternative.

Chapter IV

COST FUNCTIONS FOR INSTRUCTIONAL
RADIO AND TELEVISION

Our purpose in this chapter is to identify the variables that will determine the cost of an instructional radio or television system and to organize those variables into a total cost function in a way that will allow planners to examine the sensitivity of total cost to changes in the determining variables. Whereas the purpose of Chapter III was to present results from cost evaluations of ongoing projects, the purpose of this chapter is to discuss techniques for planning future project costs. The chapter has three sections. In the first section the variables that determine the total cost function are identified for radio and television and a general cost function is specified. In the second part, estimates for elements of the cost function are discussed in terms of costs for central administration and project start up, programming, transmission and reception; these estimates draw on the results of Chapter III. In the third part, example cost functions for radio and television are constructed from the data provided in the second part.

1. DETERMINANTS OF TOTAL COSTS

In constructing the total cost function, we assumed that total costs can be written as the sum of central costs, programming costs, transmission costs, and reception costs. This assumption, though convenient, can be restrictive as it fails to allow for tradeoffs between transmission and reception costs. This tradeoff plays a central role in assessing the economic desirability of satellite transmission.

Total costs, TC, are then given by:

(IV.1)
$$TC = C_C + C_P + C_T + C_R$$

where subscripts C, P, T and R refer to central, programming, transmission, and reception respectively. Our approach to specification of TC will be to examine each of the component cost functions in turn. The determining variables with their definitions are listed in Table IV.1. For all capital expenses the annualization factor, $a(r, n)$, discussed in Chapter II, is used.

TABLE IV.1
Determining Variables of the Total Cost Function

Variable	Definition
A. System Variables	
N	Number of students using the system each year.
h	Number of hours of programming each year. (This number could be derived by determining the average number of broadcast hours per student and multiplying by the number of distinct student groups, for example, grade levels.)
G	Area of the region to be served. (This factor could be examined in further detail by assuming several regions with different areas or geographic features.)
b	Number of pages of printed materials for each student. (The printed materials are assumed to be reusable.)
k	Number of students who will share a receiver. (This will depend upon the number of students per class and the number of classes that can share a receiver.)
e	Fraction of reception sites located in a non-electrified area.
S	Number of reception sites.
B. Cost Variables	
C_{SU}	Cost of project planning and start up.
C_{CA}	Cost of central administration.
C_{PF} (h)	Cost of production facility (land and buildings).
C_{PE} (h)	Cost of production equipment.
C_{PA} (h)	Annual cost of program production.
C_{TE} (G)	Cost of purchasing and installing a transmission system capable of serving area G.
C_{TF} (G)	Cost of transmission facility (land and buildings).
C_{TA} (G)	Annual cost of power, maintenance, and operating personnel for a transmitter capable of reaching area G.
C'_{R}	Cost of one receiver.
C_{RE}	Cost of related reception equipment (for example, antennas) for a reception site.
C_{RF}	Cost of building modifications for television reception.
C_{e}	Cost per reception site for power generation equipment (required only for TV in non-electrified areas).
C_{p}	Cost of electric power, per reception site per hour, using power lines.

TABLE IV.1 (Continued)

Variable	Definition
B. *Cost Variables (Continued)*	
C_p'	Cost of electric power, per reception site per hour, using local, power generation equipment or batteries.
C_{RM}	Cost per hour for maintenance at each reception site.
C_b	Cost of a book, per page.
C. *Capital Lifetime Variables*	
n	Life of the project.
n_p	Life of a completed program.
n_{PE}	Life of production equipment.
n_{PF}	Life of production facility.
n_{TE}	Life of transmission equipment.
n_{TF}	Life of transmission facility.
n_R	Life of a receiver.
n_{RE}	Life of related receiver equipment.
n_{RF}	Life of reception facility modifications.
n_e	Life of power generating equipment.
n_b	Life of a book.
D. *Social Rate of Discount*	
r	Social rate of discount.

CENTRAL PROJECT COSTS

Project planning and start up costs are important aspects of total costs and should be annualized over the entire project lifetime. Additionally, technology projects may require special administration costs that are distinct from administration costs for the education system. These costs, the central project costs, are given by:

(IV.2) $$C_C = a(r, n) \, C_{SU} + C_{CA},$$

where r is the social discount rate;

       n is the life of the project;

      C_{SU} is the project start up cost; and,

     C_{CA} is the annual central administration cost.

PROGRAMMING COST FUNCTION

The programming cost function is a more complicated formulation than the other equations, as the capital expenses for production facilities and equipment are annualized over the life of the program. The function is given by:

$$(\text{IV.3}) \qquad C_p = a(r, n_p) \, [a(r, n_{PE}) \, C_{PE} + a(r, n_{PF}) \, C_{PF} + C_{PA}],$$

where n_p, n_{pe}, and n_{pf}, are the lifetimes of the program, the production equipment and the production facility respectively; C_{PE} and C_{PF} are capital costs for the production equipment and the production facility respectively; and C_{PA} is annual production cost. It should be recalled that all programming costs are related to the number of programming hours. An alternative technique would be to summarize these costs into a single per hour production costs, C_{Ph}. We would then have:

$$(\text{IV.3}) \qquad\qquad C_p = a(r, n_p) \, C_{Ph} h.$$

This equation assumes a target audience with a single language and little cultural diversity, each of which could require alterations of program content for different groups.

TRANSMISSION COST FUNCTION

The transmission cost is given by:

$$(\text{IV.4}) \qquad\qquad C_T = a(r, n_{TE}) \, C_{TE} + a(r, n_{TF}) \, C_{TF} + C_{TA}.$$

where n_{TE} and n_{TF} are the lifetimes of the transmission equipment and transmission facility respectively; C_{TE} and C_{TF} are the capital costs of the transmission equipment and transmission facility respectively; C_{TA} is the annual operating cost for transmission. The costs vary with size of the region to be served. More detail could be included in the equation by assuming more than one region with different transmission requirements. There would then be a single equation IV.4 for each region and total transmission costs would be obtained by summing the equations for all regions.

RECEPTION COST FUNCTION

In writing the reception cost function, we must take account of receiver capital and maintenance expenses, power equipment and operating expenses, and printed materials cost. The reception cost function is given by:

$$(IV.5) \qquad C_R = a(r, n_R) N/_k C_R' + a(r, n_{RE}) SC_{RE} + a(r, n_{RF}) SC_{RF}$$

$$+ a(r, n_E) eSC_e + (1 - e) hC_p + ehC_p'$$

$$+ hC_{RM} + a(r, n_b) N_b C_b$$

where n_R, n_{RE}, n_{RF}, n_E and n_b are the lifetimes of the receiver, other receiver-related equipment, the reception facility, power-generating equipment for the reception facility, and printed materials respectively; C_R', C_{RE}, C_{RF}, C_e and C_b are capital costs of the receiver, receiver-related equipment, the reception facility, the power-generating equipment, and printed material respectively: C_p, C_p', and C_{RM} are hourly costs of electric power from power-lines, electric power from power generating equipment, and maintenance respectively;

- N is the number of students served by the system;
- k is the number of students sharing a receiver;
- S is the number of reception sites;
- e is the fraction of reception sites located in areas not served by power lines;
- h is the number of hours of programming each year; and
- b is the number of pages of printed material for each student.

More detail could be included in the reception cost equation by realizing that there may be some variation among reception sites. The differences in cost among sites may be small for related equipment but could be large for power costs.

COST FUNCTION RECAPITULATION

The total cost function of equation IV.1 has been described in more detail in the equations for central, production, transmission and reception costs. Even though we consider thirty-five separate determining variables, our cost function represents only an approximation; at a number of points along the way we have indicated where more detail could be provided and other instances will have occurred to the reader. The cost function provides a useful approach to a broad outline for planning. However, a detailed planning effort would be required to obtain more detailed cost information specific to local circumstances.

It is perhaps worth pointing out that equation IV.1 fits into the simple $TC = F + V_h h + V_n N$ format if one takes as given all the determining variables except N and h. Only the central costs (and perhaps the transmission costs) would be considered fixed. The variable cost per hour, V_h, could be determined by summing programming costs divided by the number of hours with the hourly reception power costs. All reception costs (with the exception of hourly power costs) would be used to determine the variable costs per student, V_n.

2. COMPONENT COSTS

Our purpose in this section is to provide background information on what actual costs for elements in the cost function have been and can be expected to be. This information can serve as a guide to planners of future systems even though the estimates presented here will generally need to be changed to reflect local circumstances.

CENTRAL ADMINISTRATION AND START UP

Project planning, feasibility studies and cost analyses are important initial steps before a project is undertaken. These costs should be included as part of the project costs. Unfortunately, many analyses often ignore these costs as they are difficult to determine. These costs may be high if the project is one of the first projects using a particular form of technology and cannot base its analysis on other project experiences. For example, Stanford was the first university to use the Instructional Television Fixed Service (ITFS) band for television with two-way audio for off-campus education. There start up costs amounted to $328,000. There are now many other systems that have followed the Stanford model and these planning costs can be minimized. In Nicaragua, initial planning expenses were $268,000. This is the first system to provide a mathematics curriculum via radio for primary school students and require forty to fifty responses from each student (in a workbook) during a thirty-minute lesson. This technique can be adapted to other Spanish-speaking countries at significantly lower cost.

Central administration is another important expense item that varies widely from project to project and is often ignored. For the Stanford ITV system, people are employed full time in an administrative capacity and their salaries are approximately $100,000 each year. Another important expense that is often not included is research and evaluation. In Nicaragua, evaluation of the programs was part of a formative evaluation process and was included within production expenses. However, an additional $118,000 was spent on other research. In the Ivory Coast, expenses for evaluation and studies have reached over $200,000 per year, and may well become higher.

PRODUCTION

Production costs vary widely and depend upon the complexity of the program being presented. As the complexity of the presentation increases, more expensive equipment and more personnel may be involved. For example, the Stanford ITV system (Chapter VIII) uses one teacher, one camera operator and two cameras in the studio. The format of the program is direct lecturing, with notes and graphs, by the teacher (the system provides a facility for student talkback), and the costs per hour for production are approximately $91. In Mexico (Chapter XI), production costs are approximately $490 per hour for a more complex production arrangement involving a teacher, a director, a camera operator, a technician, and materials produced by a graphics department. The production of programs for the Open University, which is undertaken by the British Broadcasting Corporation, costs an average of $9,600 per hour (Lumsden and Ritchie, 1975).[1]

Although production costs and program complexity vary widely, the research cited by Schramm (1972) challenges the need for professional production techniques in educational programs. Schramm reviewed the literature on program production and the impact of different production techniques on student learning. He concluded that simplicity of presentation is preferable.

> The general conclusion that emerges from the studies of simple vs. complex treatments of material in the audiovisual media is one that should gladden the heart of a budget officer or an executive producer. More often than not, there is no learning advantage to be gained by a fancier, more complex treatment (p. 55).

> Visual embellishments do not usually help learning unless (like directional arrows) they can help organize content that is not inherently well organized or (like animation) help a viewer to understand a process or concept that is very hard to understand without such simplification. In other words, visual embellishments *per se* are not especially useful in instructional material.

> No learning advantage has been demonstrated for "professional" or "artistic" production techniques such as dollying rather than cutting, key rather than flat lighting, dissolves, wipes, fades, etc.

> There is very little evidence that narrative presentation ordinarily has any learning advantage over expository or that adding humor adds to learning effect (p. 65).

His conclusion, which is relevant to the choice between television and radio, is that there is doubt that two channels (audio and visual) have an advantage over one channel (audio or visual) when the information carried by the second medium is redundant. Therefore, although he concludes that there is no advantage to spending money for complex television production, there may also be no advantage to spending money for television instead of radio if the television production merely involves lecturing. An alternative to television production utilizing graphs, charts and notes would be radio with student workbooks or printed materials.

The coordination of radio with student workbooks is especially attractive, as Schramm (1972) also concluded that active participation by the student was important.

> The chief *positive* guideline that emerges from the research is the usefulness of active student participation. Concerning that we have been able to report impressively consistent results. Participation may be overt or covert; spoken or written or done through practice with a model or a device; button pushing or asking or answering questions, or finishing what the instructor has begun to say. Different forms are more effective in different situations. Whatever the way in which students are encouraged to practice the desired responses, in most cases this activity is more effective if the students are given immediate knowledge of results—that is, told whether their responses are correct (p. 66).

> But at least two straightforward guidelines stand out from the research papers we have reviewed. Effective television can be kept as simple as possible, except where some complexity is clearly required for one task or another; students will learn more if they are kept actively participating in the teaching-learning process. Simple television: active students (pp. 66-67).

Planning a program with active student participation can easily raise the costs of production. An interesting experiment with radio production for primary grade mathematics is being undertaken in Nicaragua (Searle, Friend, and Suppes, 1975; a cost analysis of this project appears in Chapter V). The cost for program production—which includes student workbooks, teacher guides and approximately forty to fifty active responses per thirty-minute lesson—is $1,712 per hour. This cost is high for radio production (Schramm et al., 1967, estimated production costs of $250 per hour for radio programs in Thailand) and is well within the range of production costs for television. However, if one assumes a ten-year lifetime for these programs (which is reasonable considering the investment in planning, evaluation, and revision), the costs become $160 per hour per year (assuming an interest rate of 7.5%). One reason the costs are high is the use of expatriates for several phases of program production. If the expatriates could be replaced by Nicaraguans, the costs would be halved. The personnel involved in producing 150 new thirty-minute radio lessons and revising 150 other lessons are: three full time personnel for scriptwriting, three half time personnel for curriculum design, one full time artist for design and preparation of workbooks, one half full time person for writing teacher guides, three half time personnel for management, and two full time personnel for evaluation.

Table IV.2 summarizes production costs for radio and television from several projects. From these project experiences, it would seem reasonable to assume production costs of $100 to $1,200 per hour per radio.

These experiences with costs may be complemented by cost estimates for single studio facilities. Jamison and Bett (1973) estimate that a TV facility could be established for $20,000 and a radio facility for $5,000. Bourret (1973) has estimated a cost of $25,000 for equipment for a simple television studio. In the establishment of a community radio station in Canada, costs for radio station equipment were estimated at $11,000. Assuming a construc-

TABLE IV.2
Program Production Costs

	Number of Programming Hours[a]	(in 1000s of 1972 dollars)			(in dollars)
		Annualized Facility Costs[b]	Annualized Equipment Costs[c]	Recurrent Costs[d]	Average Cost per hour[e]
Instructional Television					
El Salvador	333	22.70	231.0 (38)	540.0	1153*
Hagerstown	1440	40.13	209.9 (107.7)	847.5 (68)	762
Telesecundaria	1080	12.6	44.3	472.8	490
Korea					1704
Stanford	6290	47.25	34.06	489.9 (183)	91
Open University	288				3695*
Instructional Radio					
Radioprimaria	95	0.8	2.4	29.7	133*
Nicaragua	50			160.0 (10)	1232*
Korea					96

a. This is the number of hours produced or revised in a year. It is not necessarily equal to the number of total hours broadcast to students.
b. Facility costs are annualized at 7.5% with a 20-year life.
c. Equipment costs are annualized at 7.5% with a 10-year life. Videotapes are included as equipment but assumed to have a 5 year life. The total value of videotapes is reported in parentheses.
d. The major component of recurrent costs is salaries of production personnel. Where possible, the number of full time equivalent personnel involved in production will be reported in parentheses.
e. Some projects use live program production and others rely on tapes. When programs are revised from one year to the next, a 3-year life will be assumed for all programs. Those instances where a 3-year life is assumed are marked by an asterisk (*). An interest rate of 7.5% is used.

tion cost of $50 per square foot, a television studio facility (5,000 sq. ft.) would cost $25,000, and a radio studio facility (1,000 sq. ft.) would cost $5,000. Adding maintenance costs of 10% of equipment investment and annualizing facility expenses for a twenty-year period and equipment expenses for a ten-year period, total annual costs would be $8,600 and $1,220 for television and radio respectively.

For 300 hours of programming each year, this would result in costs of only $29 per hour for television and $6 per hour for radio. However, equipment and facility costs are the smallest portion of total costs for programming. The major component of production costs is derived from personnel salaries. Assuming salaries of $5 per hour for administrators (2 hours of time per course hour), $3 per hour for teachers (10 hours of time per course hour), and $1 per hour for technicians (1.5 hours of time per course hour), personnel costs could range from $42 per hour (one administrator, one teacher, and one technician) to $173 (two administrators, five teachers, and two technicians). Total costs for television could range from $71 to $202 per hour and from $48 to $179 per hour for radio. This estimate diverges considerably from project experiences and is a result of the assumption of very simple facilities and equipment and a possible underestimation of time input and salaries. The high time input is estimated to be 55 hours. Jamison and Bett (1973) estimate ranges of 32 hours to 320 hours of personnel time for each hour of original broadcasting. The salary estimates may be changed for different circumstances.

The production costs for television are high. The high costs are incurred because of a desire for local control of programming. The cost of this local control can be estimated by comparing the production costs of Table IV.2 with program rental charges. As an example, for the 1974-1975 school year the National Instructional Television Center (1974) was charging base rates of $32 per fifteen-minute program and $48.50 per thirty-minute program with an additional charge of $1.40 per 10,000 students (in all grades in the district). This charge allows for unlimited viewing during a week. Average hourly costs for program rentals would be $100. It would appear to be useful to investigate alternative program sources for suitable courses due to the significantly lower production costs.

TRANSMISSION

Transmission system alternatives. There is a wide variety of transmission systems possible for television and radio. The transmission system delivers the signal from the broadcast origination point to the reception point. In general, transmission systems have two major components. The transmitter feeds the signal directly to the receivers. The interconnection component links the transmitters and the broadcast point.

Transmitters include satellites, airplanes, aerostats, terrestrial stations, and cables. The first four alternatives may be viewed as alternative means of increasing the altitude of the transmitter to provide a larger coverage area and reduce signal interference caused by high natural or man-made structures. An aerostat, as used in Korea, is a tethered helium-filled ballon with aerodynamical lift. Terrestrial stations rely upon transmitter towers (2,000 feet appear to be a reasonable limit for tower height), which are often mounted on mountain tops or high buildings to increase the coverage. These four choices all involve open circuit transmission of the signal. The frequency of the signal may not be the same as the frequency received by standard receivers, and frequency converters may be necessary at the reception points. This system can limit access to the broadcast by raising the price of reception. Satellite transmission is typically at higher frequencies than is standard for receivers. The Stanford ITV system deliberately broadcasts at a high frequency from their mountain-based terrestrial station to limit access. Cables are excellent means of limiting access to the programs and providing a higher quality signal by eliminating many of the causes of interference.

Interconnectors include satellites, airplanes, aerostats, microwave relays, and videotape shipment. Many combinations are possible among transmitters and interconnectors to form transmission systems (clearly some of the combinations are senseless). As an example, terrestrial stations may be connected by any of the interconnector options while satellites when used as transmitters would not require any interconnector.

Some of the important factors which affect the cost and choice of the transmission system are: quality of signal, ratio of receivers to population, percentage of population covered, population density, area, terrain, existing transmission facilities, type of educational facilities, and other telecommunication needs of the country. Butman (1972) reports that Grade A coverage (high quality signal) will be three times as expensive as Grade B coverage (moderate quality signal). Rathjens (1973) reports much higher percentage cost increases to cover low population density areas of Brazil and India with terrestrial transmitters and microwave relays than with satellite transmitters. Terrain seems to affect the choice in Korea as aerostats at altitudes of 10,000 feet provide Grade B coverage for a radius of ninety miles while Butman (1972) discusses a radius of seventy miles obtained with a 1,000-foot tower.

Basic cost information. We will not attempt to provide a detailed discussion of the costs of each transmitter and interconnector or an estimate of the sensitivity of costs to each of the factors ementioned above. However, we will provide some basic cost information for some of the choices and then discuss results of optimization and tradeoff studies of transmission systems for specific applications.

When satellites are used as transmitters (direct broadcast satellites) the satellite cost is significantly higher than the instance when satellites are used as interconnectors. The higher cost of the satellite is attributed to the higher power output required to broadcast directly to standard receivers. For India, Butman, Rathjens, and Warren (1973) estimated a cost of $25 million dollars for a direct broadcast satellite and $12 million dollars for a satellite used as an interconnector. Even though the direct broadcast satellite has higher power, special equipment is necessary at each reception point to amplify the signal and to modulate the frequency of the signal. The ASCEND (1967) study estimated a cost of $300 for this equipment. Butman et al. used the same estimate although they mentioned that costs for this equipment in India appeared to be in the range of $250-$675.

In Korea, the capital costs in 1975 for the aerostat system installation were estimated to be:

Aerostats	(2)	$2.16 million;
Television Transmitters	(4)	$1.48 million;
Radio Transmitters	(2)	$ .4 million;
Telemetry Command	(2)	$1.37 million; and
Miscellaneous		$1.10 million.

It is interesting to note that the Koreans estimated that a duplicate system would cost 75% more in 1976. The other interesting point to note is that television transmitters cost nearly twice as much as radio transmitters for the same coverage area.[2]

This relationship between costs of radio and television coverage also appears at lower power ranges. Jamison and Bett (1973) reported prices of $5,000 for a five-watt TV transmitter and $2,500 for a ten-watt FM radio transmitter. In combination with a 100-foot antenna costing $6,000, the line of sight is ten miles.

There are many variations in costs of terrestrial transmitters. For a four-channel television system, Stanford invested $134,000 for a ten-watt transmitter on top of a 2,000-foot mountain, which covers half a circle of twenty-five-mile radius with only seven watts and uses directional beams of one watt to reach fifty miles. This transmission is a very high frequency and each reception point requires special front-end equipment (antenna and converter) costing $1,350. For other terrestrial transmitters, Bourret (1973) reports that the VERTA project in the Phillipines was able to purchase a five-kilowatt transmitter and antenna for $40,000 and can cover an area with a fifty-mile radius.

The Hagerstown television system is unique in the utilization of a dedicated six-channel cable system to transmit to forty-five schools in a 268-square mile area from the central studio. The cable is leased and costs $164,000 per year.

Microwave relays are a frequent choice for an interconnector device. Butman (1972) estimated a cost of $4,000 per mile for a microwave relay in India. Butman also reported that a system in Ethiopia cost $6,000 per mile. Sovereign (1968) assumed that terrestrial transmitters would be thirty miles apart and that a one-channel television system would cost $1,733 per mile, a two-channel system $2,177 per mile, and a four-channel system $2,950 per mile for the microwave relay. Hundreds of audio channels can be carried as an alternative to one television channel.

For satellite interconnectors, Butman, Rathjens, and Warren (1973) estimated a cost of $12 million for India. However, each transmitter would require an additional $150,000 in equipment to receive the signal from the satellite. Janky, Potter, and Lusignan (unpub.) analyzed the following trade-off costs between transponder power and transmitter receive antennas for a three satellite-six transponder configuration:

Capital Cost Per Transponder	Transponder Power	Antenna Cost
n.a.	5 watts	$66,000
$4.9 million	20 watts	$ 9,300
$9.6 million	50 watts	$ 5,800

These data allow one to determine the number of transmitter sites necessary to justify additional expense on the satellite. This is one type of tradeoff decision which can be undertaken in minimizing transmission system cost. Other decisions are discussed in the next section.

Optimization and tradeoffs. It was mentioned earlier in the section on transmission that existing transmission facilities may determine the choice. For example, Radioprimaria is charged $14.40 per hour for radio facilities that are underutilized during daylight hours. Mayo, McAnany and Klees (1975) reported a cost of $2,100,000 for a one-channel television transmission system to cover a 100,000 square mile area in Mexico. However, they also reported that charges from commercial stations would be $318 per hour for the same area and $1,944 for a 767,000 square mile area (the entire country). Assuming a ten-year life at a 7.5% interest rate for the transmission system used in education, the education system should only build its own system if broadcast exceeds 964 hours per year.

Another interesting example is the Hagerstown system. Assuming a twenty-year life at a 7.5% interest rate for the cable, the total capital cost would be $1.68 million. This cost is for a transmission system to cover an area with a radius of ten to fifteen miles. According to Jamison and Bett (1973) low-power transmitters to cover the same area with six channels would cost approximately $50,000. However, the cable choice, while more costly, may still be necessary when several channels are desired and the open circuit frequency band is crowded. The Hagerstown system was begun in 1956. Technology has changed since then. The Stanford ITV system, begun in 1969, utilizes open circuit broadcast on very high frequencies and avoids the open circuit interference problem. A four-channel system for Hagerstown would cost $134,000 for the transmitter, $200,000 for a 2,000-foot tower (Butman, 1972), and $60,750 for antennas and converters for the forty-five schools. This is a significantly lower investment than for the cable system.

In a more general optimization analysis, Butman (1972) reported costs for different heights of transmitter towers and transmitter power and found that the minimum costs would occur using a 1,000-foot tower and a transmitter of sufficient power to reach an area with a seventy-mile radius. This coverage could be obtained for $35 per square mile when grade B coverage is required.

A tradeoff that is often analyzed in satellite feasibility studies is between direct broadcast satellites (D), terrestrial transmitters with satellite interconnector (R), and terrestrial transmitter with microwave interconnector (T). In analyzing these tradeoffs Rathjens (1973) used the following assumptions regarding costs:

Terrestrial Transmitter	$500,000;
Receiver for rebroadcast from satellite interconnector	$150,000;
Front-end augmentation for classroom receiver from satellite transmitter	$250;
Low-power satellite (interconnector)	$12,000,000;
High-power satellite (transmitter)	$25,000,000; and
Microwave relay	$4,000/mile.

The capital cost associated with the terrestrial transmitter covering an area of approximately 10,000 square miles is derived from Butman's (1972) optimization analysis. Assuming that the terrestrial transmitters are 100 miles apart, Rathjens derived the following equations for the capital costs of the three alternatives:

Direct Broadcast Satellite
$$C_D = 250N + 25,000,000$$

where N is the number of receivers;

Terrestrial Transmitter with Satellite Relay
$$C_R = 65A + 12,000,000$$

where A is the total area to be covered;

Terrestrial Transmitter with Microwave Relay

$C_T = 90A - 400,000.$

The tradeoffs among the three systems for different areas and number of receivers are shown in Figure IV.1. The figure reveals the combination of area size and number of receivers for which each system is optimal.[3] The solid lines dividing the three areas are the locus of points of equal cost. Super-

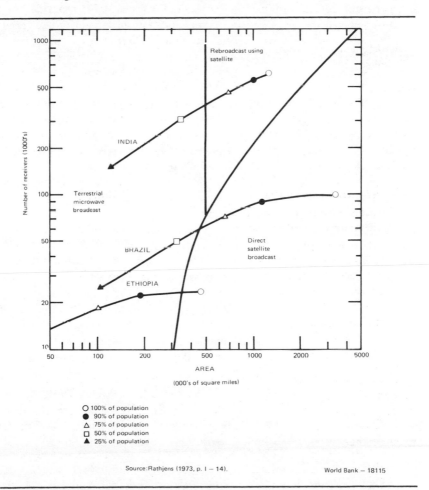

Figure IV-1: COVERAGE CURVES—BASE CASE (One T.V. Receiver per 1000 people)

Source: G. W. Rathjens. Communications for education in developing countries. In Butman, R. C., Rathjens, G. W. and Warren, C. Techno-economic considerations in public service broadcast communications for developing countries. Academy for Educational Development, Report Number Nine, 1973, p. 1-14.

imposed upon this figure, Rathjens has shown the optimal systems for varying population coverage in India, Brazil and Ethiopia. With an assumption of one receiver per 1,000 people the direct broadcast satellite is never an optimal choice in India. The terrestrial transmitter with microwave relay is optimal to the point of covering approximately 60% of the population. For higher coverage, the terrestrial transmitter with satellite relay system becomes optimal.

RECEPTION

The main components of reception costs include: receivers and related equipment such as antennas and cable; power supplies; and printed support materials.

Receivers. There is a wide variety of receivers available for television and radio signals. In choosing a receiver, consideration must be given to maintenance requirements, reception quality, and power requirements.

Receivers for radio are less expensive than television receivers. Jamison and Bett (1973) use a figure of $10 per set for radio (AM reception only) and $200 per set for a 23-inch black and white television receiver.

Consumer Reports (1975) provided an interesting comparison of AM/FM receivers in the range of $25-$60 (list price in the U.S. in 1975). This comparison gives some indication of the relationship between initial price, battery life, and three important design characteristics: tone quality, sensitivity (ability to pick up a weak signal) and selectivity (ability to receive a station without interference from another station). Sensitivity is important, as a trade off exists between transmitter power and receiver sensitivity. In planning a project and attempting to promote use of the program, it may be desirable to use a transmitter with higher power to induce the purchase of lower-cost receivers with lower sensitivity. Selectivity is important in areas with multiple channel broadcasting on closely spaced frequencies.

The general characteristics of the radio receivers tested by *Consumer Reports* are: little variance in AM sensitivity and increased FM sensitivity, AM and FM selectivity and tone quality with price. All models used four C-size batteries. The battery life was tested by playing the radio for four hours per day at high volume (conditions that would be similar to classroom use). The batteries, which have a replacement cost of approximately $1.00 for four batteries, lasted from six to twenty-four days.

Assuming a 5-year life for radios, a $60 radio would have an annual cost of $14.82 (at 7.5% interest). Annual cost for batteries would be $12.00 assuming four hours per day for 240 days, a 20-day battery life and a replacement cost of $1.00. From the Table IV.3, one can see that a reduction in price will reduce some dimension of receiver quality. The price of radios in

TABLE IV.3
AM/FM Radios: Price, Quality, and Battery Life

Model	Price[a]	FM		AM		Tone Quality	Battery Life[b]
		Sensitivity	Selectivity	Sensitivity	Selectivity		
Panasonic RF900	$60	VG	G	VG	F	G	17
Sony TFM7250W	$45	G	VG	VG	F-G	F	6
Penneys 1860	$50	G	F	VG	F	G	10
Hitachi KH1047H	$50	F	VG	VG	F-G	P	20
Sears 22696	$25	P-F	G	VG	F	P	19
Magnavox RD3035	$45	F	P-F	VG	G	F	18
Juliette FPR1286	$40	P-F	F	G	G	P	18
Lloyds NN8296	$30	P-F	F	G	F	P	21
Lafayette 1702349L	$28	P-F	P-F	VG	F	F	10
Soundesign 2298	$29	F	P-F	VG	F	P	24

KEY: P–Poor, F–Fair, G–Good, VG–Very Good

SOURCE: Consumer Reports, July 1975, pp. 438-439.
a. List price in 1975 U.S. dollars.
b. Life (in days) of four C-type batteries when set is operated for four hours per day at high volume.

this analysis is higher than the price commonly used in analyses for developing countries, as these countries often use sets which receive AM frequencies only. In choosing an AM receiver, the same consideration should be given to battery life, tone quality, selectivity and sensitivity as the comparison presented in Table IV.3.

Television receivers can be expected to cost nearly ten times as much as radio receivers. Bourret (1973) and Jamison and Bett (1973) use figures of $200 for a 23-inch black and white television set. Hagerstown (see Chapter IX) has been paying an average price of $150 per set. In the Ivory Coast, the price has been approximately $320. This price may reflect a discount from list prices. List prices are reported for television receivers as for most other equipment. Retail discounts of 10-20 percent are not uncommon and one might expect discounts on quantity purchasing directly from manufacturers.

Factors that are of importance in choosing a television receiver are picture size, set electronics and maintenance. Sensitivity for reception can be influenced by choice of antennas. Antennas have cost approximately $320 in the Ivory Coast. Jamison and Bett (1973) estimate a cost of $660 for an antenna, mount, amplifier, converter, and cable. For the Stanford ITV project (see Chapter VIII), costs for the antenna, amplifier, frequency converter, and cable have been $1,350. Costs are higher for the latter two examples as additional equipment is needed to amplify the signal and convert the signal to frequencies used by standard television receivers. Prices vary with picture size. For example, Panasonic has the following list prices for black and white, solid state receivers; $95—9-inch screen; $100—12-inch screen; $150—16-inch screen; and $160—19-inch screen. These are representative of industry prices.

The decision whether to use a set with a solid state circuit or one with heavy reliance on tubes has important implications. At present a tube set will cost approximately 30% less than an equivalently sized solid state set. Through the use of printed, modular circuits, a solid state set will be easier to maintain. In areas where alternatives to mainline power must be sought, the fact that a solid state set requires 60% of the power necessary to operate a tube set can be important. A 19-inch solid state set requires 54-60 watts whereas a tube set would require 95-100 watts. However, a solid state set is much more sensitive to fluctuations in line voltage. A solid state set, while requiring less power and being more easily maintained, has a higher purchase price and will require more expensive equipment for voltage regulation than a tube set.

The power requirements could be substantially reduced by using a set with a smaller picture tube. A 9-inch solid state set would require only 32 watts. Panasonic produces a portable television receiver with a 5-inch tube and an AM/FM radio for $200. The television and radio are operated by a rechargeable 12-volt battery which has a life of 500 hours and operates for 5.5 hours between charges. However, small tubes are totally unsuitable for regular classroom viewing.

Power sources. Many areas of developing countries receive no electrical power from mainline sources. For these communities, alternative power sources must be found if television receivers are to be used. Radio receivers are more readily available for battery operation. However, if a power source is available, it is preferable to have adaptable receivers, as battery operation tends to be expensive and radios have a low watt requirement. In the Ivory Coast, batteries used to provide power for a simple television cost approximately $500 and last for 2,000 hours; this is about sixty times as expensive as mainline power, clearly an expensive method of operating television receivers. Jamison and Bett (1973) suggest the possibility of standardizing motor vehicle batteries and using the vehicle to recharge batteries.

There are several alternative power sources that may be considered for providing power in local communities. Rao and Manjunath (1972) investigated solar cells, thermoelectric generators, fuel cells, wind power generators, water power generators, manual power generators, animal power generators, electrical power lines, engine generators, and closed cycle vapor turbogenerators in an analysis of power sources for villages in India. They dismiss the first three alternatives as impractical due to high cost, and the next four alternatives as impractical due to lack of reliability. Their cost analysis is concentrated on power lines, engine generators (gasoline, diesel and kerosene), and vapor turbogenerators.

Ayrom (1975) discussed chemical cells, solar cells, thermoelectric generators, wind power generators, vapor turbogenerators, and diesel generators for reception points in Iran. He concentrated his analysis on vapor turbogenerators and diesel generators, as the other choices were assumed to be impractical.

Jamison and Bett (1973) analyzed costs of power derived from power lines, gasoline generators, wind power generators, manual power generators, and animal power generators.

Important factors in the choice of a power source are: power requirements, capital cost, life of source, maintenance expense, and reliability of power source. Different analyses have made different assumptions regarding power requirements. Rao and Manjunath (1972) assumed a need for 170 watts to run a 65-watt television receiver, a 5-watt front end converter, and illumination of 100 watts. Ayrom (1975) assumed a continuous power need of 980 watts for four 215-watt radio receivers (a high estimate) and 120 watts for other equipment, and an intermittent need of 480 watts for illumination and 3,000 watts for air conditioning. Jamison and Bett (1973) assumed 115 watts for equipment consisting of two 40-watt television receivers, forty .2-watt radio receivers, a 5-watt radio receiver, a 10-watt front end converter, and twelve 1-watt disc players. They also considered 200 watts for a minimum lighting package and 800 watts for an adequate lighting package. It seems reasonable to assume that a need for 500 to 1,000 watts of power might be expected. When local power-generating equipment is used it may be desired to provide power for the receivers only. This would significantly reduce the power requirement.

Capital costs vary greatly for different types of equipment. For generators delivering the same amount of power (3 kilowatts) Rao and Manjunath estimated capital costs of $675 for a diesel engine generator, $400 for a kerosene engine generator, $475 for a gasoline engine generator, and approximately $3,000 for a turbo-engine generator. Capital costs also vary by country. Ayrom (1975) estimated a capital cost of $3,000 for a 2-5 kilowatt diesel generator and $10-$12,000 for a similarly powerful turbo-engine generator for Iran. While turbogenerators have higher initial costs, Ayrom (1975) and Rao and Manjunath (1972) claim substantially longer lives (twenty years for a turbogenerator, one year for a gasoline generator), and lower maintenance (one-fifth of the maintenance required for diesel generators).

Reliability of power source is determined by fuel availability for gasoline, diesel, and kerosene engine generators. Pedal generators depend upon availability of manpower. Wind is necessary for wind power generators. The unreliability of wind in Iran and India eliminated this alternative from discussion. For example, wind generators commonly need winds of twenty to twenty-five miles per hour to reach full capacity.

A final important consideration is a means of storing power developed by the source. Carter (1975) reports on the use of truck batteries for storage and estimates that ten fully charged batteries at a cost of approximately $1,000 would deliver 65 kilowatt-hours of power (enough power for a school for four to five days). The batteries used for television receivers in the Ivory Coast store approximately 100 kilowatt-hours and cost $500. However, to charge these batteries, a wind of twenty to twenty mile per hour would have to occur for thirty hours if one were using the 2,500-watt Dunlite windmill, which costs over $6,000.

Table IV.4 provides a summary of costs and requirements of alternative power systems. The following information is provided in the table: type of power source, capital cost, lifetime of equipment, maintenance costs for 1,000 hours of operation, fuel costs per hour of operation, and annual costs. Annual costs are derived by calculating annualized values of capital equipment and assuming a need for 3,750 kilowatt-hours per year (1.5 kilowatts, 10 hours per day, for 250 days).

From Table IV.4, the best choice would appear to be turbogenerators when more than three miles of power line are necessary (assuming a cost of $.05 per kilowatt-hour for powerline electricity). Turbogenerators have longer lives and require less maintenance than alternative generator sources. An additional advantage to the turbogenerators is that any type of liquefied petroleum-based fuel may be used. Using diesel fuel, assuming the use of a 1,000-gallon storage tank (a one-year fuel supply), and adding installation costs of $1,000 (annualized over a two-year period), the turbogenerator would cost approximately $1,100 per year. The wind generator would be cheaper but potentially unreliable in some areas.

The power costs have been estimated for a very high utilization rate of 2,500 hours per year and 1.5 kilowatts per hour. A more realistic estimate may be to assume a 7-hour day, 200-day school year for a total of 1,400 hours. Energy demands may be for only .5 or 1.0 kilowatts per hour. Table IV.5 gives annual costs for a few of the power sources for different demand requirements. Assuming that the placement of a powerline is unfeasible, the turbogenerator remains the optimal choice for local power generation. The costs range from $800 for a low utilization of 500 watts per hour for 1,400 hours per year to $1,100 for 1,500 watts per hour for 2,500 hours per year.

TABLE IV.4
Alternative Power Sources

Type	Power Output (in watts)	Capital Cost	Lifetime	Maintenance (per 1000 hours)	Fuel Costs[a] (per hour)	Annual Cost[b]	Remarks
Gasoline Power[c]							Additional Costs
Honda	350	$300	5,000 hours	$130	$.35	$6835	Storage tanks (annualized for 20-year life)
	800	$250	5,000 hours	$125	$.35	$2653	1,000 gallons – $ 80
	1250	$450	5,000 hours	$145	$.35	$2276	5,000 gallons – $186
	2000	$650	5,000 hours	$165	$.35	$1430	10,000 gallons – $303
	4500	$1450	5,000 hours	$245	$.35	$1707	20,000 gallons – $686
Powerline						$375 at $.10/kwhr $750 at $.20/kwhr $187 at $.05/kwhr	Installation Costs $300 per mile (annualized for 20 years) (Rao and Majunath, 1972)
Wind Power (with storage batteries)	2750	$6000	15 years	$300	– –	$1225	
		$1000	5 years		– –		
Dunlite	1500	$4000	15 years	$200	– –	$900	
		$1000	5 years		– –		
Diesel[d]	800	$375	10,000 hours	$56	.175	$1380	Additional costs – storage tanks.
	2000	$1300	10,000 hours	$195	.175	$1204	
Turbo-Generator[e]	800	$1500	20 years	$11	.175	$1224	Additional costs – storage tanks.
	2000	$5200	20 years	$39	.175	$934	

See next page for footnotes.

FOOTNOTES FOR TABLE IV.4:

a. Fuel costs are assumed to equal $1.00 per gallon for gasoline and $.75 per gallon for diesel fuel. The vapor turbogenerator is assumed to be as expensive to operate as the diesel engin. These approximate relationships in fuel prices are drawn from Rao and Majunath (1972). Honda engines use one-half gallon per 90 minutes at peak conditions. Diesel engines are assumed to have 1.5 times the fuel efficiency of gasoline engines.

b. Annual costs are calculated by determining the appropriate number of units necessary to produce the required power of 1.5 kilowatt hours for 2,500 hours of operation each year. For example, 2 Honda 800 engines would be used for 2 years and operated at full power. At 7.5% the annualized cost is $278.50. Maintenance for the year is added and is equal to 2.5 times the maintenance for 1,000 hours. Fuel costs are given per hour for peak output. A linear relationship is assumed between power output and fuel consumption. For example, to provide 1.5 kilowatts per hour, a Honda 2,000 would need to be operated at only .75 of its capacity and hence full costs would drop to .525 per hour.

c. Honda generators need a minor tuneup every 100 hours (assumed to cost $10 for all units) and a major tuneup every 1,000 hours (assumed to be 10% of initial investment).

d. Diesel engines are assumed to be 1.5 times as expensive as gasoline engines for the same power output. This is the approximate price ratio for much larger engines produced by Ford Motor Co. The diesel engines are assumed to have a longer life than gasoline engines and require a major tuneup every 1,000 hours. The engine is more complicated and the tuneup is assumed to be 15% of initial purchase price.

e. Using Ayrom's (1975) estimates for the relationship between diesel engines and turbo engines, the turbo engine is assumed to cost four times as much as a diesel, require 1/5 the maintenance of the diesel, and last an average life of 20 years. The turbogenerators may use any type of liquefied fuel including gasoline, kerosene, diesel, propane, and butane. As diesel fuel is usually the cheapest available, this fuel will be used for the calculation.

TABLE IV.5
Annual Power Source Costs and Utilization Rate

| | Total Instructional Hours | | | | | |
| | 1400 Energy demand per hour (in kilowatts) | | | 2500 Energy demand per hour (in kilowatts) | | |
	0.5	1.0	1.5	0.5	1.0	1.5
Gasoline[a]	$715	$837	$959	$992	$1,210	$1,430
Diesel[a]	$722	$783	$844	$984	$1,093	$1,204
Turbogenerator[a]	$625	$686	$747	$716	$825	$934
Powerline[b] ($.10 per kw/hour)	$70	$140	$210	$125	$250	$375

a. Annual costs exclude a 1,000-gallon storage tank costing $800, with a 20-year life and installation and construction costs of $1,000. Costs should be increased by $180 per year for each of these alternatives.

b. Powerline installation costs must be added at $300 per mile per year.

Printed material. An important fraction of the cost of instructional radio or television systems can be in the provision of the accompanying printed material. Estimates of the cost of printing a high quality hardbound book and workbook quality material are provided. We stress that the estimates in this section are for the purpose of getting a general picture of what costs are possible; analysis for any particular country would need to look in detail at local costs and opportunities. The book costs we present are those for production in Taipei, Republic of China and probably reflect the minimum feasible costs.

Table IV.6 provides a detailed breakdown of the cost of producing a high quality 500-page hardbound book in Taipei and of shipping the book 4,000 miles. The costs are recent (late 1972) estimates from a printer in Taipei and include his profits. The costs do *not* include typesetting, and assume that the material to be printed is in a form suitable for photo-reproduction. It should be kept in mind that these set up costs can be significant for small runs. Production in quantities of 1,500 results in a price of less than $160 per copy or $.0031 per page. The authors have handled books produced by this printer at the quoted price and the quality is high indeed. One of the authors purchased a lower quality two-volume set (totaling 1,800 pages) at a bookstore in Taipei several years ago at a per-page cost of $.0014. It should be stressed that at a production level of 1,500 copies most economies of scale have been realized; the price per copy would drop only about 2% if the production level were doubled to 3,000 copies.

The price per page is, however, rather sensitive to the number of pages per volume, because of relatively large fixed binding and handling charges. From information in Table IV.6 we can derive the following approximate cost equation for the cost, C_v, of a volume having P pages (with P between 250 and 750). Costs are expressed in U.S. dollars and are increased 25% from what the table would indicate, to account for probable cost changes since that time.

(IV.6) $C_v(P) = .94 + .00125P.$

The cost per page, C_p, is simply $C_v(P)/P$; for a 250-page volume C_p is $.005 and for a 750-page volume C_p is $.0025.

We have less up to date information available concerning the price of workbooks. M. Jamison (1966, pp. 76-80) surveyed printing costs at that time and concluded that a 250-page paperbound workbook with 8½" by 11" pages would cost less than $.00167 per page. This is approximately 40% of the cost estimated above for a high quality hardback of equal length. This $.00167 was estimated on what the author felt to be conservative assumptions, and he cites a study by Wilson, Spaulding, and Smith (1963) that concluded that there exist abundant, now wasted, raw materials for paper in developing countries that could be used as inputs to the production of very low-cost workbooks.

TABLE IV.6
Cost of Book Production in Taipei, Republic of China[a]

Item	Comment
1. Quantity:	1,500 copies
2. Number of pages:	500 pages
3. Size:	6 in. x 9 in. (Thickness about 1½ in.)
4. Cost of Printing and Paper:	By photo-offset, printed in black and white Paper − 80 lb. woodfree $041.02 per ream $041.02 x 40 reams = $690 $0.001 per page $0.001 x 500 pages = $.50 per copy
5. Binding:	Sewn in cloth bound $.425 per copy
6. Book Dust Jackets:	$.05 per copy (optional)
7. Plastic Waterproof Packing Bag:	$.05 per copy (optional)
8. Factory Price:	4 + 5 + 6 + 7 $.50 + $.425 + $.05 + $.05 = $1.025 per copy $1.025 x 1,500 copies = $1,537.50
9. Packing:	Packed in export standard carton boxes Each carton contains 20 copies $.50 per carton or equivalently $.025 per copy
10. Freight:	$.0625 per copy from Taiwan to U.S. West Coast
11. Miscellaneous:	Inland transportation, custom broker, loading charges, insurance, and handling charges, etc. $.0875 per copy
12. Total Price:	8 + 9 + 10 + 11 $1.025 + $.025 + $.0625 + $.0875 = $1.2 per copy

a. Source: Price quotations from a Taipei printer, 1972.

As a comparison to these estimates the cost per printed page for the television system in Korea (see Chapter X) appears to be $.0021 per page with run sizes in the tens of thousands. This cost is lower than our estimates in Table IV.6.

3. COST FUNCTIONS—EXAMPLES AND SUMMARY

In the first section of this chapter, a general cost function for educational technology systems was specified. The second section was concerned with cost estimates for many of the variables in the equation with costs drawn from project experiences and planning studies. In this section, the cost function is combined with the data, and examples are presented for a radio and a television system. The examples are meant to be realistic, although a more careful cost analysis for a specific situation may reveal differences.

The estimates of costs for the determining variable of the cost function are reported in Table IV.7. The cost function equations are repeated for convenience. The reader should refer to Table IV.1 for variable definitions.

(IV.1) $TC = C_c + C_p + C_T + C_R$.

(IV.2) $C_c = a(r, n) C_{SU} + C_{CA}$.

(IV.3) $C_p = a(r, n_p) [a(r, n_{PE}) C_{PE} + a(r, n_{PF}) C_{PF} + C_{PA}]$.

(IV.4) $C_T = a(r, n_{TE}) C_{TE} + a(r, n_{TF}) C_{TF} + C_{TA}$.

(IV.5) $C_R = a(r, n_R) N/_K C'_R + a(r, n_{RE}) SC_{RE} + a(r, n_{RF}) SC_{RF}$

$$+ a(r, n_e) e SC_e + (1 - e) HC_p + ehC'_p + hC_{RM} + a(r, n_b) Nb C_b.$$

The costs are then as follows:

Cost Element	Radio	Television
C_c	$ 89,400	$ 109,400
C_p	$140,870	$ 383,617
C_T	$140,579	$ 408,768
C_R	$102,465	$ 821,742
TC	$473,314	$1,723,527
TC/N	$2.36	$8.61
TC/120N	$ .0188	$ .0684

The costs for a television system serving 200,000 students for 120 hours per student are 3.65 times higher than costs for radio serving a similar group.

The total cost function can be put in the simple format of $TC = F + V_N N + V_h h$. Assuming central costs to be fixed; production, transmission, and reception power hourly cost to vary with the number of hours; and reception costs with the exception of hourly power costs to vary with the number of students, we have the following equations:

Radio: $TC = \$ 89,400 + 562.89 h + .51 N$.
Television: $TC = \$109,400 + 1,584.88 h + 4.10 N$.

The parameters of these hypothetical equations fall within the range of values obtained in the cases described in Chapter III and summarized in

TABLE IV.7
Example Values of Cost Components

Variable		Assumed Value for	
		Radio	Television
N	(number of students)	200,000	200,000
h^a	(total hours of programming)	500	500
G	(area of region)	31,400 sq.mi. (100 mi. radius)	31,400 sq.mi.
b^b	(printed pages per student)	200	150
k^c	(students per receiver)	70	70
e	(fraction non-electrified)	– –	.50
s^d	(number of reception sites)	1,430	1,430
C_{SU}^e	(start up costs)	$300,000	$300,000
C_{CA}^f	(annual central administration cost)	$60,000	$80,000
C_{PF}^g	(production facility capital cost)	$230,000	$2,316,000
C_{PE}^h	(production equipment capital cost)	$160,000	$1,571,428
C_{PA}^i	(annual production cost)	$320,000	$540,000
C_{TE}^j	(transmission equipment capital cost)	$480,000	$1,570,000
C_{TF}^k	(transmission facility capital cost)	$25,500	$26,000
C_{TA}^l	(annual transmission cost)	$68,000	$177,000
$C_R'^m$	(receiver capital cost)	$20	$200
C_{RE}^n	(receiver-related equipment capital cost)	– –	$320
C_{RF}^o	(reception facility capital cost)	$40	$1,100
C_e^p	(power generating equipment capital cost)	– –	$3,300
C_p^q	(hourly cost of power from power line)	– –	$.05
$C_p'^r$	(hourly cost of power from power-generating equipment or batteries)	$.025	$.186
C_{RM}^s	(hourly receiver maintenance cost)	$4	$40

TABLE IV.7 (Continued)

Variable		Assumed Value for	
		Radio	Television
$C_b{}^t$	(printed page cost)	$.005	$.005
n, n_{PF}, n_{TF}, n_{RF}	(lifetime of project and production, transmission and reception facilities)	20	20
n_p, n_b	(lifetime of programs and books)	3	3
n_R	(lifetime of receiver)	5	5
n_{PE}, n_{TE}, n_{RE}, n_e	(lifetime of production, transmission, receiver-related and power generating equipment	10	10
r	(interest rate)	7.5%	7.5%

a. Programming is assumed to be provided for 10% of the total instructional time of 1,260 hours (35 hours per week for 36 weeks) for students in four different grades.

b. Radio is assumed to require more printed materials in conjunction with broadcasts than television, due to the lack of the visual channel.

c. Each receiver may be used by 2 classes with an average class size of 35.

d. It is assumed that there is only one class for each of four grades at each reception site.

e. Start up costs are expected to be the same for both types of systems. The cost includes basic project planning, feasibility study, and cost analysis costs. The start up costs were $335,000 in Nicaragua. These costs were probably unusually high because of the unusual nature of the project (primary school mathematics via radio with 40-50 student responses per 20-minute lesson).

f. Project central administration is costing $60,000 in Nicaragua for radio and $80,000 in the Ivory Coast for television.

g. h. i. The production expenses are based upon El Salvador, which has been averaging approximately $2,900 per hour for television broadcasting. Radio production expenses are based upon the recurrent expenses for Nicaragua and an estimate of equipment expenses, which are 10% of those required for television. Schramm (1967) estimates a cost of $250 per hour for radio in Thailand and the 10% assumption will keep the relative estimates for production costs similar to project experiences.

j. Mayo, McAnany and Klees (1975) report that a transmission system to cover 100,000 sq. ml. for television in Mexico would cost $2,100,000. Butman (1972) estimates that under the best circumstances transmission for television would cost $35 per square mile. A figure of $50 per square mile is used. The VERTA project in the Philippines (Bourret, 1973) spent $20,000 for a 5 kilowatt transmitter and $20,000 for a 10 gain antenna capable of covering a 50-mile radius. Radio transmission costs are based upon the General Learning Corp. (1968) study. Costs are approximately 1/3 of the costs of television. This is fairly typical even at lower power ratings. For example, Jamison with Bett (1973) quote prices of $2,500 for a 10-watt FM transmitter and $5,000 for a 5-watt television transmitter.

k. Facility expenses include a building for transmission equipment assumed to be 500 sq. ft. at $50 per sq. ft. and installation expenses of $500 for radio and $1,000 for television.

l. Annual expenses are assumed to include 10% of equipment investment for maintenance expenses and salaries of $20,000 for four engineers and technicians.

m. Higher prices are assumed to insure good quality receivers. It is possible that these values should be $10 for radio receivers (Jamison with Bett, 1973) and $150 for television receivers (list price for receivers in the United States).

Chapter XII. If this were an actual planning study variations in the resource configurations under consideration, as well as alternative assumptions about the costs of any given resource configuration, would be tested to see their impact on system cost. Again, the more relevant variables included in the cost model, the greater the possibility of determining the sensitivity of costs to policy decisions. We turn now to apply the concepts developed to this point to a detailed analysis of the costs of a number of on-going IR and ITV projects.

NOTES

1. See Evans and Klees (1977) for an interesting analysis that combines a television production perspective with an economic one in order to analyze the organization, efficiency, and costs of ITV production in the Ivory Coast.

2. See Amid (1975) for a discussion of the application of aerostat transmission in Iran.

3. The concept of optimality used here assumes that minimization of cost/receiving site is the relevant goal, implicitly assuming that alternative transmission systems do not differ in any other important manner. For critical examination of these premises with particular attention to satellite transmission see Klees and Wells (1977c).

FOOTNOTES FOR TABLE IV.7 (Continued)

n. Radio receivers do not usually need any antennas. The figure for television receivers is derived from the expenditure in the Ivory Coast.

o. Building modifications are assumed to cost $20 per classroom for radio and require $150 per classroom for television (including a stand) and $800 for installation. These estimates are derived from Jamison with Bett (1973).

p. No electrical power equipment is necessary for the radio system. For the television system, an 800-watt vapor turbogenerator costing $1,500 is assumed to be used. This would be ample power to provide electricity for two sets as the watt requirement per set is only 60. The extra power could be used for lighting. A 1,000-gallon storage tank would cost $800 and an additional $1,000 is assumed for installation.

q. Mainline power is assumed to cost $.10 per kilowatt hour (Jamison with Bett, 1973, use $.06 and the cost in the Ivory Coast, is approximately $.11). The power requirement is assumed to be 500 watts per hour of operation.

r. Batteries for radio are assumed to have a 40-hour life and cost $1.00 to replace. The hourly operation for the television system includes maintenance at $.011 per hour and diesel fuel at .175 per hour.

s. Maintenance for receivers is assumed to cost 10% of total purchase price. There are two receivers at each reception point.

t. This number is based upon the printing costs previously discussed.

PART THREE

CASE STUDIES

In Part One of this report we discussed several methodological approaches to cost analysis and their problems, and in Part Two we applied this methodology to an examination of ongoing instructional radio and television projects and to planning such projects in the future. Here, in Part Three, we present detailed case studies of two instructional radio projects (in Nicaragua and Mexico) and five instructional television projects (in El Salvador, The United States, Korea, and Mexico), with a strong emphasis on a cost analysis of these projects. In all but one of the cases (El Salvador, where the cost data were gathered by Speagle, 1972), one or more of the authors has had firsthand exposure to the project and has gathered the cost data. An effort has been made to structure the cost analyses of the projects so that they are in as comparable a format as possible. In addition to an analysis and discussion of project costs, each case includes general information describing the system and its operation, as well as a review of any evaluations of the system's effectiveness that are available. Where possible we compare the costs and effectiveness of the instructional radio or instructional television system with those of the existing traditional educational system.

The general approach taken is the same as described in the introductory remarks to Chapter III and we repeat those remarks here for the convenience of the reader. All of the projects studied have been underway long enough to provide ongoing cost information. In all cases, however, the analysis is based on data subject to substantial error, and our divisions of costs into various categories is sometimes based on incomplete information and hence may be somewhat arbitrary. The reader should view our conclusions as approximations.

To put the costs into a form that permits the projects to be compared with one another, we have done four things. First, we converted all costs into 1972

U.S. dollars by converting from the foreign currency to U.S. currency at the exchange rate prevailing at the time the information was gathered, then used the U.S. GNP deflator to convert to 1972 dollars (see the Appendix for the exchange rates and deflators used). Due to differing relative prices in different countries and exchange rate rigidities, there may be distortions introduced by this procedure (see Vaizey et al., 1972, Chapters 15 and 16). Second, we use the same interest rates (social rate of discount) to evaluate each project. To allow examination of the sensitivity of the conclusions to the rates chosen, we use three values for the interest rate—zero, 7.5%, and 15% per year.[1] Third, we have attempted to include and exclude the same items in each cost analysis. We include central administration costs, program production costs, transmission costs and reception costs. We exclude the costs of teacher re-training and printed material. Fourth, we have assumed common capital life-times for all projects—twenty years for buildings and start up costs, ten years for transmission and studio equipment, and five years for receivers.

For each project examined we derive an annualized cost function of the linear form presented in equation in I.2 in Chapter I; that is, we assume there to be a fixed cost, F, a variable cost per student, V_N, and a variable cost per programming hour, V_h, so that total cost, $TC(N, h) = F + V_N N + V_h h$, where N is the number of students using the system and h is the number of program-ming hours provided in any particular year.[2] This simplified formulation takes *as given* the other cost determining system variable particular to each system, such as the number of grade levels served, the geographical area cov-ered, the fraction of receivers located in electrified areas, the quality of pro-gram production, the average class size. In a few cases we examine system costs as assumed changes in these variables occur. To the extent that we would want to know in detail the sensitivity of a project's costs to changes in the present configuration of these types of variables, more complex cost functions would have had to be estimated, such as those that will be de-scribed in Chapter IV for project planning uses.

To obtain the values for F, V_N, and V_h, we allocated each cost into one of six categories: fixed, capital; fixed, recurrent; variable by student, capital; variable by student, recurrent; variable by hour, capital; and variable by hour, recurrent. Capital costs were then annualized using equation I.3 of Chapter I, and the cost function was constructed by letting F equal the sum of all fixed cost components, V_N equal the sum of all variable by student cost compo-nents, and V_h equal the sum of all variable by hour cost components.

It should be noted that in some of the cost analyses that follow, the value F is quite low or even zero, as most instructional television and instructional radio system costs are assumed to vary with N and h. More specifically, most production and transmission costs are assumed to vary with h while most re-ception costs are assumed to vary with N. It is usually only central administration and start up costs (when estimates of these are available) that are assumed fixed, and sometimes even these may vary with N and h. This assumption is somewhat simplistic, but nevertheless, probably reflects the long run picture reasonably accurately; in the short run, for marginal expansion decisions, there may be sufficient excess capacity to increase N or h without increasing all related component costs. However, as the system expands, the excess capacity falls to zero, and all relevant system components need to be increased to allow further expansion (of N or h, for example). Thus the linear function that will be estimated is probably an approximation to what more realistically can be expected to be a step function, which increases in discrete increments as N and h expand to fill the excess system capacity at successive points in time.

In addition to the cost function estimation, three other pieces of cost information will be presented when possible. First, the average cost per student (AC_N) for a particular year of the project will be derived from the cost function. Second, this figure will be compared to the variable cost per student, V_N, to form a ratio, AC_N/V_N. This ratio is presented to give the reader a rough idea of the extent to which the system discussed has achieved the economics of scale available in most instructional television and instructional radio systems in their operations for the particular year in question. AC_N/V_N approaches unity as the system expands the number of students included, other things being equal. When AC_N/V_N is large, it indicates that if the system were to increase the number of students enrolled, average costs per student could be decreased substantially by enrollment expansion. Since there is no theoretical upper bound on the ratio AC_N/V_N, it is somewhat difficult to evaluate what it means for a given ratio to be "large," but an idea can be gained from examining this figure for different projects. Third, we also present average cost per student hour of each project, which is probably one of the better measures for comparison between systems, since it takes account of both N and h.

When sufficient information is available, namely, the time structure of expenditures and student usage, we present selected estimates of the average costs per student from year i to year j (AC_{ij}), a concept that was developed in Section 4 of Chapter I. As discussed in Chapter III, we believe the AC_{ij}'s form a much better summary measure or project costs than that derived from the cost function estimations. Finally, discussion of the alternatives for system expansion and considerations of system finance are presented if the relevant data are available.

Chapters V and VI analyze instructional radio projects in Nicaragua and Mexico, respectively. Instructional television projects are examined for El Savador in Chapter VIII, for Stanford, California in Chapter VIII, for

Hagerstown, Maryland in Chapter IX, for Korea in Chapter X, and for Mexico in Chapter XI.

NOTES

1. We have included an interest rate of zero *only* to show the significant difference in estimated costs due to not discounting the future; using $r = 0$ is rarely a sensible alternative in evaluating project costs.

2. To be more precise, some costs may vary with the number of programming hours produced in any year, other costs may vary with the number of hours broadcast, while still others may vary with the number of hours of instructional lessons a class receives (see the discussion in Chapter IV); the cost analysis of ongoing projects presented here is not this detailed and thus h will usually refer to the second definition, the number of hours broadcast. This yields a slightly inaccurate cost representation, but it should be recognized that each definition of h is probably roughly in proportion to the other two, and thus the estimated costs are reasonably accurate.

Chapter V

THE NICARAGUAN RADIO
MATHEMATICS PROJECT[1]

The central focus of this chapter is to provide an early assessment of what the costs of the Nicaraguan Radio Mathematics (RMP) have been and can be expected to be. Much firmer evidence is presently available for programming costs than for implementation costs. Section 2 of this chapter summarizes the cost elements of the project—central project costs, program production costs, transmission costs, and reception site costs—then presents a cost function for the project and average costs based on that cost function. Section 3 discusses the results of the cost analysis, with some of their implications. More detailed breakdowns of cost data are available for this project than for our other cases, and we include those data here to give the reader a sense of the differing levels of detail that cost analyses can provide.[1]

1. THE SYSTEM

In early 1975 a group of AID sponsored researchers and mathematics curriculum specialists began working with Nicaraguan counterparts in Masaya, Nicaragua on radio programs to teach elementary school mathematics. The Radio Mathematics Project (RMP) is now completing its first year and is reaching approximately 600 first grade students on an experimental basis. During 1976 programming will be extended through the second grade, and a carefully controlled evaluation of a large-scale implementation of the first grade curriculum will be undertaken. Present plans call for continued expansion of curriculum coverage to higher grade levels and for implementation of the radio curriculum throughout Nicaragua. Searle, Friend, and Suppes (1975) discuss in detail the RMP's activities and future plans.

2. SYSTEM COSTS

In this section we identify the cost components for the RMP and construct from them cost functions for the project. The costs fall into four categories—central project, program preparation, transmission, and reception site—and we first present information on those basic costs; since the project is in its early stages, some of these costs, particularly those dealing with reception, are estimated rather than observed. The project relies more heavily than do most on expatriate technical assistance, and for this reason programming costs in particular are relatively high. We thus also briefly discuss the cost implications of lower levels of expatriate technical assistance in the future.

CENTRAL PROJECT COSTS

We divide our central project costs into three major categories—start up, administration and research.

The RMP commenced radio program production in Masaya, Nicaragua in February, 1975; costs incurred prior to that time were for project planning, personnel moving and settling in to facilities. We thus treat those costs incurred prior to February, 1975 as being start up costs that should be annualized over the lifetime of the project. Table V.1 shows start up costs incurred at Stanford University and in Masaya.

The next aspect of central project costs is that dealing with administration. For many of the staff involved it is difficult to separate precisely their project administration efforts from other functions; at Stanford the other function is principally research; in Masaya it is principally radio program production. The estimates of time allocation that we use are, then, simply the best estimates of the project staff. Table V.2 summarizes annual project administration costs based on these best estimates; the total is approximately $47,000 per year.

The final category of central project costs is general research, which is a major purpose of the project. The research costs listed here do *not* include formative research for program development; those costs appear with other program development costs. Table V.3 shows annual expenditures on research at the present time (1975); these costs may be expected to decline as the project becomes operational.

PROGRAM PRODUCTION COSTS

The RMP is currently producing programs at a rate of about 150 thirty-minute programs per year. The first year of program production (CY [calendar year] 1975) is being devoted to programs for grade one; the second year will be devoted to revision of grade one programs and initial preparation of grade two programs. Thus a single year's activity will involve both production of a set of about 150 programs and the revision of an earlier set of 150; the output of a year's effort can thus be considered to be a produced and revised set of programs. Production here includes all steps required to plan, prepare and put on tape the radio script, as well as preparation of the student workbook materials and the teacher's guide.

TABLE V.1
Start Up Costs (through February 1975)

I.	*Start up Cost of Project at Stanford:*		
	Salaries	$46,255	
	Staff benefits	7,864	
	Travel in USA	5,745	
	Computer at Stanford[a]	19,553	
	Consulting	1,920	
	Equipment and supplies	3,066	
	Indirect costs	39,670	
	Subtotal		$124,073
II.	*Start up Cost of Project in Nicaragua:*		
	Salaries[a, b]	$23,626	
	Benefits	4,016	
	Travel	6,716	
	Moving cost (household and car)	16,131	
	Allowances[c]	19,444	
	Consulting	720	
	Expendable supplies[d]	19,002	
	Equipment[e]	18,715	
	Indirect costs	33,171	
	Subtotal		$141,542
III.	*Start up Cost Totals:*		
	1. Total start up cost		$268,000
	2. Annualized start up cost		
	(over 20-year project lifetime)		
	a. at 0% discount rate		$ 13,440/yr.
	b. at 7.5% discount rate		26,400/yr.
	c. at 15% discount rate		43,200/yr.

a. The computer was used for the production of reports, but for essentially nothing else during this period.
b. Salaries are for expatriate staff.
c. Allowances include housing allowance, post differential allowance, and children's education allowance.
d. Expendable Supplies breaks down as follows:

Office supplies	$2,906
Books	616
Postage and freight	4,868
Minor equipment	3,299 (tape recorders, etc.)
Nicaragua expenses	7,311

e. The equipment includes four cars, a mimeograph machine, an electronic scanner for making stencils, and a calculator with statistical functions.

TABLE V.2
Project Administration Costs[a]

I. *Annual Costs of Project Administration at Stanford:*
    (all figures given include direct and all indirect costs)[b]

Principal Investigator – 6% of full time	$ 2,480	
Project Manager – 50% of full time	11,680	
Secretary – 50% of full time	5,600	
Administrative services – 15% of full time		
(covered by indirect costs)	0	
University functions – purchasing, shipping,		
accounting (covered by indirect costs)	0	
Telephone, office supplies, etc.	3,520	
Computer time	3,680	
Travel to Nicaragua for administrative purposes		
(25% of four trips)	1,120	
Subtotal		$28,080

II. *Annual Costs of Project Administration in Nicaragua:*

Expatriate Advisor – 33% of full time	$12,160	
Nicaraguan Project Director – 50% of full time	4,000	
Secretary (bilingual) – 100% of full time	2,800	
Subtotal		$18,960

III. *Total Annual Costs of Project Administration* $47,040

a. Costs incurred in cordobas are exchanged into U.S. dollars at the rate of 7 cordobas per dollar.
b. Indirect costs at Stanford University are 47% of base costs.

TABLE V.3
Research Costs[a]

	Annual Amount
Principal Investigator – 17% of full time	$ 7,360
Project Manager – 50% of full time	11,680
Statistician – 50% of full time	5,760
Programmer – 100% of full time	14,880
Two graduate student assistants	8,640
Consultants	4,720
Telephone, office supplies	1,440
Computer time – 90% of computer charges	32,800
Travel to Nicaragua (7 trips per year)	7,680
Total	$94,960

a. All figures include indirect costs of 47%.

Table V.4 summarizes the cost of preparing 150 lessons; the total is $128,000. This yields a cost of $856 per thirty-minute lesson or $1,712 per hour of produced material. This is far higher than previous costs of production of instructional radio in developing countries,[2] which results from a number of factors. First, and relatively unimportant, this figure includes cost of preparation of workbooks and teacher guides. Second, preparation of programs requiring frequent student response (forty to fifty responses per thirty-minute lesson) is probably intrinsically costly. Third, careful formative evaluation is costly. Fourth, much of the cost is for expatriate technical assistance, the presence of which more than doubles the cost of production over what it would be if the same volume of production were achieved by Nicaraguan nationals. (If expatriates were replaced by nationals, the $128,000 annual cost in Table V.4 would drop to $56,800; this would reduce the cost per lesson to $376.)

Assuming a ten-year lifetime for a completed and revised lesson, the annualized cost of having a lesson available (assuming an $856 initial cost) is $86 if one assumes a zero discount rate, $128 if one assumes a 7.5% discount rate, and $170 if one assumes a 15% discount rate.

TRANSMISSION COSTS

Our estimate of transmission costs is based on the tariff of *Radio Corporacion,* a private broadcasting station whose transmitter covers all of Nicaragua. Their charge per twenty-six-minute slot between 5:00 a.m. and 9:00 a.m. is $11.60; between 9:15 a.m. and 11:45 a.m. it drops to $9.20. There is a 10% discount for a one year contract, which would be advantageous for the RMP if such contracts allowed for less frequent than daily use. For subsequent calculations we assume a cost of $12.80 to broadcast a thirty-minute lesson.

RECEPTION SITE COSTS

The present (1975) reception sites utilize cassette players because the small number of sites in the first developmental year fails to justify use of broadcasting. Current reception costs are thus little guide to future ones, and the costs presented below simply reflect present project estimates. The cost estimates we present attempt to include all elements of cost associated with operational introduction of the RMP, including teacher training costs, supervision costs and printed material costs.

Table V.5 categorizes reception site costs estimates into three parts. The first part consists of costs common to an entire school, in this case supervision costs; assuming three participating classes per school and thirty-five students per class, supervision costs come to $.59 per student per year. This number is,

TABLE V.4

Costs of Preparing 150 Radio Lessons

Item	Cost per year
1. Recording Costs	$10,080
Studio time at $11/lesson	
Artists and technicians at $34/lesson	
Director at $22/lesson	
2. Scriptwriting	32,960
2 full time equivalent Nicaraguans at $344/mo. each	
1 full time equivalent expatriate at $2,400/mo.	
3. Curriculum Design	12,960
1/2 full time equivalent Nicaraguan at $456/mo.	
1/3 full time equivalent expatriate at $2,960/mo.	
1/2 full time equivalent secretary at $208/mo.	
4. Artist for Design and Preparation of Student Workbooks	2,800
1 full time equivalent at $232/mo.	
5. Preparation of Teacher's Guides	2,400
1/2 full time equivalent writer at $400/mo.	
6. Management	15,760
1/2 full time equivalent Nicaraguan at $464/mo.	
1/3 full time equivalent expatriate at $2,960/mo.	
1/2 full time equivalent secretary at $208/mo.	
7. Formative Evaluation	15,760
1 full time equivalent Nicaraguan at $344/mo.	
1 full time equivalent expatriate at $2,560/mo.	
Data processing costs at $800/mo.	
8. Support and Facilities	6,560
Rent $232/mo.	
Utilities 72/mo.	
Maid 48/mo.	
Guard 72/mo.	
Transportation (exclusive vehicle purchase 120/mo.	
TOTAL COST	**$128,000**
TOTAL COST PER LESSON	**$ 856**

TABLE V.5
Reception Site Costs (per 150 lessons)

I.	*Costs Common to Entire School*		$62.00
	Supervisor visits (S is number of supervisor visits per school per academic year; assumed cost per visit is 1 day of supervisor time at $8.80 plus transportation at $1.60). We assume S = 6.		
II.	*Costs Common to Classroom*		30.00
	1. Radio set at $40 with 5-year lifetime	$10.00	
	a. Annualized cost at 0% = $ 8/yr.		
	b. Annualized cost at 7.5% = $10/yr.		
	c. Annualized cost at 15% = $12/yr.		
	(table uses 7.5% discount rate)		
	2. Batteries[a]	4.00	
	3. Teacher's Guide (100 pp.)	.80	
	4. Teacher training (10 hours per year at $1.60/hr.)	16.00	
III.	*Costs Individual to Student*		1.60
	1. Blank paper (0–1/2 pages per lesson; assume 40 pages per year at 1/4 cent per page)	.08	
	2. Workbook (1/2 to 1 page per lesson; assume 150 pages @ 1 cent per page)	1.50	
	3. Miscellaneous Supplies	.32	

IV. *Cost Summary (Full Program Cost Assumption)*

Assume: (1) 3 participating classrooms per school

(2) 35 students per class

Per-student reception cost	is	$3.06/yr.
	or	$ .02/lesson
	or	$ .04/hour

V. *Cost Summary (Alternative Program Cost)*

1. Teacher's Guide and training costs not imputed to radio:

Per student reception cost is	$ 2.58/yr.

2. Student workbook is replaced by additional 110 pages per year of blank paper:

Per student cost is	$ 2.09/yr.

3. Both 1 and 2 above:

Per student cost is	$ 1.61/yr.

a. This assumes an average of 10 hours of playing life per battery costing $.28; these battery lifetimes are within the range of those cited in a recent **Consumer Reports** survey (v. 40, July 1975, pp. 436-439).

of course, highly sensitive to the number of supervisor visits per school per year, and it will be important, as the project progresses, to ascertain what an adequate minimum number is. The second cost category consists of those costs common to a classroom; these costs are estimated to be $30 per classroom per year or $.87 per student. A total of $26 out of the $30 classroom costs is for teacher training and the radio set, neither of which would increase with a moderate increase in the number of currriculums broadcast. Possibilities for savings here include sharing of radio sets among classrooms, providing teacher training less frequently than annually, and undertaking teacher training by radio. The third category of costs is for materials; these are estimated to cost $1.60 per student per year. Utilizing less than one page per day of workbook material would result in substantial cost savings.

Item V in Table V.5 presents estimates of reception site costs based on alternative assumptions. The first assumption is that the costs of teacher training and the teacher guide are excluded from the accounting of costs for the radio project; this reduces the reception site costs imputed to radio from $3.06 per year to $2.58 per year. The second assumption is that the project eliminate utilization of printed workbooks; this would save $.97 per student per year.

SUMMARY OF COSTS FOR THE RADIO MATHEMATICS PROJECT

Cost function. Our cost function for the RMP will be constructed to give annualized total cost, TC, as a linear function of two independent variables— the number of lessons presented per year, h, and the number of students enrolled in a course, N. Each enrolled student would take the 150 lessons of a single year's course. The cost function we are assuming has, then, the following form:

$$TC = F + V_N N + V_h h,$$

where F, V_N, and V_h are parameters we can determine from the cost data of the preceding subsection.

The first parameter, F, consists of all cost components invariant with respect to hours of programming or student usage. That is, it consists of central project costs:

$$F = \text{annualized starting costs} + \text{project administration}$$
$$\text{costs} + (\text{research costs}).$$

We have placed research costs in parentheses because we feel it dubious that these general research costs should be included in the Nicaragua cost function. As most of the research covered by these costs has resulted directed outside

Nicaragua, we will exclude these research costs from out total cost equation; information from Table V.3 will allow those who wish to include these costs to do so. (On the other hand, we *do* include, in V_h, the cost of formative evaluation research as being directly related to program production.)

Since we annualized start up costs as three different discount rates, we have three values for F (each excluding research costs):

$$F = \begin{array}{l} \$60,500/\text{yr. if r} = 0 \\ \$73,400/\text{yr. if r} = 7.5\% \\ \$90,200/\text{yr. if r} = 15\%. \end{array}$$

The next parameter, V_h, depends on transmission costs and program production costs; it equals the annualized cost of a lesson plus the cost of transmitting it once. The annualized cost of a lesson is $86 at a zero discount rate; $128 at a 7.5% discount rate; and $170 at a 15% discount rate. The cost of transmission is $12.80.[3] Thus we have

$$V_h = \begin{array}{l} \$99/\text{yr. if r} = 0 \\ \$141/\text{yr. if r} = 7.5\% \\ \$183/\text{yr. if r} = 15\%. \end{array}$$

The final cost parameter, V_N, depends only on the cost per enrolled student per year. From Table V.5 we see that $V_N = \$3.06/\text{yr.}$[4]

Our final cost equations are, then, given by (in dollars per year)

$$TC = \begin{array}{l} 60,500 + 99\,h + 3.1\,N \text{ if r} = 0 \\ 73,400 + 141\,h + 3.1\,N \text{ if r} = 7.5\% \\ 90,200 + 182\,h + 3.1\,N \text{ if r} = 15\%. \end{array}$$

Average costs. The above equations can be used to compute the average cost of radio per student per year. AC, and the cost per student hour of exposure. PHC, as a function of the values of h and N. Table V.6 shows the results of computations of this sort for two values of h—450 and 900—and several values of N. This table uses the cost function that has a 7.5% discount rate. Since there are 150 lessons per year, a value of h = 450 implies radio coverage (in mathematics) for three grade levels; h = 900 implies radio coverage for all six elementary grades.

Even with between 10,000 and 50,000 users, the average costs remain substantially above the marginal cost of $3.06 per student per year. And, unless these high marginal costs are reduced, the costs of the RMP will remain higher than for other radio projects, and fall in the low end of the range of instructional television costs (Jamison and Klees, 1975, p. 356).

TABLE V.6
Average Costs[a]

N	h = 450 (3 grades covered)		h = 900 (6 grades covered)	
	AC[b]	PHC[c]	AC[b]	PHC[c]
	$		$	
2,000	70.20	.95	102.40	1.38
10,000	16.80	.22	23.20	.31
50,000	5.60	.07	7.20	.10
250,000	3.60	.05	3.84	.06

a. These average costs are computed from the cost function that has a discount rate of 7.5%.
b. AC stands for the average cost per student per year in dollars.
c. PHC stands for the per hour cost of instruction per student; as there are 150 thirty-minute lessons per year, PHC = AC/75.

CONCLUSIONS

Three basic points emerge from the analysis just presented of the costs of the RMP in Nicaragua: In the first place, the intensive efforts put into program preparation suggest that, unless careful effort is undertaken to make these programs available to many users, the cost per student of program production will be extremely high. The costs can be spread among users by insuring a long life (ten plus years) for the programs, by implementing the RMP through all or most of Nicaragua and by attempting to use the same programs with only slight revision for Spanish-speaking students elsewhere in Latin America or within the United States.

Second, the presently planned levels of classroom supervision, teacher training and student workbook usage result in per student reception costs of $3.06 per year, or, assuming 150 thirty-minute lessons in a year, costs of 4.2 cents per student hour. These costs are exceptionally high, suggesting the value of continued, careful experimentation with lower levels of supervision, less frequent and less intensive teacher training, teacher training by radio, and more limited workbook use.

And finally, it appears possible to reduce substantially the reception site costs and to spread programming costs over a large audience. Even if this were to be done, the project is apt to remain somewhat expensive by the standards of instructional radio projects. For this reason, principal emphasis in evaluation of the RMP must be placed on its capacity to improve the effectiveness of instruction, as indicated by its effects on mathematics achievement test scores and student repetition rates. It is too early in the project to assess its performance along these dimensions.

NOTES

1. See Jamison (1974), the study on which this case is based, for more details. Also see Wells and Klees (1978) for a recently updated study of the costs of this project, Jamison (1977b) for a study of its cost-effectiveness, and Searle, Matthews, Suppes, and Friend (1977) for a detailed analysis of effects.

2. Chapter IV reported production costs for instructional radio of about $130 per hour in Korea and in Mexico; Schramm (1973, p. 215) reports that the NHK was spending about $460 (inflation adjusted) in 1971. The cost per hour of television production is about $500 in Mexico, $1,150 in El Salvador and $2,550 in Korea.

3. This assumes that each lesson is broadcast only once per year. The relatively small cost of transmission suggests, if there were either pedagogical advantages for repeat broadcasting or advantages in shifting, that the resulting increases in transmission cost would be relatively slight.

4. Strictly speaking, $V_N = \$3.06$ if $r = 7.5\%$; we assume, however, that V_N is not dependent on r because the cost implications are so slight.

Chapter VI

THE MEXICAN RADIOPRIMARIA

Mexico, along with many other developing nations, faces a contradiction in the provision of basic education for its population; there is the desire, expressed by popular sentiment and even legislative requirement, to provide a complete primary school education to all its people, while at the same time there is a lack of teachers, classrooms and materials, especially in the rural areas, sufficient to support the school age population. Of the 32,855 primary schools in the country, only 6,440 have a full six grades complement, with most of the latter located in urban areas (see Klees, 1972).

In an attempt to meet this problem, the Mexican Secretariat for Public Education (SEP) initiated in 1969 an experimental program that utilized instructional radio to aid in the provision of fourth, fifth and sixth grade education to certain rural and semi-rural regions that lacked a complete primary school. Below we will examine Radioprimaria, with the main emphasis on the costs of the system: Section 1 will describe the system in general, its technical characteristics, organization and utilization, as well as briefly summarize evidence on its effectiveness; Section 2 will analyze the costs of the system in detail; Section 3 will compare briefly the costs of Radioprimaria with that of the traditional direct teaching system; and Section 4 will present concluding remarks. The discussion in Section 1 is based on the analysis of the structure and utility of Radioprimaria made by Spain (1973) and the interested reader is referred there for more detail; subsequent sections are the work of the authors (a somewhat less detailed cost analysis by one of the authors is included in Spain, 1973).

1. THE SYSTEM

ORGANIZATION AND TECHNICAL CHARACTERISTICS

Planning for the Radioprimaria system began in 1969. During the 1969-1970 school year, the system was used in twenty-nine schools in the Valley of Mexico and the Federal District, but was not continued in these regions after the first year, except for one classroom in the Experimental Education Center in Mexico City. At the beginning of the 1970-1971 school year, the system was tried out on a small scale in the State of San Luis Potosi and is still in use there. This case study represents an analysis of Radioprimaria as instituted in San Luis Potosi.

Radioprimaria was intended primarily to allow a school with four teachers to offer all six grades of primary schooling. Three teachers would handle the first three grades in the traditional manner; the fourth teacher would have the fourth, fifth and sixth grades in one classroom and would instruct with the assistance of radio lessons. Some instructional radio programs would be grade-specific while others would be directed to all three grades in common. When grade-specific lessons are broadcast, the students in the other two grades are supposed to engage in work on their own. It should also be noted that the above structure implies that students may be directed to listen to the same common broadcasts each year for three years.

Instructional radio lessons are prepared by a team of eight radio teachers in studios located in Mexico City. They are shipped by bus to San Luis Potosi, where they are then broadcast, by the University of San Luis Potosi radio station (at no charge to SEP), within a thirty mile radius around the capital city. Broadcasts are made every school day, Monday to Friday, from 9:00 a.m. until 12:45 p.m. In Mexico City, the programs are broadcast one hour earlier over Station XEEP, in order to be used by the experimental classroom, as well as by some traditional primary schools that use the lessons on an informal basis.

Each radio lesson lasts fourteen minutes and about five programs are broadcast each school day. The subjects of the broadcasts are taken from the official primary school curriculum and are keyed directly to the required textbooks. Emphasis is placed on Spanish, arithmetic, history, and geography, although lessons'dealing with physical education, nature study and practical activities are common. Classroom teachers receive every other week a mimeographed document that contains the radio lesson schedule and suggested activities to complement the broadcast.

UTILIZATION

In 1972, there were forty-three schools serving about 2,800 fourth, fifth, and sixth grade students receiving the radio lessons. However, contrary to the original plan, only seven of these schools, out of a possible seventy in the State, were originally incomplete schools offering fewer than six grades of primary school. Moreover, about 60% of the schools that had all six grades did not have six teachers, so often two or three of the higher grades had already been combined into one classroom with one teacher.

There is no reliable information on the number of students that participated in the system in the first year of its operation in San Luis Potosi. Furthermore, it is known that the Mexico City broadcasts are picked up and used by schools that do not formally participate in the Radioprimaria program, but again, no data are available on the extent of such use. Also, since the broadcasts are open circuit, beaming over regular radio band frequencies in both San Luis Potosi and Mexico City, it is thought that there are many adults who tune in on the lessons. Indeed, one of the original goals of the Radioprimaria system was to allow adults who had not completed primary school to participate as informal students.

Over the school year about 1,200 fourteen-minute programs are broadcast, that is, approximately 280 broadcast hours. Given that about 80% of the programs are directed at the combined fourth, fifth, and sixth grade audience, with the remaining 20% distributed among the three, we can calculate the average number of hours directed at a student in any particular grade to be 242 per year.

EFFECTIVENESS

Spain (1973) gave pretests and posttests over a semester period to a random sample of radio and nonradio students in the sixth grade. He concludes from the test results that Radioprimaria "has produced scores that are comparable to those of the children in direct teaching schools" (Spain, 1973, p. 42). However, there are some doubts as to the reliability of the results generated, which Spain himself explicitly recognizes. For example, although the rural radio classes had higher gain scores than the nonradio classes, only a few of the radio classes are that type of class for which the Radioprimaria system was originally intended. In spite of Spain's modest claims for the cognitive effectiveness of the radio system, and of the difficulty of drawing firm conclusions from the data he had available, his data suggest that students in the radio school performed better than those in nonradio schools in both Spanish and mathematics, and the difference in Spanish was statistically significant.

In many respects, Spain's evaluation of some of the other aspects of the Radioprimaria system is more enlightening than the analysis of cognitive outcomes described above. Through visiting all the radio schools and several of the nonradio schools, and by talking with system participants, a number of problems were uncovered. Spain estimated that 15% to 20% of the classes miss the first half hour of broadcast due to teacher and/or student late arrival. Furthermore, of the forty-four radio schools visited, one was inexplicably closed and eighteen others were not using the radio that particular day—either because it needed repair, or the power had failed or because the teacher had decided the lessons were useless.

No federal funds are allocated for radio purchase and consequently they must be bought and maintained by the teacher or the community; in one case no radio had been purchased because the teacher and the community could not agree on who would pay for it. Of the remaining twenty-five schools found using radios, seven had inaudible receivers. Spain reports widespread reception problems, which is not surprising given the funding arrangements which do not seem conducive to the purchase of adequate receivers and their maintenance.

Spain attributes many of the above problems to a lack of resources allocated for school supervision. Schools have been dropping out of the Radioprimaria system; in the first year of operation there were forty-nine radio schools, in 1971-1972 there were forty-four, and the following year there were only thirty-seven. Spain describes how the initial acceptance of Radioprimaria was fostered by the Director of the local Audiovisual Center, through frequent visits to the rural classrooms, using his own automobile. This individual's automobile broke down at the end of that first year and resources were not forthcoming from the federal government to support such efforts in subsequent years. Consequently, Spain feels that enthusiasm for the system has been waning.

Finally, Spain also examines the potential benefits of the Radioprimaria system's expansion of primary school education in rural areas. Contrary to the avowed government intention of the system aiding in rural development, parents and students see primary school graduation as primarily a means to leave the rural areas and compete in the urban labor market. Even more unfortunately, Spain's assessment of the employment market in the chief urban area of the State, the capital, indicates widespread unemployment and an excess supply of primary school graduates.

2. SYSTEM COSTS

Table VI.1 presents the costs of the Radioprimaria system in a format that assumes total costs vary linearly with the number of students in the system and the number of hours of radio lessons broadcast annually. That is,

$$(VI.1) \qquad TC(N, h) = F + V_N N + V_H h,$$

where   TC = total cost

      N = the number of students the system serves,

      h = the number of hours the system broadcasts,

      F = fixed costs of the system,

      V_N = costs of the system that are variable with N,

and V_h = costs of the system that are variable with h.

It should be stressed that the cost function parameters presented are only approximations. Cost data were available for only one year, 1972, and to apply the cost function that will be summarized below to rates of utilization different from those existing in 1972 requires some rather strict assumptions. First, it will be noted that there are no fixed costs of the system; all costs are assumed to be variable with N and h. For production costs this assumption is obviously not true for marginal charges in the number of hours broadcast, since, for example, sufficient personnel, studio space and studio equipment probably already exist to expand production somewhat. Nonetheless, given a longer-run view, all these cost components are to some degree variable with the number of broadcast hours produced. It should be noted that a smooth linear function as posited is only a rough approximation to what is probably a step function—that is, investments in production are lumpy in that a certain amount must be invested regardless of the extent of production and that another lump investment would be needed for expansion when there is no excess capacity left in the initial setup.

It might be thought that the transmission components would have significant fixed costs, but this will be the case only when transmission facilities are constructed, as opposed to leased or donated. In the latter cases, a cost is charged or imputed on an hourly basis that includes an allowance for capital amortization. Finally, reception costs, which include radio receivers and their maintenance and operation, may be reasonably assumed to vary directly with the number of students in the system; this assumes that class size would not be increased, although for marginal expansion this is always a possibility.

Table VI.1, based on the cost information elaborated in its footnote, calculates Radioprimaria costs for each of three social rates of discount, zero, 7.5%, and 15%. Production costs equal $110.66 per hour given no discounting for the future; $115.21 per hour at a 7.5% rate; and $121.08 per hour at a 15% rate. Although transmission costs should also vary with the discount rate, the $14.43 per hour figure given was obtained from personnel at the University of San Luis Potosi radio station without sufficient itemization to allow separation of capital and recurrent costs. Finally, reception costs are $.13 per student at a zero discount rate; $.15 per student at a 7.5% rate; and $.17 per student at a 15% rate.

TABLE VI.1
Cost of Radioprimaria[a]

Interest Rate	0%		7.5%		15%	
	Variable by		Variable by		Variable by	
	Student : Hour		Student : Hour		Student : Hour	
PRODUCTION						
Capital						
Studios		1.43		2.80		4.57
Studio equipment		2.96		5.81		9.49
Audio tapes		.34		.67		1.09
Recurrent						
Personnel		100.00		100.00		100.00
Equipment maintenance		5.93		5.93		5.93
TRANSMISSION						
Operations		14.43		14.43		14.43
RECEPTION						
Capital						
Receivers	.09		.11		.13	
Recurrent						
Operations and maintenance	.04		.04		.04	
TOTAL	.13	125.09	.15	129.64	.17	135.51

a. Cost data were gathered by Klees in 1972. Production and transmission costs are assumed to vary with the number of hours broadcast per year, which was 280 in 1972. Reception costs are assumed to vary with the number of students in the system, which was 2,800 in 1972. The basis for each cost component estimation is as follows:

Studios. The two studios and one control room cost approximately $8,000 to construct. This is annualized over an assumed 20-year life.

Studio equipment. The studio equipment cost $16,600 and is annualized over an assumed 10-year life.

Audio tapes. Audio tapes cost $6.80 for a tape of high quality; 280 such tapes are needed and their cost is annualized over an assumed 10-year life.

Production personnel. The salaries of administrators, technical personnel and radio teachers totalled $28,000 in 1972.

Production equipment maintenance. This cost is assumed to be 10% of the value of the studio equipment, or $1,660 per year.

Transmission operations. A cost of $14.43 per hour of transmission was estimated by the University of San Luis Potosi radio station for use of its 250-watt transmitter and broadcast facility.

Reception receivers. Radio receivers are assumed to cost $20 and are annualized over an assumed 5-year life. The average class size is assumed to be 45, which although somewhat higher than usual for rural areas in Mexico, reflects the use of combined grades in one classroom.

Reception operations and maintenance. This cost is assumed to equal 10% of the cost of a receiver annually.

The cost function and average cost information for 1972 may be summarized briefly below:

	Total Cost Equation	AC_N	AC_N/V_N	Cost per Student Hour
$r = 0$	TC = .13 N + 125.09 h	12.67	84.33	.052
$r = 7.5\%$	TC = .15 N + 129.64 h	13.12	77.24	.054
$r = 15\%$	TC = .17 N + 135.51 h	13.72	72.32	.057

The average cost per student (AC_N) assumes Radioprimaria utilization levels of the year 1972: 2,800 students and 280 hours broadcast. The cost per student hour figure reflects the rather unique common broadcast feature of the Radioprimaria system; that is, students receive about 242 hours of instructional radio each year, although only 280 hours are produced in total for all three grades, since 80% of the broadcasts are aimed at the combined three grades audience. The ratio of average cost per student to variable cost per student indicates that production costs dominate system costs, which is not surprising given the tentative, experimental nature of the system at this date. Average costs per student could be lowered substantially by expanding to include more students in the system. Finally, as we have noted in the other case studies, costs are quite sensitive to the interest rate. Radioprimaria costs almost 10% more if we value the future at a 15% rate than if we neglect to take time preference into account.

3. COST COMPARISON WITH THE TRADITIONAL SYSTEM

Radioprimaria was conceived of, in part, as a less expensive method than the traditional direct teaching system for providing a full six grades of primary school in rural areas. Table VI.2 examines this under somewhat hypothetical conditions. We assume the choice facing the SEP is whether to take students in a rural area and give them fourth, fifth and sixth grade education in three classrooms with three teachers or to put them in one classroom with one teacher and one radio for three years.

Even if enough teachers could be found who were willing to work in rural communities (which is a problem in Mexico), Table VI.2 indicates that the Radioprimaria alternative is a much less expensive alternative than the traditional system. The former costs about 60% less than the latter, and this advantage would be increased if student utilization were hypothesized to be greater than 2,800. The additional costs of the instructional radio components of the Radioprimaria system are more than offset by the reduced teacher and facility costs resulting from the combination of three grades into one classroom with one teacher.

TABLE VI.2
Annual Cost Per Student Comparison: Radioprimaria
Versus Traditional Instruction[a]

		Radioprimaria	Traditional Instruction
Traditional Components			
Administration		$ 50.00	$ 50.00
Classroom teacher		32.00	96.00
Facilities		6.10	18.29
	Subtotal	$ 88.10	$164.29
Instructional Radio Components			
Production		$ 11.53	$ 0.00
Transmission		1.44	0.00
Reception		.15	0.00
	Subtotal	$ 13.12	$ 0.00
Total Annual Cost Per Student		$101.22	$164.29

a. This cost estimate assumes an average of 15 students per grade, which would yield a 45-student class size for the Radioprimaria system. A social discount rate of 7.5% is used for capital amortization. The assumption on which each component is based is as follows:

Administration. This is a very rough approximation, equal to the administrative cost per student calculated for the traditional secondary school system as presented in Chapter XI.

Classroom teacher. This assumes that the salary of a primary school teacher is equal to the average for such teachers in Mexico in 1972, which was $1,440 per year.

Facilities. This assumes that the cost of a fully equipped rural classroom is $2,800 and has a life of twenty years. This figure is half that given in an untitled SEP report which estimates the cost of an urban classroom; half this estimate was used to reflect the lower cost classrooms that are usually constructed in rural regions in Mexico.

Instructional radio components. These figures follow from those given in Table VI.1, assuming a 2,800 student enrollment as in 1972.

4. CONCLUSIONS

The Radioprimaria system is an interesting attempt at meeting the problem of lack of sufficient educational opportunities in rural areas facing Mexico and most other developing nations. Although its costs may appear somewhat higher than other instructional radio projects (see Part IV), this is entirely due to its present experimental, low student utilization format; if the number of students included in the system expanded, costs per student could fall substantially. Furthermore, we have just observed in the previous section that the unique configuration of the system, which combines several grades in one classroom with one teacher, results in considerable cost savings over the traditional direct teaching system. Of course, despite a favorable cost comparison, the merits of the system must be judged by cost data combined with information on relative pedagogical effects and long run benefits.

It terms of pedagogical effects, Spain's analysis appears inconclusive, since there was not a clear comparison made of joint fourth, fifth and sixth grade classrooms with radio versus direct teaching with one teacher assigned to each grade. Spain (1973, p. 35) does indicate that there may be some problem with the grade-specific instructional radio lesson format utilized in Radioprimaria, in that the students not receiving the broadcasts "did not show a great deal of concentration" when they were supposed to be working on their own. This is not especially surprising as it is likely that the ongoing radio lesson would be difficult to ignore. In addition, it is at least questionable on a priori grounds that common fourth, fifth and sixth grade broadcasts, which are likely to be repeated to a student each year for three years, are a beneficial pedagogical tool. In short, before adopting such a system as Radioprimaria in another country, or expanding the system in Mexico, it would seem wise, as Spain suggests, to engage in a more rigorous effectiveness comparison.

Finally, it should again be emphasized that the individual and societal benefits of increasing primary school enrollment in rural areas are at least questionable according to Spain's analysis. Although this does not reflect on Radioprimaria, per se, vis-à-vis alternative instructional techniques, instructional technology systems are being used more and more frequently to extend educational opportunities to rural areas, to meet social demands and consequent political obligations. Careful attention must be given to the question of whether this social demand is based on reliable information, or whether additional education merely increases the rural exodus to overcrowded urban areas that lack sufficient employment opportunities. Increasing the educational opportunities in rural areas should involve more than the intact transfer of an urban curriculum; increased consideration needs to be given to real rural development and the meaning that this has for education, in order to allow the promise of educational benefits to become a reality.

Chapter VII

THE EL SALVADOR INSTRUCTIONAL
TELEVISION SYSTEM

El Salvador began broadcasting instructional television to a small number of seventh grade students in February, 1969. By 1972 broadcasts reached over 48,000 students in grades seven through nine with instruction in all the core subject areas. The system has continued to expand since then. The introduction of ITV in El Salvador was done in the context of an overall educational reform and was, moreover, the object of careful external evaluation from the outset of the reform. This chapter, dealing with the costs of the ITV aspect of the reform, draws on data and analysis resulting from that overall evaluation effort.

1. THE SYSTEM

The final report of the evaluation of ITV and the reform (Hornik, Ingle, Mayo, McAnany, and Schramm, 1973) contains a concise description of the reform and of television's role in it, and we quote extensively from their report by way of describing the system.

> To remedy the numerous problems that had been inherited from previous administrations and to streamline an educational system whose goals and procedures had ceased to fit the needs of El Salvador, Minister of Education Beneke set forth a comprehensive, five year reform plan in 1968. The plan was systematic and thorough in its approach, touching virtually every aspect of the educational system. The major reforms included:
>
> 1. Reorganization of the Ministry of Education
> 2. Extensive teacher retraining

3. Curriculum revision
4. Development of new study materials
5. Modernization of the system of school supervision
6. Development of a wider diversity of technical training programs in grades 10-12
7. Extensive building of new schoolrooms
8. Elimination of tuition in grades 7, 8, and 9 (in 1971)
9. Use of double sessions and reduced hours to teach more pupils
10. A new student evaluation system incorporating changes in promotion and grading policies
11. Installation of a national instructional television system for grades 7-9.

Although some of these changes were enacted immediately, most were begun with the understanding that additional planning, experimentation, and adjustment would be required and that major changes could be introduced only on an incremental basis. However, the five-year reform timetable was a strict one; it coincided with the single term of President Fidel Sanchez Hernandez and Minister Beneke was anxious to prevent the President's mandate from being undermined or stalled through bureaucratic opposition or delays.

The decision to use television as a major component of El Salvador's Educational Reform was neither imposed from the outside nor taken in a precipitous fashion. As far back as 1960, the possibility of introducing some form of educational television was being discussed, although there was no consensus and little knowledge about how television might help alleviate El Salvador's educational problems. Above all, the country lacked the capital and expertise necessary to initiate any large television project.

The initiative that led eventually to the establishment of El Salvador's national ITV system was taken by [Education Minister] Beneke in 1961. During his ambassadorship to Japan, Beneke had been impressed by the role television played in that country's correspondence high schools. Anxious to stimulate the growth of something similar in his own country, Beneke sought the help of NHK (Nippon Hoso Kyokai, the Japan Broadcasting Corporation). NHK agreed to conduct a feasibility study in El Salvador and several engineers were dispatched for that purpose in 1962. The results of this study confirmed what Beneke had suspected; El Salvador possessed excellent topographical conditions for the installation of a national television network.

The initiative taken by Beneke was supported by former President Julio Adalberto Rivera, who established the first Educational Television Commission in the fall of 1963. The Commission was supposed to evaluate alternative uses for educational television with the goal of proposing a national plan. However, the Commission met sporadically and little progress was made until Beneke returned from Japan in 1965.

Under Beneke's chairmanship, weekly meetings were instituted, and the Commission made a fresh start toward defining a specific proposal for the use of television. . . .

By the end of 1966, the Commission had reached a consensus on a number of basic points. First, acknowledging the fact that their country had neither a reservoir of trained people nor sufficient economic resources to embark upon a large television project, the Commission decided that its initial efforts would have to be limited in scale, but flexible enough to permit expansion should circumstances permit. Second, the Plan Basico (grades 7-9) was selected to be the first level served by television, for it was the lack of opportunity and low quality of instruction at this level that was believed to constitute the "bottleneck" to El Salvador's development. Instructional television, the Commission members believed, would compensate for the many unqualified secondary school teachers who, in turn, could be trained in a short time to become effective monitors within television classes. Third, the Commission concluded that ITV should be administered by an autonomous institute directly under the President with freedom to set its own personnel policies and to import the vast array of technical equipment that would be required. Finally, the Commission resolved to seek foreign financial and technical assistance so that ITV could be put on as firm a footing as possible from the outset (pp. 8-11).

With the preceding principles as guidelines, ITV has developed into a major component of middle level education in El Salvador.[1] In what follows we report on the cost of the ITV aspect of the reform.

2 SYSTEM COSTS

This section applies the methods of Chapters II and III to analysis of the cost data that were gathered by Speagle (1972). First, a cost tableau is presented, and then, based on the cost tableau, total cost functions and average cost values are developed.

Table VIII.1 presents the basic cost tableau. The table presents costs in various subcategories of production, transmission and reception on a year by year basis. The figures for 1966 to 1973 are based primarily on Speagle's comprehensive analysis and the figures from 1974 on are projections based on the planned growth rate of enrollment. All costs in the table are inflation corrected and are expressed in 1972 U.S. dollars.

Year by year figures for total (all inclusive cost) are presented below the costs by category. Underneath the row giving total cost is the row showing foreign aid and debt repayment. The numbers in parentheses in this row show the total amount of grant or loan money received that year for the ITV system. The number in parentheses is then subtracted from the all-inclusive cost

TABLE VII.1
Cost of Instructional Television in El Salvador for Third 'Cycle Schools[a]
(thousands of 1972 U.S. dollars)

	1966	1967	1968	1969	1970	1971	1972	1973	1974	1975	1976	1977	1978	1979	1980	1981	1982	1983	1984	1985	1986	1987	1988
Production																							
Facility					234	108	36	36							36	36							
Equipment			50	270	40	966								270	40	966							
Operations				300	370	410	490	490	490	490	540	540	540	540	540	540	540	540	540	540	540	540	540
Start up	50	50	380	360	260	210	200	200	100	50													
Videotape				51	51	51			51	51	51		51	51		51			51	51	51		
Transmission																							
Facility					26	12	4	4							4	4							
Equipment						644										644							
Operations				20	20	40	10	10	10	10	10	10	10	10	10	10	10	10	10	10	10	10	10
Reception																							
Classroom Remodeling			1090																				
Equipment			50		120	120	120	53	62	80	13	13	13	18	13	18	18	18	13	18	18	22	18
Replacement								50		120	120	120	103	62	200	133	133	116	80	213	151	151	134
Total Costs	50	50	1570	1001	1121	2561	860	843	713	801	734	638	716	951	934	2402	701	684	694	832	770	733	702
Foreign Aid and Debt Repayment			(190)	(680)	(300)	(1980)	(320)	(320)							45	45	45	45	45	45	45	45	45
Total Cost to Government	50	50	1380	321	821	581	540	523	713	801	734	638	716	951	979	2447	746	729	739	877	815	768	747
Number of Students (in thousands)				2	14	32	48	60	72	86	104	107	110	113	117	120	124	128	131	135	139	144	148

See next page for footnote a.

to give the cost to the government for the given year. Beginning in 1980, the numbers in this row represent loan repayment. Costs to the Salvadoran government are computed by adding the loan repayment to the total incurred expenditures. The values for loan repayment were computed using the methods described in the preceding subsection.

The final row of Table VII.1 shows past and projected future student usage of the system. Usage increases rapidly until 1976, when most of the relevant age population is assumed to be covered. Thereafter, usage increases at the school age population growth rate of approximately 3% per year.[2]

The footnote to Table VII.1 provides somewhat more information on the source of the figures in the various categories. Readers interested in a detailed discussion of the various cost components should consult the comprehensive

---

FOOTNOTE FOR TABLE VII.1

a. Cost data are based mainly on Speagle (1972) for 1966 to 1973.

Production facility. Ninety percent of the costs of the Santa Tecla facility were allocated to production and 10% to transmission, with the life of the air conditioning assumed to be 10 years and the facility life to be 25 years.

Production equipment. This assumes a 10-year life, with the cost of the Santa Tecla equipment allocated 60% to production and 40% to transmission.

Production operations and start up. These are the same as Speagle's until 1974 when start up costs are assumed to decrease over two years to a $50,000 level. After 1975 they remain at this level and are included in the cost of operations which are based on Speagle's projection.

Videotape. It is not clear whether these costs are included in Table 2.1 of Speagle. They are added here, purchased as needed, under the assumption of a 5-year tape life, 300 hours of programming a year, and a cost of an hour length videotape of $170.

Transmission facility. This is explained under production facility.

Transmission equipment. This is explained under production equipment.

Transmission operations. This represents the rental charge through 1971 for the use of commercial broadcast time. Beginning in 1972 operations are estimated to cost 25% of the 1971 rental charge.

Classroom remodeling. This is the same as in Speagle, with an assumed 25-year lifetime.

Reception equipment. Beginning in 1973 this is based on the number of students added to the system, an average class size of 45, and a cost per receiver of $200.

Foreign aid and debt repayment. Through 1973 this represents the actual size of foreign grants and loans. The loan portion of this aid is paid off with a 10-year grace period during which interest accumulates at 2% and a 30-year repayment period during which interest accumulates at 2.5%. With our assumption of a 4% annual rate of inflation these effective interest rates become −2% and −1.5% respectively. If there were no inflation present, value of the repayment amount would be almost three times as large. The repayment is scheduled as if the 40-year period for the total loan began in 1970.

Number of students. This is assumed to grow rapidly from 1972 to 1976 (about 20% per year) after which a 3% growth rate is accounted for mainly by population growth.

The cost data do not include teacher training (not considered by Speagle as part of ITV costs), the distribution and printing of teacher's guides and student workbooks, nor maintenance and power costs for reception equipment. Speagle says the latter is extremely small.

treatment by Speagle (1972). This chapter will provide no further discussion of these component cost estimates except to expand briefly on the cost of program production.

Program production costs are high and account for a substantial fraction of foreign exchange costs. It is for this reason important to examine these costs in some detail and Speagle (1972, pp. 72-78) provides a breakdown of the operating costs of program production. However, a very substantial proportion of program production costs are capital costs and it is important, particularly for planners from other countries, to obtain an estimate of total production costs, not just the operating costs of program production. Table VII.2, using cost data from Table VII.1, presents the component and total costs of program production, including annualized capital expenditures at a 7.5% discount rate; the total of $979,000 per year is almost twice the recurrent cost of $540,000 per year. At the estimated production rate of 1,000 twenty-minute programs per year, the cost per hour of program production comes to about $2,940.

THE TOTAL COST FUNCTION FOR ITV

Using the data from Table VII.1, it is possible to obtain a cost function for ITV in El Salvador. In this chapter the program production and transmission costs are considered fixed while reception costs are variable with the number of students. The cost function we use is, then, $TC(N) = F + V_N N$. Start up costs were treated as an initial capital investment in the system. They were annualized over the assumed twenty-five-year lifetime of the system and included in F. The 1972 student enrollment estimate of 48,000 was used along with the assumption of an average of 170 hours of program pre-

TABLE VII.2
Costs of Program Production[a]

Cost Category	Amortization Period[b]	Cost	Annualized Cost[c]
Facility (building)	25 years	342	31
Facility (air conditioning	10 years	72	10
Equipment	10 years	1326	193
Start up	25 years	1860	167
Videotape	5 years	153	38
Operations (recurrent)	– –	– –	540
TOTAL			979

a. These costs are expressed in thousands of 1972 dollars.
b. The amortization period is the number of years the cost item is assumed to last; start up costs are amortized over an assumed 25-year life for the project.
c. The annualization was done with a social discount of rate of 7.5% per annum.

sentation per year. The enrollment figures allow calculation of AC and AC/V_N; the program presentation assumption allows computation of costs per student hour of viewing. The total cost equation (expressed in 1972 U.S. dollars) for the system is as follows, assuming a discount rate of 7.5%.[3]

Total Cost Equation	AC	AC/V_N	Cost per Student Hour
TC(N) = 1,116,000 + 1.10N	24.35	22.14	.143

With twice as many students using the system (N = 96,000), average costs fall to $12.73, and per student hour costs fall to $.075. This substantial reduction is possible because of the initially high value of AC/V_N.

The above total cost equation is for all inclusive costs. It is also of value to compute a cost equation that includes only costs to the Salvadoran government.[4] To do this one must reduce the fixed cost components of the above equation by an annualized equivalent of the grants and loans. To find this equivalent, the present value of the thirty-year loan repayment series was calculated, and this was subtracted from the total amount of the foreign grants and loans (the total amount was assumed to occur in the year 1970). The resulting figure was annualized over the twenty-five-year assumed lifetime of the project and subtracted from the fixed costs. The Government of El Salvador cost equation is as follows:

Government of El Salvador Cost Equation	AC	AC/V_N	Cost per Student Hour
TC(N) = 799,000 + 1.10N	17.75	16.13	.104

It should be observed that the net grant and loan contribution to the ITV system is substantial. At the 7.5% social rate of discount, foreign contributions cover about 27% of the system's cost. This 27% is based on 48,000 students per year using the system. Since the entire cost of expanding the system is borne by El Salvador, the percentage of foreign contribution will decline as usage increases. Because of the high value of AC/V_N though, the decline is only to a little over 25% when the student usage reaches the 104,000 projected for 1976.[5]

The cost equations of the preceding paragraphs provide a reasonably clear picture of system costs as a function of N, the number of students per year using the system. In order to assess accurately the actual average costs incurred, account must be taken of the time structure of student usage, and this is done in the computations of values for AC_{ij} that follow.

AVERAGE COSTS

The data in Table VII.1 suffice to calculate values of AC_{ij} for El Salvador for the years 1966 to 1988. Letting 1966 equal year one (and therefore 1973 equals year eight), one can use the methods of Chapter II to compute all possible values of AC_{ij} both for all inclusive costs and for costs to the government. These computations depend of course, on the accuracy of the enrollment projections in the last row of Table VII.1, and deviations from those projections would induce corresponding deviations in average costs.

Figure VII.1 displays values of AC_{ij} graphically. One can see from that graph that if the social discount rate is 7.5%, the average costs through year twelve of the project (that is, through 1977) will have been about $24 per student per year. What this means is that total expenditures up to 1977 divided by total student usage up to 1977 (each properly discounted) will equal $24. If one extends the time horizon to twenty-three years (1988) the results comes to about $17. The bump in the curve that occurs near year fifteen

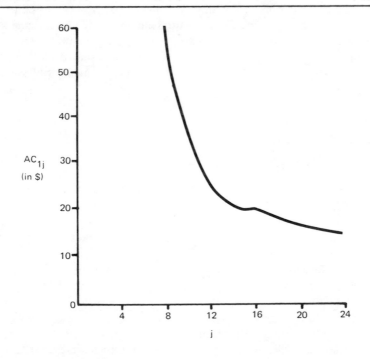

Figure VII.1: AC_{ij} FOR THE TOTAL COST OF INSTRUCTIONAL TELEVISION IN THIRD CYCLE

(1980) results from the need to replace production and transmission equipment at that time.

Figure VII.2 displays the same information as Figure VII.1, except that costs are viewed from 1973 rather than from the beginning of the project. Notice that the scale on Figure VII.2 differs from the one on Figure VII.1 and that values of AC_{8j} for j less than eight are undefined (indicated by the flat part of the curve). From the perspective of 1973, average costs through year twelve (1977) are, of course, much less than the $24 of $AC_{1,12}$; the value of $AC_{8,12}$ is about $8.50 for a 7.5% discount rate. This $8.50 is the total projected expenditure between 1973 and 1977 divided by the projected number of years of student use between now and 1977, each properly discounted. The small bump at year fifteen on Figure VII.1 is much magnified in Figure VII.2; this is both because the fixed replacement costs are a larger fraction of average costs viewed from 1973 and because they are less discounted, since by 1973 they are much nearer in the future.

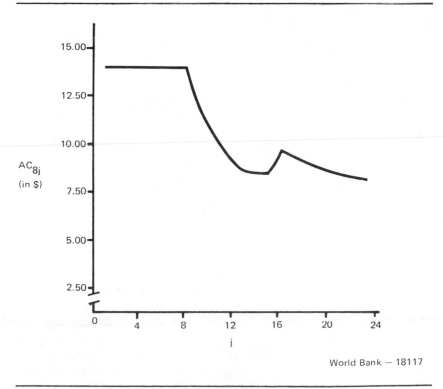

World Bank — 18117

Figure VII.2: AC_{8j} FOR THE TOTAL COST OF INSTRUCTIONAL TELEVISION IN THIRD CYCLE

Table VII.3 presents exact computations of AC_{ij} based on a 7.5% discount rate and the figures in Table VII.1 for total cost. The top row of Table VII.3 corresponds to the graph in Figure VII.1 and its fifth row corresponds to the graph in Figure VII.2. Table VII.4 presents the same computations for costs to the Salvadoran government instead of all inclusive costs; except in the lower right hand corner, costs in Table VII.4 are lower than corresponding costs in Table VII.3. The appropriate cost to use depends on one's vantage point. At the time of El Salvador's initial decision, the long-run average cost to the government, $AC_{1,23}$[6] in Table VII.4, was the most useful number for El Salvador to consider; by 1973, for long-term planning, the values of $AC_{8,23}$ are perhaps most useful. On the other hand, for present short term expansion or contraction decisions, the marginal costs are the appropriate ones to use.[7] If El Salvador had not had grant and loan opportunities, the all inclusive costs of Table VII.3 would be more appropriate.

In terms of what others can learn from El Salvador's experience, the most useful number is perhaps the long-term average cost viewed from when El Salvador commenced expenditure. At the 7.5% discount rate, this number, $AC_{1,23}$, is seen from Table VII.3 to be $14.97 (say, $15.00). If the students view an average of 170 hours of ITV per year, the cost per student hour is $0.09. It should be kept in mind that these costs assume that the system continues through 1988 and, more importantly, that the rapid expansion of enrollments projected in Table VII.1 is in fact attained.

The cost of ITV is necessarily an add-on to whatever else may be provided the students. The introduction of ITV may, however, facilitate reduction of other costs and the next subsection considers very briefly the factors that may allow offsetting of ITV costs.

3. FACTORS OFFSETTING THE COST OF ITV

This subsection presents a very brief analysis of how ITV costs have in part been offset by reduction of other input factors to the schooling process. The principal cost of conventional instruction is, of course, teachers' time, and the offsetting factor to be considered here is reduction in teacher time per student. The amount of teacher time expended per student depends on class size, C, and the relative length of the student and teacher school weeks. If h_s is the number of hours in school per week of a full-time student and h_t is the number of hours per week of a fulltime teacher, the student to teacher ratio, S, can be defined to equal $(h_t/h_s)C$. Thus, if teachers teach two full shifts $(h_t/h_s = 2)$ and the average class size is forty, the student to teacher ratio will equal eighty. ITV costs can be offset by increasing that ratio through increases in C or h_t or through decreases in h_s. If the mechanism is through increases in teacher hours, teacher salary increases must be less than proportional to those hour increases.

TABLE VII.3
Average Total Costs From Year i To Year j For Third Cycle Schools
Interest Rate = 7.5%

Year i \ Year j	1968	1970	1972	1974	1976	1978	1980	1982	1984	1986	1988
1966		254.95	82.72	44.49	29.84	23.11	20.01	18.38	17.14	15.95	14.97
1969		134.63	60.50	34.24	23.71	18.73	16.53	15.96	14.59	13.67	12.89
1971			43.71	24.90	17.75	14.35	13.02	13.00	11.99	11.33	10.75
1972			17.92	13.55	10.95	9.45	9.15	9.80	9.18	8.80	8.44
1973				11.78	9.69	8.46	8.37	9.21	8.64	8.31	7.98
1974				9.75	8.52	7.58	7.73	8.77	8.23	7.92	7.61
1975					8.00	7.12	7.43	8.66	8.08	7.77	7.45
1976					6.95	6.48	7.09	8.58	7.95	7.63	7.30
1977						6.23	7.13	8.90	8.11	7.72	7.34
1978						6.51	7.55	9.57	8.47	7.96	7.50
1980							7.89	11.17	8.98	8.15	7.53
1984									5.21	5.58	5.32
1988											4.74

TABLE VII.4
Average Government Costs From Year i To Year j For Third Cycle Schools
Interest Rate = 7.5%

Year i \ Year j	1968	1970	1972	1974	1976	1978	1980	1982	1984	1986	1988
1966		177.52	44.19	25.37	18.39	14.93	13.56	13.52	12.51	11.84	11.25
1969		70.79	24.48	16.28	12.96	11.04	10.47	10.92	10.25	9.81	9.40
1971			13.99	11.20	9.85	8.78	8.68	9.43	8.94	8.63	8.33
1972			11.25	9.84	8.98	8.10	8.15	9.03	8.57	8.29	8.01
1973				9.26	8.56	7.74	7.87	8.87	8.40	8.13	7.85
1974				9.75	8.52	7.58	7.78	8.89	8.38	8.09	7.80
1975					8.00	7.12	7.49	8.79	8.25	7.96	7.65
1976					6.95	6.48	7.16	8.73	8.14	7.84	7.52
1977						6.23	7.22	9.07	8.32	7.95	7.58
1978						6.51	7.68	9.78	8.72	8.22	7.77
1980							8.27	11.55	9.33	8.51	7.88
1984									5.56	5.92	5.64
1988											5.05

In El Salvador the introduction of ITV has tended to reduce costs by increasing both teacher hours and class size; counterbalancing these cost reductions are, of course, the costs of providing the ITV. This subsection provides approximate estimates of the instructional expenditures[8] per student as we assume it would have been if ITV were not introduced, E(no ITV), and as it was after the introduction of ITV, E(ITV). These estimates are based on occasionally shaky or inconsistent data but are probably accurate to within 15%.

After the Reform instituted changes in the school week, students attended twenty-five hours of classes per week. A full load for teachers who were not assigned to double sessions was also twenty-five hours ($h_s = h_t = 25$). Prior to the great expansion in the numbers of students attending Third Cycle, which began in 1971, average class size was no more than thirty-five. If we use that as an estimate for class size, and twenty-five hours as estimates of both student week and teacher week, the student-teacher ratio was 35:1. At a salary of $1800 per year[9] for a twenty-five-hour work week, which was the 1972 cost, the instructional expenditure per student was $52 per year. If the Reform had been mounted without ITV and traditional class size had been maintained, that would have been the cost per student.

However, ITV was introduced, and accompanying it were two other changes affecting cost per student. Average classroom size was increased, as smaller Third Cycle schools were closed and more students matriculated at the schools remaining open. At the same time, teacher load was increased from twenty-five to thirty-five hours (an increase of 40%) while teacher salaries were only increased by 20% to $2,165.[10] While one cannot say definitively that such changes would not have occurred unless ITV had been introduced, that may be a reasonable assumption. Certainly the Ministry planners believed that one of the advantages of extending ITV to primary schools would be "to help the teacher who sees himself as overburdened by his work day with double sessions."[11]

Given the longer work week, the teacher cost per student equals the teacher wage divided by the student to teacher ratio; that is, it equals $2,165/S; since $S = (h_t/h_s)C = (35/25)C$, the teacher cost per student equals $1546/C, where C is the class size after the introduction of ITV. In addition to teacher costs, one must consider television costs per student to the government; the equation giving costs to the government summarized these expenditures. The annualized ITV costs per student are seen from that equation to equal $799,000 + $1.10N, where N is the number of students using the ITV system. The sum of this plus teacher costs give the per student costs with ITV, E(ITV):

$$E(ITV) = \$1,546/C + \$799,000/N + \$1.10.$$

It is not yet clear what the average class size will become after El Salvador's Educational Reform is fully implemented. In order to illustrate how class size and N jointly affect the per student costs, Figure VII.3 shows how E(ITV) varies with N for three values of C: C = 35; C = 40; C = 45.

Figure VII.3 also shows E(no ITV), the assumed instructional cost if ITV had not been introduced, of $52. E(no ITV) does not, of course, vary with N. All points on the E(ITV) curves that lie below the E(no ITV) curve indicate combinations of class size and total enrollment that result in having instructional costs per student be less with ITV than without. For example, if C = 40 in Figure VII.3, this indicates that with more than 60,000 students using ITV, the cost per student per year would be less with the ITV system than without the changes in class size and teacher hours which accompanied the introduction of ITV. It thus seems quite possible that the use of ITV in the Reform in El Salvador will be accompanied by a reduction in unit costs.

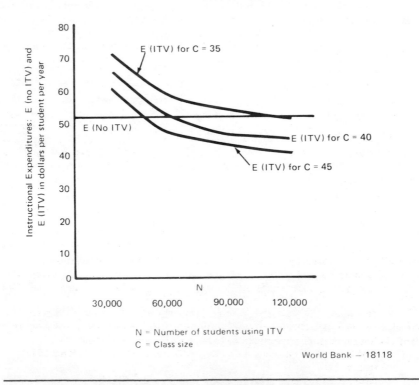

Figure VII.3: INSTRUCTIONAL COSTS PER STUDENT PER YEAR

NOTES

1. For an up-to-date discussion of ITV and the educational reform see Mayo, Hornik, and McAnany (1976); their book also describes results of the extensive pedagogical evaluation to which the ITV system has been subjected. Students in the reform did as well or better in most subjects than did nonreform students; this is probably at least in part due to the ITV component of the reform.

2. Recent planning estimates indicate that the enrollment estimates in this table for the late 1970s may be 10% to 15% too low.

3. Jamison and Klees (1975) examined the sensitivity of the cost estimates to the value chosen for the social discount rate; increasing it from 7.5% to 15% increases AC by about 20%. This is a substantial amount, due to the highly capital intensive nature of the project.

4. In order to adjust all-inclusive costs for grants one simply subtracts the amount of the grant in the given year from the all-inclusive costs of that year. Loans are somewhat more complicated because they must at some point be paid back. The loans negotiated by El Salvador have a ten-year grace period before repayment begins. Thus, in early years of the project the loans in a given year are, like the grants, simply subtracted from the all-inclusive costs. In later years the repayments must be added to the all-inclusive costs in order to obtain costs to the government.

Computing the amount to be repaid in each of the later years is complicated by lack of knowledge of the inflation rate of the dollar. The loans are negotiated in fixed dollar terms so the higher the rate of dollar inflation the lower the real value of the loan repayments, that is, the lower the value expressed in fixed dollars (1972 dollars are used as the base in this report). The situation is exactly analogous to that of a homeowner with a mortage; in times of high inflation he gains because the value of his debt is fixed in dollar terms. Inflation rates for the dollar are unpredictable even, it now appears, several months, much less ten years in advance. For this reason, the value used in this chapter, 4%, should be regarded as only a conservative estimate. Given the value of the loans, the interest rates they bear, their repayment schedules, and the rate of inflation for the dollar, one can use standard accounting formulas to determine the annual repayment in terms of 1972 dollars. These repayments begin in 1980 and as of that year costs to the Salvadoran government must be determined by adding the loan repayments to the all inclusive costs.

5. In comparing the average costs in total with those to the Salvadoran government, it is an interesting fact that the latter is totally insensitive to the social discount rate. This results from a coincidental balancing of two factors: on the one hand increasing the social discount rate increases capital costs, but on the other hand it increases the value of foreign loans.

6. 1966 corresponds to year one and 1988 corresponds to year twenty-three.

7. A more detailed analysis of El Salvador ITV costs, including discussion of expanding the system to the first through sixth grades, may be found in Jamison and Klees (1975).

8. This report uses the term "instructional expenditures" to denote the costs of the teacher and television. It thus excludes costs for school administration, classroom space and student supplies, which are assumed to be the same with or without ITV.

9. ODEPOR, "Plan Quinquenal de Ramo Education 1973-1977." (June, 1972).

10. Ibid, p. 33.

11. Ibid, p. 33.

Chapter VIII

THE STANFORD INSTRUCTIONAL TELEVISION SYSTEM

The Stanford Instructional Television System, established in 1968, is one of a number of ITV systems in the United States with a clientele consisting of full-time employed professionals. These systems are typically operated by universities and provide undergraduate and graduate higher education. Students who are part of the system receive all of their instruction via the ITV system. For example, students in the Stanford system may receive a Master of Engineering degree from Stanford or a Master of Business Administration from Golden Gate University.

This system was established to extend learning to persons for whom classroom attendance was difficult because of either commuting distances or interference with normal work activities. By reducing these problems, it is possible to extend continuing education to professionals who might ordinarily forgo further education. In addition, the system reduces the loss in work time for companies which ordinarily allow students to attend classes during work. Pettitt and Grace (1970) mentioned that one company estimated a savings of 2.5 man years during one academic year when the ITV system was used. Unfortunately, they did not report the number of students from this company.

The system differs from typical formal education programs, where a receiver (television or radio) is in a classroom and viewed by a group of students and from distance learning, where students view or hear programs at sites of their own selection. Several companies in the area near Stanford have established themselves as reception points by equipping one or more rooms in their buildings with receivers. A typical Stanford engineering class has an instructor and on-campus students in a studio classroom and one or more off-campus students in several of the company classrooms with no instructors in these classrooms.

The original decision to establish the system included the objective of providing an equivalent quality education for off-campus students. The companies which joined the Stanford ITV system in the early years established talkback facilities. The video portion is a one way broadcast from the studio classroom to the company classrooms, but the audio portion is a two-way process allowing the students in the company classrooms to ask and respond to questions. The response of a student is rebroadcast to the other company classrooms. Although the students are geographically separated, the system has been established to duplicate the more traditional setting.

Two organizations utilize the Stanford ITV system. The first broadcasts Stanford engineering courses which are part of the normal graduate program at Stanford. The second organization, the Association for Continuing Education (ACE) broadcasts a variety of programs designed to serve the interests of the companies which are members of the Stanford ITV system. In 1974 there were thirty-seven member companies and thirty of these had established classrooms. There were 2,142 students for the Stanford engineering courses and 2,800 for the ACE courses.

1. THE SYSTEM

TECHNICAL CHARACTERISTICS

In 1963 the FCC designated a band of thirty-one TV channels to be used by educational institutions and called it ITFS (Instructional Television Fixed Service). The band extends from 2,500 to 2,686 mHz with each channel occupying 6 mHz. Channels are usually allocated in groups of four with 6 mHz in between each channel. The maximum power of any station is 10 watts, and, because of the high frequencies of the broadcast, special equipment is required to convert the signal to the lower frequencies used as input to a standard television monitor. In response to a proposal by Stanford, the FCC in June 1969 set aside an additional band of 4 mHz (2686-2690 mHz) to allow for FM radio talkback.

Broadcasts originate on the Stanford campus and the signals are sent from the master control room to a mountain top transmitter 7.9 miles from campus via a 12 GH microwave link. On the mountain, 7 of the 10 available watts are utilized for a $160°$ omni-directional transmission and a coverage of twenty to twenty-five miles is possible. The $160°$ beam is utilized since all receiving sites are located on one side of the mountain range. The remaining three watts of power are focussed into higher gain beams to areas thirty-five to forty miles from campus.

On campus there are four classrooms and one auditorium equipped for transmission. There is a control complex of five control rooms for the classrooms and the auditorium and a separate master control for all of the rooms. The control complex and the master control room are linked by cable. The auditorium has 200 seats, five 23 inch monitors for viewing in the auditorium and two GPL-1000 Vidicon cameras (one rear and one overhead). Each classroom has 45 seats with one 9 inch monitor for every 2 seats, 2 cameras, and an instructor's desk (with facilities for showing slides, transparencies, etc.). Attached to each of the classrooms is an overflow room of 25 seats with one 9 inch monitor for every 2 seats and no broadcast facilities. The monitors in the classrooms and auditorium are utilized to enable on-campus students to view diagrams, charts and notes broadcast by the overhead camera.

At each receiving site a special antenna and a down converter are required, in addition to standard television monitors for reception of the video and audio broadcasts. There may also be from one to four classrooms each independently switchable to receive broadcasts from any one of the four channels. Two types of talkback facilities are possible: a system which allows simultaneous talkback from any of the classrooms at a given location on different frequencies or a time-shared talkback system which allows for talkback on only one frequency from a given location, regardless of the number of classrooms. The first option allows students at a location with more than one classroom to simultaneously ask questions in different courses. The second option allows only one student to speak from a given location even if four courses are being viewed. Different frequencies are alloted to each of the courses being broadcast. Special equipment is utilized which allows only one off-campus student to speak on each frequency.

While broadcast is possible on four channels simultaneously, most of the receiving sites have fewer than four classrooms as it is unlikely that four courses being broadcast simultaneously would all be of interest to individuals at a given company.

ORGANIZATION AND UTILIZATION OF
STANFORD ENGINEERING COURSES

The broadcast of Stanford engineering courses is a continuation of the Stanford Honors Cooperative Program (HCP), which was begun in 1953 to allow students with full time positions in local companies to pursue graduate education in engineering and science. Prior to the advent of the television system, these students had to commute to campus. Regular Stanford admission procedures and privileges apply to these students. As tuition was calculated to cover approximately one-half of the costs of education, the HCP students are required to pay a matching fee equal to the amount of the tuition. The courses that are received via television also have an additional surcharge of $20 per unit.

Students may also take the course on a noncredit basis (nonregistered option—NRO) and pay the matching fee and the TV surcharge. These students may later apply for admission to a regular degree program if their grades are high enough and may, by paying the tuition, apply the credit towards a degree. Since the courses that are broadcast are regular university courses, the admission from the above categories of students is limited to 50% of total class enrollment with priority given to students in the Honors Cooperative Program. The remainder of the enrollments consists of regular full time Stanford students.

A third category of students consists of auditors who receive class material but who are not graded. In order to encourage increased auditor enrollment and raise revenue, Stanford in 1971 established the following pricing schedule for each company:

Total number of auditors per quarter	Fee for each auditor
1–20	$75.00
21–40	$ 0.00
41–80	$37.50
81–150	$ 0.00
>150	$20.00

Under the previous system of charging $135.00 per auditor, there was an average of 30 auditors per quarter; this figure climbed to 450 by autumn, 1973. Since the auditor only receives printed material, there is a small drain on resources of the system, and revenues have more than doubled.

Regular Stanford faculty members are used in these courses, and instead of teaching the class in a regular classroom, the course is taught in one of the TV classrooms and broadcast live from that facility.

Utilization of the Stanford engineering courses for 1968 (academic year 1968-1969) through 1987 is reported. Enrollment and broadcast schedules are used for 1968 through 1974, and projections were undertaken from 1975 on. Stanford has broadcast an average of 40-45 courses each quarter during the autumn, winter and spring quarters, and 20 during the summer quarter. During the past two years (1973 and 1974), a total of 150 courses has been broadcast, and as no expansions are planned, it has been projected that 150 courses per year will continue to be broadcast.

A Stanford engineering course is typically 30 hours in length. The broadcast of 150 courses involves 4,500 hours of broadcast time. When one considers that these courses are normally scheduled from 8 a.m. to 12 p.m. and 1 p.m. to 5 p.m. on Mondays to Fridays, then for four ten-week quarters there is a total of 6,400 hours available for broadcasting of engineering courses and the system is under-utilized.

HCP and NRO students are considered to be registered students in Table VIII.1, and auditors are considered separately. When the new fee schedule for auditors was instituted in 1971, the number of registered students dropped by one-third (from 939 to 622 students), while the number of auditors increased dramatically from 98 to 737. However, in the last two years there has been an upsurge in the number of registered students (658 in 1972 to 962 in 1974) and a decline in the number of auditors (1,321 in 1972 to 1,180 in 1974). The projection of utilization for 1975 and beyond involved conservative assumptions of 25 students transferring from auditor status to registered status each year and an additional 25 students joining the system as registered students each year. With these assumptions, total enrollment is projected to increase from 2,142 students in 1974 to 2,467 in 1987.

ORGANIZATION AND UTILIZATION OF ACE COURSES

The Association for Continuing Education (ACE) was formulated to meet the needs of local industry, and a wide variety of courses is presented, including courses leading to a Master of Business Administration degree from Golden Gate University, preparatory courses for the MBA degree from the College of Notre Dame, technical courses in Cybernetic Systems in cooperation with California State University at San Jose, four courses leading to a certificate in Supervisory Management, and special courses designed to meet specific needs of the member firms. ACE rents office space on Stanford's campus and pays $18.00 per hour for use of the studio classrooms, broadcasting equipment and technicians. Courses are presented Mondays to Fridays from 7 to 8 a.m., 12 to 1 p.m., and 5 to 7 p.m. In this manner air time that would be unusable for broadcasting the Stanford engineering courses is used.

The Association for Continuing Education has two arrangements with companies and several different arrangements with the universities that are of particular interest, since the Stanford and ACE organizational arrangements have inspired proposals on other campuses (College of Engineering, 1972). Committed companies pay an annual fee of $12,000, and in addition to receiving reduced tuition for most of the courses, they are entitled to request four four-week courses each year that meet their own requirements. Students from these companies pay $75 per course for Golden Gate MBA courses to ACE and no fee to ACE for courses designed by ACE or the College of Notre Dame. Students from uncommitted companies that pay no fee are charged $174 per course for MBA courses and $50 for ACE and Notre Dame courses. Students from all companies pay $15 per course to the College of Notre Dame for Notre Dame courses and regular tuition for San Jose State University courses.

For the Golden Gate MBA courses, ACE pays a fee of $2,500 per course,

TABLE VIII.1
Utilization of the Stanford ITV System

	1968	1969	1970	1971	1972	1973	1974	1975	1976	1977	1978	1979	1980	1981	1982	1983	1984	1985	1986	1987
STANFORD[a]																				
Number of:																				
courses		120	146	143	145	150	150	150	150	150	150	150	150	150	150	150	150	150	150	150
hours		3,600	4,380	4,290	4,350	4,500	4,500	4,500	4,500	4,500	4,500	4,500	4,500	4,500	4,500	4,500	4,500	4,500	4,500	4,500
registered students		798	939	622	658	762	962	1,012	1,062	1,112	1,162	1,212	1,262	1,312	1,362	1,412	1,462	1,512	1,562	1,612
auditors		101	98	737	1,321	1,246	1,180	1,155	1,130	1,105	1,080	1,055	1,030	1,005	980	955	930	905	880	855
student hours (in thousands)																				
no auditors		23.9	28.2	18.7	19.7	22.9	28.9	30.3	31.8	33.4	34.9	36.4	37.9	39.4	40.9	42.4	43.9	45.4	46.9	48.4
with auditors		27.0	31.1	40.8	59.4	60.2	64.3	65.0	65.8	66.5	67.3	68.0	68.8	69.5	70.3	71.0	71.8	72.5	73.3	74.0
students		899	1,037	1,359	1,979	2,008	2,142	2,167	2,192	2,217	2,242	2,267	2,292	2,317	2,342	2,367	2,392	2,417	2,442	2,467
ACE[b]																				
Number of:																				
courses		24	34	53	60	73	80	85	90	95	100	105	110	115	120	125	130	135	140	145
hours		770	1,089	1,270	1,664	1,717	1,790	2,040	2,160	2,280	2,400	2,520	2,640	2,760	2,880	3,000	3,120	3,240	3,360	3,480
students		1,365	1,475	1,975	2,100	2,550	2,800	2,975	3,150	3,325	3,500	3,675	3,850	4,025	4,200	4,375	4,550	4,725	4,900	5,075
student hours (in thousands)		43.8	47.2	47.3	58.2	60.0	62.6	71.4	75.6	79.8	84.0	88.2	92.4	96.6	101.0	105.2	109.4	113.6	117.8	122.0
STANFORD + ACE																				
Number of:																				
students																				
no auditors		2,163	2,414	2,597	2,758	3,312	3,762	3,987	4,212	4,431	4,662	4,887	5,112	5,337	5,562	5,787	6,012	6,237	6,462	6,687
with auditors		2,264	2,512	3,334	4,079	4,558	4,942	5,142	5,342	5,542	5,742	5,942	6,142	6,342	6,542	6,742	6,942	7,142	7,342	7,542
student hours																				
no auditors		64.8	72.3	72.0	76.4	82.8	91.9	101.7	107.4	113.2	118.9	124.6	130.3	136.0	141.9	147.6	153.3	159.0	164.7	170.4
with auditors		67.9	75.3	94.1	116.1	120.1	127.3	136.4	141.4	146.3	151.3	156.2	161.2	166.1	171.3	176.2	181.2	186.1	191.1	196.0
hours		4,370	5,469	5,560	6,014	6,217	6,290	6,540	6,660	6,780	6,900	7,020	7,140	7,260	7,380	7,500	7,620	7,640	7,760	7,880

a. **Stanford.** The number of courses available and the number of registered students and auditors for 1969 through 1974 are derived from course schedules and enrollment records. All courses are 30 hours in length and students are counted by number of course registrations. A student enrolled in two courses is counted twice. Projections for 1975 through 1987 were undertaken by assuming no growth in number of courses, a continuation of the trend from auditor to registered status at 25 students per year and an additional gain of 25 registered students per year (an increase in total students of approximately one percent per year). As there is now a start in the use of videotapes, this increase in utilization is probably extremely conservative.

b. **ACE.** The number of courses, number of hours, and number of registered students for years 1969 through 1974 were derived from course schedules and enrollment records. Student hours for these years were calculated by assuming each student is in a class of average length (total hours divided by number of courses for a given year). Projections were calculated by assuming class size to remain at 35 students per class (the average class size for 1972, 1973 and 1974), an additional five courses per year, and an average course length of 24 hours. These extensions are not unreasonable as the system with four channels is still underutilized.

and Golden Gate is responsible for hiring the instructors, printing materials and designing the course. ACE receives all student fees for the MBA courses. San Jose also hires its own instructors and designs the course, but they pay ACE a fee of $60 per unit per student. For the College of Notre Dame courses, ACE hires instructors and bears all other expenses. The College of Notre Dame receives $15 per student per course and grants credit for the course.

Utilization of ACE courses is reported in Table VIII.1. The number of courses has increased by an average of eleven per year from twenty-four in 1969 to eighty in 1974. It has been assumed that ACE will continue to add five courses per year through 1987.

While the number of courses has increased, the average course length has decreased from approximately 32 hours in 1969 to an average of 22.5 hours in 1974. For purposes of projection, the average course length has been assumed to be 24 hours for 1975 through 1987. Because ACE can use the television system only during hours not reserved for Stanford engineering courses, there is a total of 2,880 hours available during the four ten-week quarters. If Stanford continues at the same utilization rate, than an additional 1,900 hours are available during times normally reserved for Stanford. If one designs short courses for the twelve weeks of the year for which no courses are broadcast for Stanford, an additional 2,784 hours become available. Thus, a total of 7,564 hours is potentially available for ACE courses. The projections for utilization result in only 3,480 hours in 1987.

While the number of students enrolled in all ACE courses has more than doubled from 1,365 in 1969 to 2,800 in 1974, the average class size has declined from 57 to 35 students. For purposes of projecting utilization, it has been assumed that class size will remain at an average of 35 students. This results in an assumed enrollment of 5,075 students in 1987.

EFFECTIVENESS

This system utilizes one-way video transmissions with two-way audio so that students may ask questions of the instructor. While the two-way audio adds to the cost of the system, there is no convincing evidence that it contributes to the effectiveness of the courses; Martin-Vegue, Morris and Talmadge (1972) suggested that the major reasons for including two-way audio may have been to gain faculty acceptance and to allow off-campus students not to feel like second class students. However, at present Stanford University does not require newly joining companies to install two-way audio as a systems component.

Dubin and Hedley (1969), in a review of the effectiveness of ITV at the college level, concluded that while there were no significant differences in the effectiveness of one-way television with conventional face to face instruction (for example, lecture and discussion), television with two-way audio was inferior to conventional instruction. Dubin and Hedley based their conclusions on a summarization of the results of ninety-three studies comparing televised and conventional instruction. However, of the twenty-six studies comparing conventional instruction with two-way television, twenty-five came from one school (Los Angeles City School District, 1959) and the results may indicate poor organization or some other deficiency of the particular system rather than ineffectiveness of two-way television per se.

Chu and Schramm (1967) concluded that: "The lack of opportunity for students to raise questions and participate in free discussion would seem to reduce the effectiveness of learning from instructional television, particularly if the students are fairly advanced or the material is relatively complicated" (p. 91). However, while they cited evidence that students are less dissatisfied when two-way audio is available (Stuit et al., 1956 and Southwestern Signal Corps Training Center, 1953), the evidence they cited regarding the effectiveness of two-way audio (Wolgamuth, 1961 and Greenhill, 1964) leads to a conclusion of no significant differences with respect to conventional instruction.

In studies of students utilizing the Stanford system, Jamison and Lumsden (1975) found no significant differences in learning among students in the classroom, students utilizing the two-way audio facility and students viewing the lectures on videotape.

Wells (1976), in an analysis of student opinions regarding the Stanford system, found that students felt that the two-way audio system was necessary, although they were less inclined to use the two-way audio than speak in a traditional classroom setting.

2. SYSTEM COSTS

YEAR BY YEAR COST

Costs for the Stanford ITV system are presented in Table VIII.2 in 1972 U.S. dollars. The total investment in production and transmission equipment, on-campus classroom reception, construction, and personnel in planning and construction was approximately $850,000. This compares with $825,000 spent by the University of Southern California in the construction of a similar facility. The USC facility was recently built, and it is expected that equipment costs have risen. However, since Stanford was the first system to utilize this technology, USC probably benefited from the experience and was able to reduce planning costs. This figure may also be compared with the estimate given by Martin-Vegue et al. (1972) for a similar four channel ITV system with audio talkback. Their estimate of $535,000 for equipment and personnel is lower than the experiences of Stanford and USC, since Martin-Vegue et al., ignored instruction costs. The costs for reception are borne by the participating companies and are not included in the above investment figures. The costs to the companies for reception equipment in Table VIII.2, $337,800 in 1968 and $35,400 in 1972, are derived from the estimated equipment and installation expenses for the different types of reception equipment presented and the configurations for companies presented in Table VIII.3. The costs of reception are underestimated, since there is no estimate available for construction expenditure by the companies to prepare classrooms. While there are thirty-seven members of the Stanford system, there are classrooms at only thirty locations, and the number of classrooms and the type of equipment utilized varied among the locations.

Administration for the Stanford ITV system consists of a manager, two secretaries and two engineers. Their salaries and fringe benefits are actual expenses for 1969 through 1974 and are assumed to increase by 5% per year from 1975 through 1987. This estimate may be high, because the pattern seems to have been relatively constant salaries with an overcompensation for inflation in 1974. The administration for the ACE system consists of a manager, an assistant and a secretary. When teacher salaries are excluded from the analysis, the administrative salaries and office expenses (rent, supplies and a courier service between companies and Stanford to distribute course materials and collect student papers) account for nearly 70% of annual expenses.

The technicians who operate the cameras during the classes are hired on an hourly basis. Their pay with fringe benefits averages to $3.80 per hour. Stanford students are given a short amount of training and hired as camera operators.

If one merely examined the expenses for the Stanford engineering courses, the costs of a similar ITV system for institutions wishing to replicate the system would be understated. All instructor salaries are excluded from the budget of these courses as the network simply broadcasts regularly scheduled Stanford engineering courses. Therefore, in calculating the costs of the system, there are three possible approaches to instructor costs:

(1) assume the cost is $0 since the ITV system is a marginal operation; that is, the engineering courses would be scheduled for on-campus students, and having these classes meet in studio classrooms instead of regular classrooms does not affect the class but allows more individuals to participate;

(2) prorate the instructor cost based on the number of off-campus and on-campus students; and

(3) assign the full cost to the television system.

The first and last of these alternatives are considered and the assumption is made that instructors would be paid $2,000 per course.

TABLE VIII.2
Costs of the Stanford ITV System (in thousands of 1972 U.S. dollars)

	1968	1969	1970	1971	1972	1973	1974	1975	1976	1977	1978	1979	1980	1981	1982	1983	1984	1985	1986	1987
ADMINISTRATION[a]																				
1. Staff—Stanford		69.5	72.2	74.2	73.7	87.0	104.2	109.5	115.0	120.7	126.7	133.0	139.7	146.7	154.0	161.7	169.8	178.3	187.2	196.5
2. Office and related—Stanford		8.5	8.7	8.9	9.8	11.5	9.8	10.0	10.0	10.0	10.0	10.0	10.0	10.0	10.0	10.0	10.0	10.0	10.0	10.0
3. Staff—ACE		21.5	22.4	27.4	27.9	30.9	35.9	37.7	39.6	41.6	43.7	45.9	48.2	50.6	53.1	55.8	58.6	61.5	64.6	67.8
4. Office and related—ACE		10.3	10.5	12.3	9.4	10.5	9.9	10.0	10.0	10.0	10.0	10.0	10.0	10.0	10.0	10.0	10.0	10.0	10.0	10.0
PRODUCTION[b]																				
5. Facility	482.2										51.7									
6. Equipment	233.3	4.4	5.5	5.6	6.0	6.2	6.3	6.5	6.7	6.8	6.9	7.0	7.1	7.2	7.4	7.5	7.6	7.6	7.7	7.9
7. Maintenance		240	296	286	290	300	300	300	300	300	300	300	300	300	300	300	300	300	300	300
8. Instructors—Stanford		12.7	15.4	14.6	14.0	18.7	17.0	17.0	17.0	17.0	17.0	17.0	17.0	17.0	17.0	17.0	17.0	17.0	17.0	17.0
9. Technicians—Stanford		48	68	106	120	146	160	170	180	190	200	210	220	230	240	250	260	270	280	290
10. Instructors—ACE		2.7	3.8	4.3	5.3	7.2	6.7	7.2	7.6	8.1	8.5	9.0	9.4	9.9	10.3	10.8	11.2	11.7	12.1	12.6
11. Technicians—ACE		15.2	21.4	22.9	29.7	29.4	27.7	29.6	31.4	33.3	35.1	37.0	38.8	40.7	42.8	44.7	46.5	48.4	50.2	52.1
12. Studio rental—ACE																				
TRANSMISSION[c]																				
13. Equipment	134																			
14. Maintenance		3.3	3.3	3.4	3.2	3.3	4.4	4.8	4.8	4.8	4.8	4.8	4.8	4.8	4.8	4.8	4.8	4.8	4.8	4.8
RECEPTION[d]																				
15. Equipment	337.8	8.8	11.0	11.2	35.4			15.6	15.6	15.6	134.5	15.6	15.6	15.6	33.3	15.6	15.6	23.4	23.4	23.4
16. Maintenance					12.0	12.4	12.6	13.0	13.4	13.6	13.8	14.0	14.2	14.4	14.8	15.0	15.2	15.2	15.4	15.8
TOTAL COST[e]																				
17. Stanford (no teachers)	1187.3	107.2	116.1	117.9	154.1	139.5	154.3	176.4	182.1	188.5	365.4	201.4	208.4	215.7	240.8	231.2	239.6	255.9	265.1	275.0
18. Stanford (teachers)	1187.3	347.2	412.1	403.9	444.1	439.5	454.3	476.4	482.1	488.5	665.4	501.4	508.4	515.7	540.8	531.2	539.6	555.9	565.1	575.0
19. ACE + Stanford (no teachers)	1187.3	141.7	152.8	159.6	198.6	187.9	206.8	231.3	239.3	248.1	427.6	266.3	276.0	286.2	314.2	307.8	319.4	339.1	351.8	365.4
20. ACE + Stanford (teachers)	1187.3	429.7	515.8	509.9	564.1	634.1	666.8	701.3	719.3	738.0	927.6	776.3	796.0	816.2	854.2	857.8	879.4	909.1	931.8	955.4

See next page for footnotes.

The situation with instructor salaries is more complicated for the ACE courses, since some instructors are paid by the ACE and others are paid by universities. However, for simplicity the same assumptions are made for ACE courses as for Stanford courses; instructor salaries are excluded or equal to $2,000 per course. As ACE courses tend to be of shorter length than Stanford courses, this amount is probably high for the ACE courses.

FOOTNOTES FOR TABLE VIII.2

a. **Administration.** Administrative expenses for Stanford and ACE for years 1969 through 1974 were derived from budgeted expenses for each organization. Office and related expenses include paper, mailings, a courier vehicle for distribution and collection of course-related papers, actual office space rent for ACE and an imputed rent for Stanford. Projections were accomplished by assuming annual increases of 5 percent in salaries (which may be high as this would be a real increase above inflation rates) and constant streams of $10,000 for office expenses for each organization.

b. **Production.** The initial expense for the facility is the amount spent for personnel and construction during the planning and completion of the master control room, and the studio complex. This facility will not need replacement. The equipment includes a specially constructed master control console, cable, control consoles for each of the five classrooms, 10 cameras, and 145 classroom monitors for use by students in the classroom. It is assumed that cameras and monitors will be replaced after 10 years. Maintenance for years 1969 through 1974 is slightly higher than reported amounts and assumed to be equal to $1 per hour for the life of the project. Instructors are assumed to receive a salary of $20,000 per course to cover salary and benefits. This is a reasonable assumption for the Stanford courses as professors at Stanford normally teach five courses per year and have other responsibilities. Technicians are assumed to continue a salary of $3.78 per hour as in 1974. The studio cost to ACE is an internal accounting mechanism between ACE and Stanford whereby ACE has been charged $18 per hour for use of the system (inflation between 1969 and 1974 has caused this figure to be higher in this table for 1969, 1970 and 1971 and lower for 1973 and 1974). Since Stanford pays all technicians this represents a net revenue of $11.70 per hour of ACE broadcast in 1974 and if this were included it would reduce the Stanford cost. If one were calculating costs to ACE the studio cost would be included and the technician, equipment and facility cost excluded.

c. **Transmission.** Transmission equipment was purchased in 1968 and is assumed to have a 20-year life. Maintenance is reported amounts for 1969 through 1974 and as the amounts did not vary in this period maintenance is assumed to remain constant for the remainder of the project although at a higher amount.

d. **Reception.** Equipment amounts for 1968 and 1972 are estimated amounts based on 1972 equipment costs from Table VIII.3 and the types of equipment purchased by the companies in those years. From 1975 two companies per year are assumed to be added to the system; one with four classrooms and no talkback and one with four classrooms and time-shared talkback. This may be a slightly high assumption as new companies are often utilizing preexisting facilities at nearby companies and are tending to opt for no talkback if they purchase equipment. However, there is no cost included for arrangement of viewing areas in the companies. It is assumed that conference rooms are used for this purpose. Due to the varying use of the reception equipment, the relative infrequent use of talkback equipment, and the long life of antennas, cables, masts, etc., it is assumed that 25 percent of the equipment is replaced every 10 years. Maintenance is assumed to be $2 per hour for all reception equipment.

e. **Total cost.** Total cost is calculated for the Stanford engineering courses only by assuming all equipment is necessary for Stanford courses and ignoring the possibility of renting facilities to other users when capacity is available. The total for Stanford without teachers is the sum of item 1 + 2 + 5 + 6 + 7 + 9 + 13 + 14 + 15 + 16. When the system is considered as a whole, items 3, 4 and 11 are also added. If one were calculating the costs for ACE only one would use items 3, 4 and 12.

TABLE VIII.3
Company Reception Cost[a]

	1 classroom switchable to 4 channels	2 classrooms independently switchable to 4 channels	3 classrooms independently switchable to 4 channels	4 classrooms independently switchable to 4 channels
RECEPTION				
10 in. mast, 2 in. parabola antenna, down converter, VHF amplifier, power supply, cable	1,350	1,350	1,350	1,350
TV receiver and mounts	795	1,590	2,385	3,180
TALKBACK				
A. Independent for each classroom (transmitters, antenna, cable)	4,190	7,040	9,990	12,640
B. Time-shared (transmitter, antenna, cable, receiver, mod)	4,930	5,460	5,990	6,520
TOTAL				
A. Reception only	2,145(4)	2,940	3,735(1)	4,530(1)
B. Reception and independent talkback	6,335(2)	9,980(4)	13,725(2)	17,170(12)
C. Reception and time-shared talkback	7,075	8,400(3)	9,725	11,050

a. Number in parentheses are the number of companies with that particular equipment set up.

The production of courses on the Stanford ITV system is probably one of the simplest possible for a television system: one instructor and one technician. Yet by using the overhead camera or the projectors, it is possible to utilize many of the advantages of the television technology.

The final production cost in Table VIII.2 is the studio cost of $18 per hour charged to ACE for use of the facilities. When the total costs of the system are calculated, this cost is ignored as it is merely a transfer of funds from one part of the system to another. If one wanted to calculate the costs to ACE, then technicians' salaries would be ignored as this is paid for from the Stanford engineering budget and the studio cost would be included. Since the Stanford engineering portion does not utilize the full system capacity, one would expect that the rational decision for efficient allocation of resources would be to charge a price equal to marginal cost (the extra cost to utilize the system for one more hour). This aspect of the system will be analyzed in the next section.

In summary, one can see from the cost tableau (Table VIII.2) that for a total initial investment of $1,187,300, an ITV system was established which allowed for simultaneous broadcast of four courses with audio talkback capabilities to an area with a radius of approximately twenty miles. The system included: four studio classrooms and one auditorium, each equipped with two cameras and several monitors; four on-campus overflow classrooms with monitors; and approximately seventy classrooms in twenty-five different locations with monitors and talkback capabilities.

COST FUNCTIONS

Cost data from Table VIII.2 are used to calculate a cost function for the project where TC, total cost, is a function of N, number of students and h, the number of broadcast hours. This cost function, whish is assumed to be linear, takes the general form:

(VIII.1) $$TC = F + V_N N + V_h h$$

This equation may then be used to calculate average costs per student (AC_N). In the equation, F is a fixed cost of the system; V_N and V_h are the variable costs per student and per hour respectively.

For purposes of calculation, the cost function data from 1974 are used. In Table VIII.4 all expenses labelled "recurrent" are actual expenditures in 1974, and all expenses labelled "capital" are annualized values of capital expenses occurring prior to and including 1974. Capital expenses are annualized at three different interest rates: zero, 7.5% and 15%. Assumptions regarding the lifetime of equipment are explained in Table VIII.4. To determine variable costs per student, the total enrollment (including auditors) of 4,942

TABLE VIII.4
Total Cost Function, Stanford ITV System 1974[a] (in thousands of 1972 U.S. dollars)

Interest rate	0% Fixed	0% Variable Student	0% Variable Hour	7.5% Fixed	7.5% Variable Student	7.5% Variable Hour	15% Fixed	15% Variable Student	15% Variable Hour
Administration[b]									
Recurrent	159.8			159.8			159.8		
Production[c]									
Recurrent									
Teachers			.0730			.0730			.0730
Other			.0048			.0048			.0048
Capital	9.644		.0023	37.129		.0040	72.33		.0060
Transmission[d]									
Recurrent			.0007			.0007			.0007
Capital			.0011			.0021			.0030
Reception[e]									
Recurrent			.0020			.0020			.0020
Capital		.0056			.0092			.0135	
Total Cost	169.44	.0056	.0839	196.922	.0092	.0866	232.130	.0135	.0895

a. The cost function is calculated from cost data through 1974 for the Stanford ITV system. The utilization in 1974 was 4,942 students and 6,290 hours. Recurrent expenses are expenses during 1974. Capital expenses are annualized values of investment prior to 1974.

b. **Administration.** All administration expenses (salaries and office and related expenses) are assumed to be fixed.

c. **Production.** Although teachers are hired to teach courses of 30 or 24 hour lengths it is assumed for simplicity that these teachers may be hired by the hour. The technicians are hired by the hour and are represented by the recurrent expense of $3.80 per hour. Maintenance is also included in the recurrent expenses. The fixed capital expense is the production facility which is assumed to have a 50-year life. Of the variable capital expenses, $181,600 is assumed to have a 20-year life and $51,700 is assumed to have a 10-year life. The 20-year equipment includes the master control unit, the five classroom control units, and connecting cable. The 10-year life equipment is the monitors and cameras.

d. **Transmission.** Recurrent expense is transmitter maintenance. Capital expense is the annualized value of the transmitter equipment which is assumed to have a 20-year life.

e. **Reception.** Recurrent expense is the maintenance expense. Capital expense is calculated by assuming that half of the equipment has a 20-year life and half has a 10-year life.

students in 1974 is used. The total number of broadcast hours (6,290) is used to calculate variable costs per hour.

Production and transmission equipment are assumed to vary with the number of hours of production. The reception equipment is assumed to vary with the number of students. This is obviously a simplifying assumption, since the purchases are lumpy; that is, the cost of equipment is a step function with respect to number of hours or number of students. An additional simplifying assumption is that teachers may be hired by the hour, although in fact they are hired by the course. The average variable teacher cost is $73 per hour and it accounts for approximately 80% of all variable costs at a zero interest rate and 70% at a 15% interest rate.

A summary of the total post functions (TC), the average cost per student (AC_N), average cost per student hour, and the ratio of average cost to variable cost for students (AC_N/V_N) is given below.

	Total Cost Equation	AC_N	AC_N/V_N	Cost per Student Hour
0%	$TC = 169,400 + 5.60N + 83.90h$	146.60	26.18	5.70
7.5%	$TC = 196,900 + 9.20N + 86.60h$	159.20	17.30	6.20
15%	$TC = 232,100 + 13.50N + 90.10h$	175.10	12.97	6.80

Several interesting facts emerge from this analysis. As expected, the average costs increase as the interest rate increases. The average cost per student at 7.5% is $159.20. While this may appear to be high, it should be borne in mind that this ITV system is not an addition to an educational system but has the main burden of instruction. The figure of $159.20 includes costs for instructors and annualized capital and is for a system with only twenty-one students per class on average. Using the same methodology, the average costs per student, including auditor enrollment, for the Stanford engineering courses at only 7.5% interest would be $268.60 when teacher costs are included and $128.54 when teacher costs are excluded.

If auditors are not included, these average costs become $598.07 and $286.22 respectively. One can see that the inclusion of teacher costs and the decision on whether or not to include auditors in the analysis have profound effects on costs. However, as expensive as the system might appear, it should be noted that if one can assume that tuition covers approximately half of all expenses for the entire university and tuition for a three unit engineering course is approximately $270, then only for the highest figure of $598.07 (an average class size of only seven students), does the television become more expensive than the traditional system.

One can also use the cost functions to determine the appropriate charge to ACE for use of the facilities. Excluding the instructor cost of $73 per hour and the reception maintenance cost of $2 per hour from the variable hourly cost, the marginal hourly cost of the system is only $11.60 at 7.5% and $15.10 at 15%. This hourly cost includes a charge for the capital equipment and actual marginal costs would be even lower. It would appear that the charge of $18 per hour for use of the system is too high. However, one should note that the calculated costs do not include any charge for engineers' time, because this is considered a fixed expense of the system. If it were necessary to pay for additional hours of engineers' time, as is currently done for technicians' time, the charge of $18 per hour would not appear to be high.

A final interesting piece of information is the ratio of average costs to variable costs. In a very broad sense this figure gives one an idea of the excess capacity of the system. When the ratio is very high, a great deal of capacity exists. At 7.5% the average cost for 4,942 students is $159.20 per student, but the approximate cost of adding another student is only $9.20. As more students are added, the average cost per student will diminish. One should realize that $9.20 is a long-run marginal cost per student. In the short run, the cost of adding an additional student is nearly zero.

AC_{ij}

The use of cost functions is a reasonable approach to the determination of average costs. An alternative approach is to calculate a summary average cost from year i of the project to year j, AC_{ij}. This type of calculation makes full use of the yearly utilization data in Table VIII.1 and the yearly cost data in Table VIII.2. The average cost, AC_{ij}, is calculated by discounting costs and utilizations, such that

(VIII.2)
$$AC_{ij} = \frac{\sum_{k=i}^{j} C_k/(1 + r)^{k-i}}{\sum_{k=i}^{j} N_k/(1 + r)^{k-i}}$$

where r is an interest rate and C_k and N_k are costs and utilizations (students or student hours) in year k respectively.

When k = i we calculate the average costs of the project from its inception to different points in time (possible project termination dates with an assumption of no recovery costs for equipment). Table VIII.5 presents the AC_{ij} information for Stanford engineering courses only with teacher costs excluded, auditor enrollment included, and using an interest rate of 7.5%. The first row of the figure provides the information of the average cost per student for different project lengths. Due to the large initial investment in capital

TABLE VIII.5
Average Costs Per Student From Year i To Year j
Interest Rate = 7.5%
(Stanford courses only, teacher costs excluded, auditor enrollment included)

Year i \ Year j	1968	1969	1970	1971	1973	1975	1977	1979	1981	1983	1985	1986	1987
1968	0.0	1540.16	800.06	523.42	205.72	255.18	193.74	182.58	170.93	163.61	158.48	156.58	155.03
1969		121.36	115.36	103.63	87.68	83.81	83.64	90.51	90.47	91.23	92.01	92.52	93.05
1970			110.61	96.47	82.06	79.95	80.70	88.52	88.77	89.75	90.70	91.26	91.83
1971				85.50	75.75	75.81	77.79	86.88	87.40	88.65	89.76	90.43	91.07
1973					68.23	73.35	76.88	88.96	89.26	90.50	91.60	92.27	92.99
1975						81.08	82.29	98.16	96.27	96.68	97.24	97.76	98.34
1977							84.30	111.11	103.61	102.39	102.17	102.52	102.97
1979								87.87	89.63	92.93	94.93	96.10	97.22
1981									91.89	95.97	97.77	99.00	100.23
1983										96.11	99.20	100.82	102.32
1985											104.22	105.15	106.40
1986												106.80	107.88
1987													109.49

equipment, average costs decline as the project length increases and more students use the same equipment. If the project had been terminated after the current year (1974), the average cost of the system for that time period, $AC_{1,7}$, would have been $252 per student. If the project runs a full twenty years, the average cost, $AC_{1,20}$, declines to $155 per student.

Another interesting row is the one using the next year of the project (1975) to help the planner determine future possibilities of the project. As soon as the initial year of the project is excluded, the initial investment costs are treated as sunk costs and not included in the analysis. From Table VIII.5 the average cost from the present to the end of the planning horizon, $AC_{8,20}$, is $98.

Other interesting questions can be answered with this average cost analysis. If one calculates the costs to Stanford excluding the reception costs, $AC_{1,20}$ becomes $122 assuming no growth and $AC_{8,20}$ becomes $53. If one excludes auditors from the analysis, $AC_{1,20}$ from Table VIII.6 for the Stanford engineering courses becomes $287, a substantial increase above the $155 average cost, when auditors are excluded. The impact of adding teacher cost is also substantial. The average cost $AC_{1,20}$ is $571 when auditors are excluded and $309 when auditors are included.

Two additional tables are included, Table VIII.7 and VIII.8, which are average costs for the entire ITV system with teacher costs excluded in Table VIII.7 and included in Table VIII.8. Auditor enrollment is included in both tables. When the ACE courses are added to the Stanford courses, there is a sharp drop in average costs. Adding the ACE courses results in a division of capital equipment over more students. The ACE courses have an average enrollment of 35 students whereas the Stanford engineering courses have average enrollments of 15 students with auditors and 8 without auditors. $AC_{1,20}$ becomes $72 with teacher costs excluded and auditors included, as compared with $155 for the Stanford engineering courses only. When teachers are included, the costs for the length of the project, $AC_{1,20}$, rise to only $164 for the entire system as compared with $309 for the Stanford courses. Finally, when auditors are excluded from the analysis, $AC_{1,20}$ for the entire system is $88 when teacher costs are excluded and $201 when teacher costs are included.

In analyzing costs, great care must be given to the assumptions of the analysis and the types of decisions which are made. The major assumption for the cost analysis was the growth 'assumptions for all years after 1974: an additional 25 students for Stanford courses, an additional five ACE courses and 175 students, an additional four classroom locations with reception only capabilities, and an additional four classroom locations with time-shared talkback. The growth assumptions result in higher average costs compared with an assumption of no growth for Stanford courses and lower costs for a no growth assumption for the entire system.

TABLE VIII.6
Average Costs Per Student From Year i To Year j
Interest Rate = 7.5%
(Stanford courses only, teacher costs excluded, auditor enrollment excluded)

Year j	Year i 1968	1969	1970	1971	1973	1975	1977	1979	1981	1983	1985	1986	1987
1968	0.0												
1969	1735.09	136.72											
1970	892.03	128.63	122.15										
1971	720.00	142.55	146.28	186.82									
1973	548.22	162.54	171.09	197.52	179.79								
1975	438.74	163.29	169.43	183.32	170.18	173.62							
1977	380.84	164.42	169.22	179.09	169.43	170.15	168.08						
1979	356.89	176.92	182.34	192.31	188.65	196.67	214.70	164.36					
1981	330.33	174.82	179.25	187.15	183.28	187.47	194.66	163.01	162.27				
1983	311.85	173.89	177.67	184.41	180.67	183.50	187.51	164.76	165.23	161.12			
1985	297.75	172.85	176.17	182.03	178.38	180.34	182.84	164.47	164.49	162.48	166.60		
1986	292.06	172.57	175.66	181.25	177.64	179.36	181.50	164.72	164.77	163.37	166.27	166.97	
1987	287.12	172.33	175.22	180.53	177.10	178.60	180.45	164.94	165.12	164.10	166.52	166.91	167.56

TABLE VIII.7
Average Costs Per Student From Year i To Year j
Interest Rate = 7.5%
(Stanford and ACE courses, teacher costs excluded, auditor enrollment included)

Year j \ Year i	1968	1969	1970	1971	1973	1975	1977	1979	1981	1983	1985	1986	1987
1968	0.0												
1969	626.77	63.43											
1970	339.04	61.51	60.27										
1971	226.61	55.97	52.91	47.36									
1973	140.46	50.34	48.00	44.98	40.72								
1975	108.95	48.00	46.23	44.18	42.26	44.85							
1977	93.97	47.17	45.77	44.25	43.07	44.54	44.50						
1979	87.85	49.36	48.35	47.39	47.38	50.17	54.29	44.45					
1981	81.72	48.66	47.75	46.91	46.79	48.69	50.63	44.51	44.69				
1983	77.62	48.37	47.55	46.82	46.71	48.22	49.50	45.16	45.72	45.11			
1985	74.61	48.14	47.39	46.73	46.62	47.88	48.84	45.39	45.83	45.72	46.92		
1986	73.44	48.09	47.39	46.75	46.65	47.83	48.71	45.59	46.05	46.07	47.09	47.33	
1987	72.43	48.08	47.40	46.79	46.68	47.82	48.63	45.79	46.25	46.35	47.27	47.50	47.80

TABLE VIII.8
Average Costs Per Student From Year i To Year j
Interest Rate = 7.5%
(Stanford and ACE courses, teacher costs included, auditor enrollment included)

Year j	Year i 1968	1969	1970	1971	1973	1975	1977	1979	1981	1983	1985	1986	1987
1968	0.0												
1969	754.02	190.64											
1970	475.03	197.79	205.18										
1971	350.69	180.21	175.83	152.43									
1973	250.21	160.20	154.54	142.24	138.57								
1975	213.09	152.12	147.60	139.41	136.42	136.25							
1977	194.64	147.82	144.03	137.79	135.35	134.50	132.89						
1979	186.01	147.46	144.39	139.46	138.11	138.83	141.40	130.28					
1981	177.92	144.81	142.05	137.71	136.27	136.19	136.60	129.20	128.26				
1983	172.22	142.91	140.38	136.50	135.04	134.65	134.45	128.85	128.30	126.68			
1985	167.83	141.31	138.96	135.40	133.98	133.40	132.89	127.99	127.54	126.47	126.73		
1986	166.06	140.66	138.39	134.97	133.56	132.92	132.33	127.99	127.36	126.41	126.47	126.33	
1987	164.48	140.08	137.86	134.57	133.18	132.51	131.87	127.79	127.17	126.32	126.30	126.13	126.03

The other important decisions from the standpoint of decision makers at Stanford are: accounting for teacher costs, inclusion or exclusion of auditor enrollment and inclusion or exclusion of ACE courses. All of these considerations have important impacts on the average costs of the system.

3. EXPANSION ALTERNATIVES

A major expansion alternative which has been discussed is the addition of courses and new students within the Stanford area. However, even with the assumption of increased production, 35% of the capacity from 7 a.m. to 7 p.m., Monday to Thursday, and 7 a.m. to 5 p.m. on Fridays still remains. This time could be utilized at a cost of approximately $84 per hour counting maintenance, technician salaries and teacher salaries. Many more students could be added by utilizing existing facilities. Considering the investment in additional reception equipment, more students could be added at a cost of approximately $9 per student.

An additional and important expansion possibility is the use of videotapes. The Stanford ITV system has already begun the distribution of videotapes to areas which are unable to receive direct transmissions. The only loss in utilizing videotapes instead of direct broadcast is the lack of talkback facilities. The costs of expanding the system may be conservatively estimated to be $50 per hour for recording and mailing a one-hour one half-inch tape. Stanford already owns five video taping machines. At reception locations the investment would be much lower and require the purchase of videotape playback machines only. A videotape playback machine with a monitor would cost approximately $800; adding a camera would raise the cost to $1,500.

4. SYSTEM FINANCING

All Stanford engineering and ACE courses are open to member companies only. Stanford has established a schedule of membership fees based on the size of the company. The purpose of the fees is to help Stanford recover the costs of the capital investment. There is a variety of payment plans but the one-time lump sum fees are the following:

Annual Gross Revenue	Lump Sum
$5 million	$ 2,200
$5 − $20 million	$ 8,800
$20 − $50 million	$17,600
$50 − $100 million	$26,400
$100 million	$39,600

The operating costs of the system are financed through the $20 television surcharge for HCP and NRO students for the Stanford engineering courses and through the fee schedule for auditors. The ACE courses are financed through a variety of means depending on the course: fees of $50 per student per course, lump sum payments of $12,000 by companies and direct payments from other universities.

From the viewpoint of the Stanford administration, to determine the viability of the system in terms of recurrent expenses, the revenues would include the $20 surcharge, auditor fees and the studio charge to ACE. For 1974 this revenue was approximately $82,000, assuming an average of $30 per auditor. However, to this total one should also add the matching fees for the NRO students who are not matriculated and are not receiving credit. The annual operating budget is approximately $140,000.

Chapter IX

THE HAGERSTOWN INSTRUCTIONAL
TELEVISION SYSTEM

The instructional television system in Washington County, Maryland has perhaps the longest continuous history of any ITV project in the world. The project began transmission in September 1956, with service to schools in the immediate area of Hagerstown, Maryland and was gradually extended to all schools in Washington County. The network reached 6,000 students in 1956-1957, 12,000 students in 1957-1958, 16,500 students in 1958-1959, and 18,000 students (nearly 100% coverage of all twelve grades) by 1959-1960. Initial equipment for production and reception, valued at approximately $300,000, was donated by the Electronics Industries Association. The Fund for the Advancement of Education and the Ford Foundation contributed a combined total of $200,000 per year for the first five years of the project. The county has funded the project since the sixth year (1961-1962). The Chesapeake and Potomac Telephone Company installed and maintains the six channel coaxial cable which connects all county schools with the studio facility in Hagerstown. The telephone company charges a rental fee for the use of the cable. The fee is based upon the amount of cable and not the utilization time.

The system has been described in county reports (Washington County Board of Education, 1963; 1973; and Washington County Instructional Television Evaluation Committee, 1973). These documents include costs of the system, evaluations of the system comparing the academic performance of students using television with those not using television in Washington County and the performance of these students with average scores on standardized national achievement tests in a variety of subjects, and an attitude survey of students and teachers.

1. THE SYSTEM

ORGANIZATION AND TECHNICAL CHARACTERISTICS

A standard studio crew employs a teacher, two technicians, a director, a floor manager, and two camera operators. Many of the technical positions are filled by students from the local junior college, and it is estimated that training of a novice can be completed in two weeks. The system has its own engineering and maintenance staff, which serves the needs of the central facility and the schools.

In 1972-1973 there were 31 TV teachers, 23 persons employed on a full time basis in engineering and production, 32 junior college and other production personnel employed on a part time basis (equivalent to 5.1 full time personnel) and 9.3 full time equivalent personnel from support services such as, cinematography, graphics, audiovisual, and instructional materials.

The teachers for television were originally drawn from the classroom teacher supply in Washington County. The TV teachers have an organizational structure similar to traditional schools, except that the teachers report directly to the subject area administrators for the entire school district. The studio teachers have not been rotated back to the classroom, and several of the teachers have been teaching on television since the beginning of the project. The most striking difference between classroom teachers and studio teachers is the instructional load and hence the availability of preparation time. A studio teacher teaches three twenty-minute classes per *week* while a classroom teacher typically teaches five forty-five-minute classes each *day*. The instructional time requirement for studio teachers is also satisfied by the use of videotapes of their courses from previous years with the studio teacher providing necessary updating and revisions.

There are five television studios at the central facility in Hagerstown. These studios are connected with classroom television monitors in the schools by the dedicated six-channel coaxial cable installed by the telephone company. In 1972-1973 there were approximately 800 receivers in the schools. Most of the receivers are for black and white broadcasts only. The system has, however, begun to move toward production in color.

One of the most interesting features of the system, from the technical standpoint, is the relatively long life of equipment in the system. Videotapes which were purchased in the earlier years of the project are still being used. Through careful maintenance the television monitors, ordinarily assumed to function for five years, have been in use for many years. Of the 342 receivers purchased in 1955, over 140 were still in use in 1973.

UTILIZATION

With six channels available and assuming a 35-hour school week for 36 weeks, there is a total of 7,560 hours available for television production. Of these hours, only 1,400 hours were used for original production in 1972-1973, while 1,900 hours were used in earlier years. There is clearly a great deal of capacity for additional original programming or use of programs from other distributors such as, National Instructional Television, Learning Corporation of America, and the Maryland State Department of Education's Division of ITV. Excess capacity has been used for repeat broadcasts of junior and senior high school programs to reduce scheduling conflicts.

The Washington County school system is small. In 1972-1973 there were only 22,000 students enrolled in all twelve grades. Televised instruction has been available to all students since 1959-1960. The utilization of these courses by students is reported in Table IX.1. There are no expansion possibilities for increasing the numbers of students serviced by the system. Students outside of Washington County can view open circuit broadcasts from the Maryland State Department of Education.

The only possible expansion possibility is more programming hours. However, the trend in recent years has been to reduce the number of broadcast hours. Additionally, televised courses are no longer required for twelfth grade students. County officials have estimated that 60% of these students do view the elective courses.

Television course schedules reporting the number of broadcast hours per week for each grade level available for most years from 1958-1959 on. The enrollment figures were combined with broadcast schedules when available to determine the total number of student hours each year. The total number of student hours reported in Table IX.1 was calculated by summing the products of enrollments and instructional time for each grade level, i.e.,

$$(IX.1) \qquad SH_p = \sum_{q=1}^{12} Epq \times ITpq$$

where SH_p is the total number of student-hours in year p, Epq is the enrollment in grade level q in year p, and ITpq is the instructional time via television for grade level q in year p. When broadcast schedules were not available, a broadcast time for each grade level was assumed and equation IX.1 was used to determine student hours. The utilization has fluctuated from 2,954,000 student hours in 1959 to a high of 3,255,000 in 1968. There has been a general decline since 1968. In 1972 only 2,588,000 student hours of utilization occurred. At this utilization level the average student is receiving 117 hours of instruction each year. Assuming a 35 hour instructional week for 36 weeks, this figure represents 0.3% of total instructional time for each student.

TABLE IX.1
Costs and Utilization for the Hagerstown ITV System[a] (in thousands of 1972 U.S. dollars)

	1955	1956[b]	1957	1958	1959	1960	1961	1962	1963	1964	1965	1966	1967	1968	1969	1970	1971	1972	1973[c]	1974
ADMINISTRATION[d]																				
General		30	35	40	40	43	47	50	54	56	58	60	60	60	60	"60	60	60	60	60
A-V subject area		4	4	5	5	6	6	6	6	8	9	10	10	10.3	9.3	14.7	11.5	10.5	11	11
PRODUCTION[e]																				
Facility	409.5	250	250	300	300	300	300	300	300	300	285	300	300	329.0	404.2	415.6	415.8	398.3	400.0	400.0
TV teachers		100	100	125	125.0	132.0	139	146	152.0	156	160	164	168	172.0	202.4	224.8	236.1	228.5	230	230
Engr., Prod., and Technicians		25	25	30	30.0	33	36	39	43.2	44.7	46.1	47.5	48.9	50.2	50.3	54.8	57.9	58.6	58	58
Support personnel					32.4	16.5	0.6	5.2	108.5	6.7	17.8	79.0	100.5	7.1	2.3	35.1	6.8	7.8	10	10
Equipment	461.0																			
Video tapes	81.4								3.5	1.8		15.0	28.1	6.8	13.9	9.5	5.7	5.0	6	6
Power		3.0	3.0	3.0	3.0	3.0	3.0	3.0	3.0	3.0	3.0	3.0	3.4	3.3	4.5	4.3	5.1	5.0	5.0	5.0
Other		40	45	50	64.6	65	66	68	69.7	70	70	72	73	75.2	89.1	102.3	110.4	147.1	150	150
Maintenance		5.0	5.0	10.0	10.0	10.0	10.0	10.0	10.9	10.0	10.0	10.0	9.6	6.4	8.0	7.5	9.3	10.0	10.0	10.0
TRANSMISSION[f]																				
Cable rental	97.8	50	110	136	136	158.7	181.3	203.8	226.5	215.3	201.8	190	180.7	183.7	180.5	163.0	163.4	164.0	164	164
RECEPTION[g]																				
Equipment		1.0	1.0	20.8	7.3	7.5	9.7	9.1	32.1	16.0	13.8		7.3	6.2	1.5	8.3	3.1	3.2	3.0	3.0
Power				1.5	1.5	1.5	1.5	1.5	1.5	1.5	1.5	1.5	1.5	1.5	1.5	1.5	1.5	1.5	1.5	1.5
Maintenance		1.0	2.0	3.0	3.0	3.0	3.0	3.0	3.6	3.0	3.0	3.0	3.2	2.2	2.7	2.5	3.1	3.0	3.0	3.0
TOTAL COST	1049.7	509.0	629.0	724.3	757.8	779.2	803.1	844.6	1014.5	892.0	879.0	955.0	994.2	913.9	1030.2	1103.9	1089.7	1102.5	1111.5	1111.5
UTILIZATION[h]																				
Number of students (in thousands)	6.0	6.0	12.0	16.5	18.0	18.2	18.6	19.3	19.8	20.4	20.4	20.7	21.1	21.5	21.9	21.9	22.0	22.0	22.0	22.0
Number of student hours	950	950	1,900	2,612	2,954	2,844	2,630	2,664	2,718	2,889	2,968	3,314	2,974	3,255	2,859	2,757	2,839	2,588	2,500	2,500

See next page for footnotes.

EFFECTIVENESS

Achievement results for students in the earlier years of the project have been reported in Washington County Board of Education (1963) and repeated in Wade (1967). In the first year of utilization (1956-1957), fifth grade students gained an average of 1.9 grade equivalents on a national test. Achievement gains for students in mathematics for urban and rural students in grades 3, 4, 5, and 6 exceeded the national norm of 1.0 grade equivalents. Additionally, within Hagerstown, students in a given grade had higher average

---

FOOTNOTES FOR TABLE IX.1

a. The year given in the column is the year of the start of the academic year, e.g., 1958 means 1958-1959. Detailed records of equipment purchases for all years were available and figures in the table are accurate. A detailed county cost study (Washington County Board of Education, 1973) was undertaken for most costs from 1967 through 1972 and the results of that study were used here. A county report (Washington County Board of Education, 1963) was also available with some cost information for 1959 and 1963. Wade (1967) was used for cost information during 1965. Other data are estimated by the authors. Costs are reported in 1972 U.S. dollars. Current costs were converted to constant costs by using the GNP price deflator. Current prices for years 1955 through 1974 were multiplied by 1.82, 1.80, 1.78, 1.76, 1.68, 1.63, 1.60, 1.51, 1.45, 1.38, 1.29, 1.21, 1.18, 1.12, 1.10, 1.09, 1.06, 1.00, 0.95 and 0.86 respectively.

b. Costs for years 1956 and 1957 were based upon utilization patterns for those years and the relationship with utilization in 1958. Production costs and administration were assumed to be a higher percentage of 1958 costs than the relative utilizations would indicate as some start-up and planning time must be assumed.

c. Costs for 1973 and 1974 are slightly higher than 1972 costs with no growth assumed.

d. **Administration.** Data was available for total administration expenditures for years 1959 and 1965 and for audio-visual (AV) and subject area administration for years 1968 through 1972.

e. **Production.** Facility expense is estimated value of buildings assigned to TV and is derived from Washington County (1963). Teacher salaries were available for 1965 and for 1968 through 1973. Engineering, production and technician salaries and support personnel (graphics, audio-visual, photographic, secretarial, etc.) salaries were available for 1959, 1963 and 1968-1973. Equipment and videotape expenses are all from county records. Equipment includes cameras, tape machines, etc. Power expenses were available for 1963, 1965 and 1967 through 1971. Other expenses include salary fringe benefits for all production personnel, travel, custodial service, and workshops. Maintenance expense was known for 1963 and 1967 through 1971 and was allocated 75 percent to production and 25 percent to reception based upon approximate equipment value ratios.

f. **Transmission.** Cable rental expenses were known for 1959, 1963, 1965 and 1968 through 1973. County records were available for information for 1960, 1961, 1962, 1964 and 1967.

g. **Reception.** All equipment expenses are from county records and represent the purchase of approximately 1,050 black and white television sets and 50 color sets. In 1955, 342 sets were purchased. Approximately 200 sets are no longer in use. Power is estimated by assuming 1,000 sets in operation, 100 watts per set, 750 hours per set per year, and $.02 per kilowatt-hour.

h. **Utilization.** Utilization patterns were derived from county enrollments and published production schedules. Enrollments were available for all years of the project and were used to estimate numbers of students receiving televised instruction. A county report indicated that utilization was lower than enrollments for the first three project years and these figures are reported. To determine utilization in terms of student hours, enrollment levels for all 12 grades were used in conjunction with weekly broadcast schedules by grade level.

test scores than their predecessors at that grade level with less exposure to television. For example, students in rural schools in grade 5 scored: 5.34 in May 1958 with no television; 5.71 in May 1959 with one year of television; 6.03 in May 1960 with two years of television; and 6.11 in May 1961 with three years of television.

Attitude surveys were also undertaken in the earlier years of the project. There was a general decline in teachers' opinions from primary school to senior high school as reported by Wade (1967). For example: 76.9% of primary teachers and only 40.9% of senior high school teachers felt that television provided help in instruction; 98.4% of primary teachers and 76.3% of senior high teachers felt that television provided a richer experience, and similar numbers felt that television enriched and expanded the curriculum.

Criticisms of the system in recent years have led to a county report (Washington County Instructional Television Evaluation Committee, 1973) on the attitudes of parents, teachers and students toward the system. It is unclear what sampling procedure was used for the attitude surveys but the results have been published in local papers and have been rather negative. For example, 2,439 students felt that they learned more from the classroom teacher, while 707 felt that they learned more from the TV teachers; 2,111 of 3,360 felt that television did not motivate them to learn; and 2,201 of 3,244 students felt that they would rather learn without television. A total of 180 responses was obtained from the general public. Approximately 60% of this sample felt that television did not contribute to learning, did not motivate students and did not belong in the schools. The majority of these people also did not favor an increase in the use of television even if a benefit to student learning could be demonstrated or if costs would remain the same. The use of television was more favorably viewed by teachers, although their opinions declined relative to the earlier survey. Approximately 50% of elementary and secondary teachers responding to the survey felt that ITV did not improve quality of instruction. Additionally, 50% of secondary and 75% of elementary teachers felt that their students were losing by the use of TV.

2. SYSTEM COSTS

YEAR BY YEAR COSTS

Complete cost data were available for several years of the project and records of all capital equipment expenses were available for all years of the project. As opposed to many other ITV projects which have operated for only a few years, it is possible to analyze detailed costs for an eighteen-year period for the Hagerstown ITV system. Projections of costs were undertaken for only two years. The cost data for each year of the project are reported in Table IX.1.

The initial investment in equipment for the studios and classrooms and construction of the central facility was $1,049,700. In other years of the project, new capital expenses rarely exceeded 10% of total expenses and have usually been approximately 3%. Annual expenses have increased from $724,300 in 1958 to $1,102,500 in 1972. Salaries for TV teachers have been 30-35% of total expenses; engineering, production and support salaries have been 20-25% of total expenses; administration salaries have been 7-8% of total expenses; and cable rental has been 15-20% of total expenses.

Two items from the cost table are of special interest. The long history of this project allows one to examine changes in relative prices of different elements of the system. In general, salaries have increased at the general rate of inflation and have remained fairly constant in 1972 U.S. dollars. Technology costs have, however, been declining. The average price of television receivers has remained at $150 in current dollars. This results in an even larger decline in price in constant dollars. In current dollars only $53,783 was spent in 1955 for 342 black and white television sets. With an adjustment for inflation, this figure becomes $97,800 in 1972 dollars. In 1972, $1,340 was spent on 11 black and white television sets.

The second item of interest is the impact of maintenance. The decline in relative prices for the equipment components of the system gives a more favorable picture of replacement expenditures than the true situation. More money, in constant dollars, was spent in 1955 than in all the remaining years of the project. If one examines the the amount of equipment purchases, a clearer picture of the replacement needs emerges. According to records kept by the maintenance department, only 200 sets have been replaced during the entire life of the project. As there were 342 sets originally purchased, at least 140 sets are still functioning after twenty years.

COST FUNCTIONS

Cost functions for the Hagerstown ITV project have been estimated for 1972. Total cost is assumed to be a function of the number of original programming hours (1,440 in 1972) and the number of students served by the system (22,000 in 1972). The cost function is given by the following equation:

(IX.2) $$TC = F + V_N N + V_h h$$

where TC is total cost,
      N is the number of students,
      h is the number of hours,
      F is fixed costs, and
     V_N and V_h are variable costs per student and per hour respectively.

The data for the cost functions are drawn from Table IX.1 and reported in Table IX.2. Recurrent costs in Table XI.2 are expenditures during 1972. Capital costs are annualized values of equipment expenses from the beginning of the project in 1972. Three interest rates are used (zero, 7.5% and 15%). Production equipment is assumed to have a twenty-year life and was assumed to be variable with the number of hours of production. Reception equipment was assumed to be variable with the number of students and has a fifteen-year life. Transmission equipment is normally assumed to have a given life and to be variable with the number of hours. However, Hagerstown only leases the cable used for transmission. The charges are not variable with the number of hours and have been treated as fixed, recurrent expenses.

The assumptions of costs varying with the number of students or the number of hours are undertaken to represent the long run variable costs. In the short run another student could be added to the system at a cost of virtually zero. However, over the long run, new receivers would have to be added.

The cost functions calculated in Table IX.2 are used to calculate average costs per student (AC_N), average cost per student hour (there were 2,588,000 student hours in 1972), and the ratio of average costs to variable costs for students (AC_N/V_N). These calculations are summarized below:

	Total Cost Equation	AC_N	AC_N/V_N	Cost per Student Hour
0%	TC = 234,500 + .50N + 617h	51.54	103.08	.44
7.5%	TC = 234,500 + .90N + 652h	54.23	60.25	.46
15%	TC = 234,500 + 1.50N + 697h	57.78	38.52	.49

As the interest rate increases, all annualized variable costs and all average costs increase. The average costs per student ($54.23 at 7.5%) are the costs to Hagerstown for providing an average of 117 hours of instruction to each student via television.

The ratio of average costs to variable costs gives a rough approximation of the excess capacity of the system. When the ratio is high, excess capacity exists. For the addition of students, the long-term variable cost is only $.90 (at 7.5% interest). However, the average cost is $54.23. As more students are added to the system, average costs will decline.

AC_{ij}

An alternative methodology for analyzing the costs of the project and providing information for project planners is to calculate the average cost (per student, per hour or per student hour) from year i of the project to year j, AC_{ij}. This calculation utilizes cost and utilization information for all years of the project from i to j. Costs incurred prior to year i are treated as sunk costs.

TABLE IX.2
Total Cost Function, Hagerstown ITV Project 1972[a] (in thousands of 1972 U.S. dollars)

Interest rate	0%			7.5%			15%		
	Fixed	Variable Student	Hour	Fixed	Variable Student	Hour	Fixed	Variable Student	Hour
Administration[b]									
Recurrent	70.5			70.5			70.5		
Production[c]									
Recurrent			.578			.578			.578
Capital			.036			.071			.116
Transmission[d]									
Recurrent	164.0			164.0			164.0		
Reception[e]									
Recurrent			.003			.003			.003
Capital		.0005			.0009			.0015	
Total Cost	234.5	.0005	.617	234.5	.0009	.652	234.5	.0015	.697

a. The cost function is calculated from cost data through 1972 for the Hagerstown ITV project. The utilization in 1972 was 22,000 students and 1,440 hours. Recurrent expenses are expenses during 1974. Capital expenses are annualized values of investment prior to 1974 with the assumption of a 20-year life.

b. **Administration.** All administration expenses are assumed to be fixed.

c. **Production.** Recurrent expenses include all teacher, engineering, production and support staff salaries. Although these people are hired on a yearly basis it is assumed that in the long run the number of employees would vary with production levels.

d. **Transmission.** The recurrent expenses are simply the cable rental charge for 1972 and is not variable with the number of students or the number of hours. The charge is based on the length of the cable and hence the geographic distribution of schools.

e. **Reception.** Recurrent expenses include maintenance and power which are assumed to vary with the number of hours of production.

The calculation allows the planner to determine an average cost of the project from the first year to different potential termination dates or allows the planner to analyze the costs of continuing a project.

The equation for the calculation of AC_{ij} is given by:

$$(IX.3) \qquad AC_{ij} = \frac{\displaystyle\sum_{k=i}^{j} C_k/(1+r)^{k-i}}{\displaystyle\sum_{k=i}^{j} N_k/(1+r)^{k-i}}$$

where C_k is the cost in year k; N_k is the number of students in year k (or hours or student hours); and r is an interest rate.

When k = 1, average costs are calculated from the beginning of the project to different termination dates. This calculation is reported in the first row of Table IX.3. As one can see, as the project operates for more years, average costs decline. The steady decline is attributable to the spread of capital costs over increasing numbers of students. As expected, average cost per student would be very high if the project were terminated in earlier years. For Hagerstown the average costs declined rather rapidly to $60.53 ($AC_{1,8}$) per student in 1962 and then declined to only $53.37 by 1972 ($AC_{1,18}$). This slow decline occurs because of the rather high expenditure each year on recurrent costs; that is, capital costs, although spread over more students, are an increasingly less important portion of total costs.

To compare the AC_{ij} calculation with the cost function, one should use $AC_{1,18}$, which is the average cost per student for the first 18 years of the project; this cost is $53.37. The average per student cost from the cost function is $54.23 at 7.5%, which is a comparable figure.

Average costs per student hour have also been estimated and are reported in Table IX.4. In examining the average costs from the project inception, one observes a rather rapid decline from $1.72 per student hour (for j = 1957, that is, $AC_{1,2}$) to $.37 per student hour (for j = 1962, that is, $AC_{1,8}$). The interesting difference between the calculations for costs per student and per student hour is the different picture presented to decision makers in the present. The calculations for $AC_{18,j}$ present the expected average costs for continuation of the project beyond 1972. The average costs per student are lower than previously; that is, $AC_{18,18}$ is $50.11, whereas $AC_{1,18}$ is $53.37. However, in terms of average costs per student hour, $AC_{18,18}$ is $.43, whereas, $AC_{1,18}$ is $.35. Continuation costs appear to be higher per student hour and lower per student than the average costs for the life of the project. The

TABLE IX.3
Average Costs Per Student From Year i To Year j
Interest Rate = 7.5%

Year i \ Year j	1955	1956	1957	1958	1960	1962	1964	1966	1968	1970	1972	1973	1974
1955	0.0	272.69	129.40	90.57	67.83	60.53	57.72	55.61	54.25	53.69	53.37	53.27	53.18
1956		84.83	63.74	54.71	48.89	47.26	47.32	46.87	46.61	46.81	47.05	47.17	47.27
1957			52.42	47.61	44.88	44.42	45.12	45.02	45.00	45.38	45.74	45.91	46.06
1958				43.90	42.90	43.10	44.23	44.28	44.36	44.83	45.27	45.47	45.64
1960					42.81	43.22	44.82	44.75	44.77	45.31	45.78	46.00	46.18
1962						43.76	46.20	45.59	45.41	45.98	46.49	46.72	46.91
1964							43.73	44.25	44.47	45.49	46.25	46.56	46.81
1966								46.14	45.29	46.51	47.31	47.61	47.85
1968									42.51	46.46	47.66	48.06	48.34
1970										50.41	50.00	50.11	50.18
1972											50.11	50.28	50.34
1973												50.52	50.49
1974													50.52

TABLE IX.4
Average Costs Per Student-Hour From Year i To Year j
Interest Rate = 7.5%

Year i \ Year j	1955	1956	1957	1958	1960	1962	1964	1966	1968	1970	1972	1973	1974
1955	0.0	1.72	0.82	0.57	0.43	0.39	0.38	0.37	0.36	0.36	0.37	0.37	0.37
1956		0.54	0.40	0.35	0.31	0.31	0.31	0.31	0.31	0.32	0.32	0.33	0.33
1957			0.33	0.30	0.28	0.29	0.30	0.30	0.30	0.31	0.32	0.32	0.32
1958				0.28	0.27	0.28	0.30	0.30	0.30	0.31	0.31	0.32	0.32
1960					0.27	0.30	0.31	0.31	0.31	0.32	0.33	0.33	0.33
1962						0.32	0.33	0.32	0.32	0.33	0.34	0.34	0.35
1964							0.31	0.30	0.30	0.32	0.33	0.34	0.35
1966								0.30	0.31	0.33	0.35	0.35	0.36
1968									0.28	0.34	0.36	0.37	0.38
1970										0.40	0.40	0.41	0.42
1972											0.43	0.43	0.44
1973												0.44	0.44
1974													0.44

difference is attributable to the treatment of all previous capital expenses as sunk costs in the calculation of $AC_{18,18}$ but the general decline in student hour utilization (the last row in Table IX.1) results in an increase in average costs per student hour.

DISCUSSION

The costs of the Hagerstown project have remained high because of the relatively low number of students involved in the system and the rather high costs of programming derived from teacher and staff salaries.

The length of the experience of the Hagerstown project allows us to see one important advantage of technology in the past; the declining relative price of equipment. The importance of maintenance in extending equipment life has helped to keep costs lower on this project relative to a situation in which receivers are replaced every five years.

In 1972 the county (Washington County Board of Education, 1973) estimated the cost of replacing the television system. The report estimated a need for an additional sixteen high school teachers, nineteen middle school teachers, and forty-eight elementary school teachers for an annual cost of $846,600, and, further, that approximately twenty-seven new classrooms would be needed at a capital cost of $357,500 ($32,175 for a 7.5% interest rate and a life of only twenty years). This compares with annual operating costs of $1,084,000 in 1972. If this cost differential could be expected to continue and if television instruction, compared with traditional instruction, could not be demonstrated to be more effective for student learning, then it may be wise to terminate the project.

Although the project is expensive, the recommendations from the evaluation committee have been to continue using the system but to attempt to modify it to increase effectiveness and reduce negative reactions. Their recommendations, which will probably increase costs, include the following:

1. The use of "direct" televised instruction for art, music and language for elementary levels and as a supplement for other elementary subjects;

2. The use of ITV as a supplement only for secondary courses;

3. The introduction of new "direct" ITV use only when:

   a. there is evidence of a positive effect upon learning;

   b. an investigation has been made to determine if other material may be leased or purchased; and

   c. a continuing evaluation for modification or cancellation of the course has been established;

4. The use of videotapes to allow time for editing and improvements prior to presentation;

5. An investigation of the cost and feasibility of other instructional media to provide classroom teachers with a wide variety of resources;

6. The establishment of a system to rotate TV teachers back to the classrooms;

7. The replacement of classroom receivers on a regular basis with consideration given to the use of color receivers; and

8. The development by the studio teacher of a test of the performance of students, to be used as a measure of his or her effectiveness.

Chapter X

THE KOREAN ELEMENTARY/
MIDDLE SCHOOL PROJECT

In the period 1970-1971 the Republic of Korea undertook a major systems analysis of its educational sector, the purpose of which was to ascertain the feasibility of improving the internal efficiency of the educational system and of making the system more responsive to Korea's economic and social needs.[1] Two important conclusions of the analysis were that a single entity within Korea should take responsibility for educational reform activities and that an important initial target for reform would be the elementary (grades one through six) and middle (grades seven through nine) schools.

1. THE SYSTEM

In August, 1972 the Government of Korea responded to recommendations by establishing the Korean Educational Development Institute (KEDI) under the direction of Dr. Yung Dug Lee. One of the first major tasks facing KEDI was development, and final plans for implementation remain to be decided on. The E/M project will, however, use ITV and, to a lesser extent, radio to provide instruction. Present plans call for students in grades two through nine to receive about six twenty-minute television lessons per week by the time the operational phase of the project begins in 1978; more intensive use of ITV will be considered if funds become available. Plans call for students in grades one through nine to receive about ten twenty-minute radio lessons per week. In addition to use of ITV and IR, the E/M project will involve reform of curriculum and textbooks and may involve use of differentiated staffing,[2] use of individualized instruction and maintaining the overall student-to-teacher ratio with multiple grouping of students, such as small (thirty to forty students), medium (forty to sixty) and large (sixty to eighty). The impact of the reform will be assessed as one aspect of an analytical case study of KEDI activities that will be undertaken by a team from the University of Pittsburgh (Masoner, 1975); thus the process and outcomes of the reform will be well documented from near the outset.

At the time of this writing (September, 1975), the E/M project is at a critical juncture. The first phase of its activities—initial planning for and tryouts of the new instructional approaches—is nearing completion. Its transmission facilities and new studios are scheduled to become operational within a few months, thereby allowing the second major phase of the project —comprehensive demonstrations in thirty schools—to begin, and a third phase in forty-five schools. The demonstration phases will continue through February, 1978. A fourth phase, that of nationwide implementation, will begin in the course of the demonstration,[3] and in parallel with it, implementation is planned to occur in the period 1976-1980.

The KEDI E/M project is ambitious in the comprehensiveness of the reform it plans to implement and in the extent to which, like Nicaragua's Radio Mathematics Project (Searle, Friend, and Suppes, 1975), it will attempt to utilize research results from educational psychology in its instructional design. The project is, in addition, utilizing the most recent technical advance in transmission systems, the tethered aerostat, for signal distribution; KEDI's use of an aerostat will be the first use made of this technology for television broadcasting. For all these reasons, then, the E/M project will be closely observed and its costs will be important to ascertain. The cost information we shall present in this paper is based in part on costs that have been incurred, and in part on present KEDI plans. The results are thus tentative.

In the next section we offer present estimates of the costs of various components of the system—development and start up activities, program production, program transmission, and reception. In the third section we use this information to obtain cost functions for the media aspect of the E/M project.

2. SYSTEM COSTS

In this section of the chapter we will present information on the various components of the costs of the media aspects of the E/M project. We first discuss development and start up costs, then production costs, next transmission costs and, finally, reception site costs.

SYSTEM DEVELOPMENT AND START UP COSTS

Table X.1 shows system development and start up costs. These costs total $3,111,200. The table also shows the annualized value[4] of these start up

TABLE X.1
System Development and Start Up Costs

Item	Amount
System development (including book writing and curriculum preparation)	$2,411,200
Training and technical assistance	419,200
Contingency	280,800
TOTAL	$3,111,200
Total, Annualized at 0%[a]	$155,200/yr.
Total, Annualized at 7.5%[a]	$304,800/yr.
Total, Annualized at 15%[a]	$496,800/yr.

a. These annualizations are based on spreading costs over a hypothetical 20-year project lifetime.

costs assuming the costs to be spread over an estimated twenty-year project lifetime. These start up costs are the total estimated to be incurred during the period September, 1972 through February, 1978.

PROGRAM PRODUCTION COSTS

KEDI is now completing the construction and installation of equipment in a large new studio and research facility. The facility will have two radio studios and two TV studios (one of 3,600 square feet, the other of 2,400). Table X.2 shows construction costs for the entire facility and apportions those costs among the TV studios, radio studios and research center. It also shows the costs of studio equipment, including shipping. The table shows annualized values of these capital costs using KEDI's lifetime estimates and interest rates of zero, 7.5%, and 15%. The estimated total cost of the TV studios, including equipment, is $2,032,000; that for the radio studios is $194,400. Table X.3 shows estimates of the recurrent costs per program; these total $439 per twenty-minute TV program and $22 per fifteen-minute radio program.

In order to obtain a rough estimate of the *total* cost per program, the recurrent cost per program (from Table X.3) must be added to the cost per program of capital facilities. To compute this we assume that the capacity of the TV studios is 1,860 programs per year and that of the radio studios is 9,620. The annualized capital costs of the TV and radio facilities (item C, Table X.2) are then divided by these production rates to obtain an estimate of capital costs per program. Table X.4 shows the total production costs per program, that is, the sum of the capital plus recurrent costs; assuming a 7.5% discount rate, the cost per TV program is $568; per radio program $24.

TABLE X.2
Capital Costs of Studio Facilities

A. *Construction and Installation*

Land		$ 44,000
Construction of studios and research center		1,528,000
TOTAL		**$1,572,000**

	Discount Rate		
	0%	7.5%	15%
Annualized construction cost[a]	$31,440	$121,200	$236,000
TV studios' share[b]	16,800	64,240	125,120
Radio studios' share[b]	1,920	7,280	14,160
Research center's share[b]	12,880	49,680	96,800

B. *Studio Equipment Cost, Including Shipping*

TV studio equipment[c]	$1,200,000
Radio studio equipment	100,000
TOTAL[d]	$1,300,000

	Discount Rate		
	0%	7.5%	15%
Annualized TV equipment cost[e]	$120,000	$175,200	$239,200
Annualized radio equipment cost[e]	10,000	14,560	19,920

C. *Total Costs, Construction Plus Equipment*

	Total Cost	Annualized Cost		
		0%	7.5%	15%
TV studios	$2,032,000	$136,800	$239,200	$364,000
Radio studios	194,400	12,000	21,600	34,400

a. This annualization assumes a 50-year lifetime for the facilities.

b. The share of total cost borne by the TV studio facility is assumed to equal 53%; that of radio studio facility 6%; and that of the research center 41%. These percentages were computed under the following assumptions: (i) studios constitute 48% of the total area of the facility, (ii) radio studios constitute 10% of the total studio area, and (iii) the cost of construction of studio facilities is half again as expensive as that of research facilities per unit area.

c. The principal items of TV studio equipment include six videotape recorders (2-inch) at $73,600 each; four studio camera chains at $40,000 each; three telecine chains at $48,000 each; two lighting systems at $66,400 each; four TV control units at $76,000 each; and two radio control units at $17,600 each.

d. This total cost may go up if purchase is made of an additional $431,200 worth of equipment in 1976, as is now tentatively planned. Further, there is some indication that the KEDI equipment purchase was on exceptionally favorable terms; the winning bid was lower than expected and less than 75% of the alternative bid.

e. This annualization assumes a 10-year equipment lifetime.

TABLE X.3
Recurrent Costs of Program Production[a]

A. *TELEVISION*

Broadcasting program development[b] (producers, editors, engineering and studio personnel)	$194
Scriptwriting and actors	165
Films, videotapes, sets	80
TOTAL	**$439**

B. *RADIO*

Broadcasting program development[b] (producers, editors, engineering and studio personnel)	$10
Scriptwriting and actors	8
Tapes and setting	4
TOTAL	**$22**

a. The costs in this table are per program. TV program duration is 20 minutes; radio program duration is 15 minutes.

b. KEDI has budgeted $570,000 to the E/M project for broadcasting program development in the period 1972-1978. Assuming that 14,600 radio programs are produced in this period, 2,205 TV programs are produced, and that broadcasting program development costs for television stand to those for radio as do the other recurrent costs (that is, 20:1), one obtains the numbers in the table.

TABLE X.4
Total Production Costs Per Program[a]

	Recurrent Cost Plus Capital Costs Annualized at		
	0%	7.5%	15%
Television	$513	$568	$635
Radio	23	24	25

a. The costs in this table are per program. Television program duration is 20 minutes; radio program duration is 15 minutes.

TRANSMISSION SYSTEMS COSTS

From the technical point of view, a principal source of interest in the KEDI E/M project is that it will be the first to use a tethered aerostat as the platform for its television and radio transmitters. An aerostat is a dirigible-shaped lighter-than-air craft lifted by helium gas and the aerodynamic force of the wind. A steel tether, less than an inch in diameter, links the aerostat to the ground station; in Korea the aerostat will be tethered at an altitude of 10,000 feet. The Korean installation, which is located in the village of Bong

TABLE X.5
Capital Costs of Transmission System

A. *Construction and Installation*

Aerostat site,[a] including equipment installation		$280,800
Relay station sites (4)		65,600
TOTAL		$346,400

	Annualized at		
	0%	7.5%	15%
Annualized construction cost[b]	$11,520	$29,360	$65,900

B. *Equipment, Including Shipping*

Aerostat[a, c]	$2,632,000
Relay stations (4), including equipment installation	66,000
TÓTAL	$2,698,000

	Annualized at		
	0%	7.5%	15%
Annualized equipment cost[d]	$269,800	$393,040	$537,600

C. *Total Costs*

		Annualized at		
	Total	0%	7.5%	15%
Total Capital Cost	$3,044,800	$281,600	$422,400	$590,400

a. KEDI allocates 47% of total aerostat costs to its own activities; the number in the table are for this 47%.

b. The construction costs are annualized assuming a 30-year site lifetime.

c. An Export-Import Bank loan of U.S. $5,600,000 financed the transmission site equipment, which was purchased from the TCOM Corporation, a subsidiary of Westinghouse Electric. The $5,600,000 purchased two aerostats (at $864,000 each), four UHF TV transmitters (at $296,000 each), two FM radio transmitters (at $162,400 each), two elemetry command systems (at $548,800 each), and miscellaneous equipment, services, and transportation totaling $1,263,200. A total of 47% of this $5,600,000 expenditure is attributed to KEDI in Korean Government accounting (footnote a). Estimated costs for a second aerostat transmission site are 75% higher than were costs for the first one.

d. The equipment costs are annualized assuming a 10-year equipment lifetime.

Yang, will have two aerostats—one for regular use and one for immediate backup in case of failure of the first. Each will carry two UHF TV transmitters and one FM radio transmitter. In addition to these broadcasting packages, carried for KEDI, the aerostats will carry telecommunications equipment.

The KEDI complex in Seoul will beam the TV and radio signals to the operating aerostat at Bong Yang, seventy miles away, by a C-band (four to six GHz) microwave link; the aerostat will receive these signals, shift their frequency and retransmit them. Wankel motors connected to a generator will supply the power to operate the on-board electronics package; the operations crew will lower the aerostat every several days to refuel the motor and to undertake regular maintenance. Standard UHF television sets will receive the signals with an estimated FCC Grade "A" signal quality at distances up to sixty miles from Bong Yang; a Grade "B" signal should be obtainable at distances of ninety miles. At some additional expense (about $480) one can add a higher gain antenna and a low noise preamplifier/ converter to a standard UHF receiver, increasing the coverage radius substantially. Present plans call for installation of four UHF relay stations to provide coverage beyond the reach of the aerostat, and transmission cost estimates here are based on that assumption. KEDI is examining the possibility of acquiring a second aerostat site as an alternative to the relay stations.

As of September, 1975, the aerostats were installed at Bong Yang, and preliminary tests were under way to ascertain whether actual signal strengths would match predicted ones to various parts of Korea.

Table X.5 presents the capital cost of the transmission system, including site preparation and construction.[5] The costs in that table are based on an assignment of 47% of the aerostat system costs to KEDI's broadcasting facilities; this is the figure used for Korean government accounting. While allocation of fixed costs among alternative uses of an installation is inevitably somewhat arbitrary, this allocation seems reasonable enough.

Table X.6 presents current estimates of the recurrent costs of the transmission facilities; these costs include operations, maintenance and spare parts, power, and helium[6] for the aerostats. An earlier analysis (Lee, 1975) suggested that recurrent costs would be about 40% higher than these estimates, which are based on the most recent KEDI planning figures. It is probably fair to say that, until KEDI has had several years of experience with the system, there will remain substantial uncertainty concerning the recurrent costs of the transmission facility.

Table X.7 presents estimates of the costs per channel per year, based on the cost information from Tables X.5 and X.6. To allocate costs among the

TABLE X.6
Recurrent Costs of Transmission System

At aerostat site[a]	$159,200/yr.
At relay transmitter sites	8,800/yr.
Total	$168,000/yr.

a. KEDI allocates 47% of total aerostat costs to its own activities; the number in the table is for this 47%.

TABLE X.7
Total Annual Costs Per Channel Per Year[a]

	Recurrent Cost Plus Capital Costs Annualized at		
	0%	7.5%	15%
A. UHF Television (channels 20 and 26)	$176,800/yr.	$232,800/yr.	$299,200/yr.
B. FM Radio (104.9 MHz)	$95,200/yr.	$124,800/yr.	$160,000/yr.

a. The system will transmit two channels of UHF television and one channel of FM radio; the costs indicated for television are per channel, and include the costs of the four off-the-air relay stations for reaching areas in the south. The FM radio signal is planned to reach far enough to cover the south from the Bong Yang aerostat site.

TABLE X.8
Reception Site Costs (television and radio)

A.   *Capital Costs (per 3 classrooms)*

UHF color television receiver (1)	$413
Television receiver installation	22
Radio set (1)	25
TOTAL	$460

	Annualized At		
	0%	7.5%	15%
Annualized capital cost[a]	$92	$114	$137

B.   *Recurrent Costs (per 3 classrooms)*

Television operating costs—power, spares, and maintenance[b]	$82
Radio operating cost—power, spares, and maintenance[b]	5
TOTAL	$87

C.   *Total Annualized Cost (per 3 classrooms)*

	Recurrent Cost Plus Capital Cost Annualized At		
	0%	7.5%	15%
For television	$170/yr.	$190/yr.	$212/yr.
For radio	10/yr.	11/yr.	12/yr.
TOTAL	$180/yr.	$201/yr.	$224/yr.

a. These annualizations assume lifetimes of 5 years for the radio and television receivers.
b. KEDI's plans assume that the annual operating costs (power, spares, and maintenance) of television and radio receiving equipment will equal 20% of initial cost.

one radio and two TV channels, we allocated KEDI's fraction of the aerostat facility costs in proportion to the transmitter costs per se (footnote c, Table X.5). As the TV transmitters cost $299,000 each and the radio transmitters cost $160,000, the fraction of total KEDI aerostat cost allocated to the radio transmitter is 22%, and the fraction allocated to *each* TV transmitter is 39%. Half the cost of each TV relay station was then added to each television channel's fraction of aerostat costs to obtain total annual cost per television channel; at a 7.5% discount rate the cost is $232,800 per channel per year. At the same discount rate, the radio channel costs $124,800 per year.

Assuming that the channels transmit for 8 hours a day six days a week (or 2,500 hours per year) the cost per hour of transmission of UHF television is $72 at a discount rate of zero; $93 at a discount rate of 7.5%; and $120 at a discount rate of 15%. The cost per hour of FM radio transmission is $38 at a discount rate of zero; $50 at a discount rate of 7.5%; and $64 at a discount rate of 15%.

RECEPTION SITE COSTS

There are two principal components to the reception site costs; the first is the purchase, installation and maintenance of the TV and radio receivers, and the second is the purchase of printed materials. Table X.8 shows the television and radio costs; Table X.9 shows the printed material costs, based on presently planned levels of print usage.

TABLE X.9
Reception Site Costs (print)

A. *Elementary*	
Teacher's guide, including tests (1,600 pages per teacher per year @ $.0021 per page)	$2.60 per teacher per year
Student workbooks (1,000 pages per student per year)	$2.00 per student per year
B. *Middle School*	
Teacher's guide, including tests (1,300 pages per teacher per year)	$2.20 per teacher per year
Student workbooks (1,200 pages per student per year)	$2.60 per student per year
C. *Total Print Costs Per Student Per Year*[a]	
Elementary school	$2.10 per student per year
Middle School	$2.60 per student per year

a. These costs assume a class size of 60 students.

TABLE X.10
Annual Reception Site Costs Per Student[a]

	Recurrent Costs Plus Capital Costs Annualized At		
	0%	7.5%	15%
Television only	$0.94	$1.06	$1.18
Radio only	$0.06	$0.06	$0.06
Television plus radio plus print[b]	$3.08	$3.20	$3.32

a. These costs assume an average of 60 students per class and that television and radio receivers are shared among three classes.

b. These include the print costs for elementary school students from Table X.9; the cost for middle school students would be $.56 per student per year higher.

Current plans call for three classes to share reception equipment; assuming an average class size of 60, reception equipment will be shared among 180 students. Table X.10 shows annual reception site costs per student per year under this assumption. At a discount rate of 7.5%, these costs total $3.20 per student per year;[7] of this amount printed materials account for 65%, television accounts for 33%, and radio accounts for 2%. Even with the low costs per printed page that KEDI plans for, the high planned utilization of printed materials causes print to be a dominant factor in reception site costs.

TOTAL COST FUNCTIONS

Based on the information presented in the preceding section, we can prepare an annualized total cost function for both the television and the radio components of the E/M project, as well as one for the project as a whole. These cost functions are of the following form:

$$TC(N, h) = F + V_N N + V_h h,$$

where TC = total system costs, per year,
N = the number of students reached,
F = fixed system costs,
V_N = variable cost per student, and
V_h = variable cost per hour.

Table X.11 shows the values of the cost parameters—F, V_N, and V_h— for the television, radio and print components of the E/M reform, each considered separately.

For example, the cost function for only the television aspect of the reform, assuming a 7.5% discount rate, can be seen from Table X.11 to be:

$$TC(N, h) = \$213,600 + 1.06N + 1797h.$$

TABLE X.11
Total Cost Functions

		Annualized At		
		0%	7.5%	15%
Television				
	F^a	$108,000	$213,600	$348,000
	V_N^b	.94	1.06	1.18
	V_h^c	1,609	1,797	2,026
Radio				
	F^a	$32,800	$64,000	$104,000
	V_N^b	.06	.06	.06
	V_h^c	131.20	145.60	163.20
Print				
	F^a	$13,600	$27,200	$44,800
	V_N^b	2.08	2.08	2.08
	$V_h^{c,\,d}$	0	0	0
Total (Television + Radio + Print)				
	F	$155,200	$304,800	$496,800
	V_N^b	3.08	3.20	3.32

a. The fixed costs, F, are from the annualizations given in Table X.1. The fixed cost for print is 9% of the total and is the entire 'purchase of books and contingency' item. The remaining 91% of the fixed costs are divided, somewhat arbitrarily, between radio and television in the following way: television, 70%; radio, 21%. The method for assigning costs to television and radio is the same as that described in footnote b of Table X.3.

b. V_N is the variable cost per student of television, radio, print, and the total of the three, respectively. In the case of print, the amount given is for elementary school students; for middle school students it is $.55 higher.

c. V_h is the variable cost per **hour** of programming broadcast; that is, it is the sum of the annualized cost of an hour of production (i.e., production of three television or four radio programs) and the cost of an hour of transmission time.

d. For print we have $V_h = 0$, which is impossible; the number of different workbooks and teacher's guides that need to be prepared will probably be roughly proportional to the number of hours of programming, and certain costs of preparation would vary accordingly. We have no information that would allow us to separate these costs from the fixed costs of print and from the costs that are variable with respect to number of students.

KEDI now plans to provide 70 hours of TV per year at each of eight grade levels, resulting in a value of h of 560; putting this value of h into the above equation we obtain:

$$TC(N) = 1,220,000 + 1.06N.$$

If N = 1,000,000 the average cost is $2.27 per student per year or 3.3 cents per student per hour. On the other hand, if N is "only" 100,000, the average cost is $13.32 per student per year or 19 cents per student per hour. Similarly one can examine properties of the cost functions for radio and print.

It is also possible to construct a cost function for the reform as a whole.[8] Here we use the "total" entry at the bottom of Table X.11 and consider separately the number of hours of television and radio programming. Let h_T equal the number of hours of TV programming and h_R equal the number of hours of radio programming. With a 7.5% discount rate we then have:

$$TC(N, h_T, h_R) = \$305,000 + 3.20N + 1797h_T + 146h_R.$$

As before, we let h_T = 560. KEDI currently plans to broadcast 1,095 hours of radio per year to students in grades one through nine, so the cost function becomes, in terms of N only:

$$TC(N) = \$1,469,000 + 3.20N.$$

If N = 100,000 the average cost per student per year is $17.90; if N = 1,000,000, this cost drops to $4.70. This cost includes television, print and radio. In our previous example we computed the cost per student per year of television alone to be $2.30; television costs are thus about 49% of the total.

3. CONCLUSION

In concluding this chapter it is perhaps worth stressing once again the preliminary status of the figures reported here. It is far too early in the E/M reform for the costs reported here to reflect actual experience; on the other hand, enough equipment has been purchased and installed for at least some of the figures reported here to reflect more than planning estimates. In part one we discussed problems of error in cost estimation in the planning and early phases of instructional technology projects and noted an almost universal tendency for estimates to understate actual costs. Time alone will tell whether the planning estimates reported here will follow the general pattern. Our predictions are, however, the following:

1. The construction and installation cost estimates for studio and transmission facilities will prove to be accurate or slightly low.

2. The transmission equipment cost estimates will prove accurate; the operations and maintenance costs will prove to have been major underestimates (see note 5).

3. The studio equipment estimates of this chapter will prove low because additional equipment will be purchased. Studio operation and maintenance costs will either prove to be quite low or substantially fewer programs will be produced annually than is here assumed.

4. The TV and radio receiver purchase, installation and maintenance cost estimates will prove to be slightly high.

5. The cost of printed materials will be perhaps twice as high as is estimated here.

NOTES

1. Florida State University provided technical assistance for the sector analysis, and the report on their effort (Morgan and Chadwick, 1971) presents the methods and conclusions of the analysis.

2. Bostick (1975) provides a detailed analysis of the economic impact that differentiated staffing would have on the E/M reform.

3. Present KEDI planning calls for operational installation of 6,950 TV receivers in over 20,000 classrooms in 1976; these are in addition to 168 receivers (1 receiver per 2 classes) to be installed in demonstration schools. Final budget authorization remains to be made for the operational installations.

4. As discussed in Chapter II, we annualize capital costs by using the standard accounting annualization formula; if we are given an initial cost, C, for an item of capital (start up activities as well as equipment are considered capital), its period of usefulness in years, n, and an interest rate of cost of capital, r, the *annualized cost* of the capital is given by $a(r,n)C$. The annualization factor, $a(r,n)$, is in turn given by: $a(r,n) = (r (1 + r))^n / ((1 + r)^n - 1)$.

5. The authors have learned, subsequent to the preparation of this case, that there is reason to believe that aerostat costs have become much higher than here reported. Additionally, the technical problems experienced with the aerostat subsequent to this writing makes its present utility doubtful.

6. Each aerostat uses about 190,000 cubic feet of helium, the current price for which in Korea is at present $.27 per cubic foot—substantially above the world market price. Thus the value of the helium in the two aerostats is about $103,000. The permeability of the aerostat membrane (which is extremely low), inevitable small tears in the membrane, and occasional dumps of helium for flight control cause a steady loss of helium. Site engineers hope this loss can be kept to 200 cubic feet per aerostat per day which would result in a total cost to the installation of $40,000 per year.

7. This would be $.56 higher for middle school students; see footnote b to Table X.10.

8. This cost function will be only for the direct instruction aspect of the reform; all teacher training costs are excluded.

Chapter XI

THE MEXICAN
TELESECUNDARIA

Mexico, along with many other developing nations, faces a bottleneck at the secondary school level; there are not sufficient places in the present secondary school system to allow all those students who complete primary school to continue their education if they so desire. This problem is most acute in rural areas since few secondary schools are located in these regions, and consequently most rural youths who want to pursue their education must leave their homes and go to school in the cities. In recent years, the Mexican government has made political commitments to provide universal primary and secondary schooling and in 1966 began experimenting with a system of instructional television called Telesecundaria, as a means of extending the secondary school system in rural areas.

Below we will examine Telesecundaria, with a primary emphasis on system costs: Section 1 will give an overview of the system—its organization and technical characteristics, the extent of its utilization and a summary of evidence on its effectiveness; Section 2 will analyze system costs; Section 3 will compare Telesecundaria's costs with those of the traditional direct teaching system; Section 4 will examine the costs of expansion alternatives for Telesecundaria; Section 5 will comment briefly on system financing; and Section 6 will summarize and conclude. This case study is based almost entirely on previous work in which one of the authors participated, and has been reported on more fully in Klees (1975) and Mayo, McAnany, and Klees (1975). The interested reader is referred to these sources for more complete details of the analysis, especially with regard to system effectiveness.

1. THE SYSTEM

ORGANIZATION AND TECHNICAL CHARACTERISTICS

Telesecundaria began on a small scale in September, 1966, with closed circuit broadcasting to an experimental school in Mexico City. Eighty-three seventh graders, divided into four classes, received televised instruction in the standard subjects. The following year, open broadcasting began to 6,569 seventh grade students in 304 classrooms scattered throughout eight states.

While retaining the identical curriculum and goals of the traditional Mexican secondary school system, the Telesecundaria employs a mix of national and community resources. In place of large, federally financed school buildings, Telesecundaria classes customarily meet in space provided by the local communities. Such space consists of one, two or three rooms donated by the municipal government, local cooperatives or other social service agencies. Occasionally, space is given by a local patron or by one of the students' families. In communities where interest in the Telesecundaria runs particularly high, parent organizations have been instrumental in raising money for the construction and maintenance of permanent facilities.

Instead of fully accredited and specialized secondary school teachers, the Telesecundaria relies upon classroom coordinators to oversee all instruction. The coordinators are drawn from the ranks of fifth and sixth grade primary school teachers, and they are paid by the federal government. Unlike their counterparts in the traditional system who specialize in one subject, Telesecundaria coordinators are assigned to one class of students whom they must instruct in the whole range of seventh, eighth or ninth grade subjects. The coordinators are supplied with a monthly outline and schedule of the topics to be covered in each telelesson. Workbooks to assist students in the daily utilization of teleclasses have been specially designed and are distributed at low cost through commercial bookstores.

The television teachers and producers who are responsible for the development and presentation of the broadcast lessons are recruited from the traditional school system on the basis of their subject specialties, pedagogical skills and, in the case of the television teachers, their poise on camera. Television teachers are hired on an hourly basis and given special training in elocution, the techniques of television teaching, scriptwriting and the use of audiovisual aids. Approximately thirty television teachers were utilized in 1972. Producers are given extensive technical training in audiovisual instruction as well as studio management. Their selection and training reflects a basic Telesecundaria policy that it is better to train academic specialists to be television producers than to expect experienced producers to become academic specialists.

Television carries the primary instructional burden of the system. In a typical week, students receive about thirty televised lessons divided among the various subjects and vocational activities. Teleclasses average twenty minutes in length, with the remaining forty minutes of each class divided between preparation and follow-up activities supervised by the classroom coordinators. Teleclasses are broadcast between 7:45 a.m. and 2:00 p.m., Monday through Friday and for one hour on Saturday morning with the rest of that morning being reserved for broadcasts to the classroom coordinators. To accommodate a very tight broadcast schedule, transmissions to the three secondary grades are staggered so that a twenty-minute lesson to the seventh grade is followed immediately by one to the eighth grade, and finally by one to the ninth grade.

The system was initiated and run, until very recently, under the auspices of the Audio Visual Department of the Mexican Secretariat of Public Education (SEP). Production activities of the Telesecundaria are centered in four studios maintained by SEP in Mexico City. Two strong incentives for using studio time efficiently are the fact that a large number of subjects are broadcast and that they are almost all televised live. Each teleteacher has only one hour in the studio to rehearse and deliver a twenty-minute lesson.

All Telesecundaria lessons are transmitted over XHGC-TV, Channel 5 in Mexico City or over XHAJ-TV, Channel 6, a repeater station in Las Lajas, Veracruz. Mexican law requires commercial broadcasters to donate 12.5% of their broadcast time for government use, although this rule has rarely been enforced. Channel 5 has far exceeded this requirement, donating over 40% of its broadcast day to Telesecundaria. The growth of the Telesecundaria system, however, has been limited by the fact that it must rely solely on that channel. Coverage has been confined to those areas able to receive Channel 5's signal: the Federal District, and the states of Mexico, Hidalgo, Morelos, Oaxaca, Puebla, Tlaxcala, and Veracruz. A project was initiated in 1969 to send taped lessons by plane to the northern state of Sonora, but this effort was discontinued because of administrative and scheduling difficulties.

UTILIZATION

Table XI.1 reports student enrollment in Telesecundaria from its inception through the 1971-1972 school year. Expansion proceeded by adding one grade to the system each year, and by 1970 Telesecundaria was serving about 5% of the total secondary school enrollment in its eight state region or approximately 3% of the entire Mexican secondary school population. There have been more requests by communities to establish Telesecundaria facilities than the Audio Visual Department has been able to handle, due primarily to limitations in the funds available from SEP to hire classroom teachers.

Since the television lessons are broadcast over an open circuit commercial network, there is the possibility of utilizing the system to provide secondary

TABLE XI.1
Student Enrollment in Telesecundaria

Grade	1967-1968	1968-1969	1969-1970	1970-1971	1971-1972
Seventh	6,569	10,916	12,175	14,499	12,432
Eighth		5,324	8,240	9,459	9,194
Ninth			5,473	6,997	7,350
Totals	6,569	16,240	25,888	30,955	28,976

schooling on an informal basis to adult members of the populace. Some efforts were made towards this end early in Telesecundaria's history, but the substantial administrative apparatus needed to monitor such an activity discouraged its continuation. At the present time any such informal work is not monitored or credited, and its extent is unknown.

As mentioned previously, the production level of the Telesecundaria system is high, as television is used to transmit a large amount of the formal instruction. Each year a typical student receives approximately 1,080 twenty-minute programs, that is, about 360 hours of televised instruction.

EFFECTIVENESS

As reported in both Klees (1975) and Mayo, McAnany, and Klees (1975), pretests and posttests in Spanish, mathematics and chemistry were administered to a large random sample of ninth grade students in the Telesecundaria and traditional systems over a semester period in 1972. Both groups scored at almost the same levels on the pretests, and the gains for the Telesecundaria group were somewhat larger than those for the direct teaching group (the difference in gain scores was statistically significant at the .01 level) in all three subjects. However, since student, teacher and general system characteristics differ substantially between Telesecundaria and the traditional system, in addition to the television, nontelevision difference, a simple comparison of means is not an adequate comparison of relative effectiveness. Klees (1975, Chapter V) compares the two systems through regression analysis, controlling for a large number of variables including community characteristics, student background, attitudes, and aspirations, teacher education, experience, and classroom behavior, and class size and still finds that television contributes significantly to student learning. This finding holds true for both low ability and high ability students, although the effect is somewhat stronger for middle level students.

The results above were especially interesting in the light of the many casual judgments that had been made as to the low quality of Telesecundaria's instructional program. Because the broadcasts are open circuit, anyone may tune in and form an impression of program quality; the simple "talking head" nature of the presentations had caused many doubts as to the adequacy of such an instructional technique. Further problems were caused by the inclusion of the Telesecundaria system within the Audio Visual Department of SEP, which is administratively separate from that division which is responsible for the traditional secondary school system administration. This separation caused some rivalries and probably contributed to the lack of expansion of Telesecundaria in recent years. Quite recently, after the above studies were completed, the administration of the Telesecundaria system was transferred to the regular secondary school division within SEP and serious consideration is being given to alternative expansion possibilities.

Looking at system effectiveness at a more macroscopic level, both Klees and Mayo, McAnany and Klees report on the relative potential of the two systems to enroll and graduate students and thus to satisfy an increasing social demand for secondary schooling. Both systems were found to have identical dropout, repetition, promotion, and graduation rates. Given the relatively lower costs of the Telesecundaria that will be discussed in Section 3, it follows that Telesecundaria could enroll and graduate almost 60% more students than the traditional system, given equal budgets.

Unfortunately, no information reflecting relative system long-run benefits exists. Mayo, McAnany, and Klees attempted to do a follow up survey of system graduates, but administrative problems and resource constraints made this task too difficult to complete. The Telesecundaria graduate receives a regular secondary school diploma, which does, however, state whether it was awarded by a teleschool or a traditional one. Whether the Telesecundaria diploma will have the same marketability as that of the traditional system is still an open question.

Finally, one important point relevant to long-run benefits, that does not necessarily reflect on the effectiveness of Telesecundaria vis-à-vis other alternative instructional techniques, centers on the problem of rural education and rural development. From responses to questions on their attitudes and aspirations, it is evident that many rural youths look on secondary schooling as a means to leave the rural areas for the city, to compete in the urban employment market. Most urban areas of Mexico, especially the capital city, are already overcrowded and unemployment is a serious problem. Unfortunately, it seems likely that the urban migration of these youths will often be met by a lack of sufficient employment opportunities.

2. SYSTEM COSTS

YEAR BY YEAR COSTS

Estimates of the historical and projected costs of the Telesecundaria system are given in Table XI.2 on a year by year basis, for the twenty years following project inception. The costs presented are total costs to Mexico as a whole, including costs incurred by local communities, students and their families and other groups within the private sector, as well as direct governmental outlays. The projected costs are based on the assumption that student enrollment grows at a rate of 5% annually and continues to function only within the eight state region which is presently reached by the signal of Channel 5. The detailed assumptions on which the cost estimates are based are found in the footnote to the table.

ANNUALIZED COST FUNCTIONS

Based on the information presented in the previous subsection, we can derive an approximate annualized cost function for the instructional television component of Telesecundaria, of the following form:

$$TC(N, h) = F + V_N N + V_h h,$$

where   TC = total system costs,
$\qquad$ N = the number of students enrolled in the system,
$\qquad$ h = the number of hours of programming broadcast,
$\qquad$ F = fixed system costs,
$\qquad$ V_N = variable cost per student, and
$\qquad$ V_h = variable cost per hour.

A long-run point of view is taken below in that it is assumed that there are no fixed system costs (that is, $F = 0$)—all costs vary directly with the number of hours broadcast or the number of students in the system. For short-run, marginal, expansion alternatives, such may not be the case; that is, for example, there may be sufficient excess capacity to expand production without building a new studio or having new teleteachers. However, for the long run, and in terms of planning information for initiating a similar project, the assumption that all costs are variable is reasonable. Below we will examine the cost functions for each ITV system component—production, transmission and reception—at alternative social rates of discount of zero, 7.5%, and 15%. All calculations are based on the information presented in Table XI.2 and its footnote.

Production costs are all assumed to vary directly with the number of hours the system broadcasts, which in 1972 was approximately 1,080. Treating the studios and studio equipment as capital costs to be annualized over their

TABLE XI.2
Costs of the ITV Components of Telesecundaria and Utilization[a] (in thousands of 1972 U.S. dollars)

	1966	1967	1968	1969	1970	1971	1972	1973	1974	1975	1976	1977	1978	1979	1980	1981	1982	1983	1984	1985	1986
Production																					
Facility	64	64																			
Equipment	162	162	60	60	60	60					102	102	29	29	29	29	29	29	29	29	29
Operations	108	228	337	444	444	444	444	444	444	444	444	444	444	444	444	444	444	444	444	444	444
Transmission																					
Operations			17	35	52	52	52	52	52	52	52	52	52	52	52	52	52	52	52	52	52
Reception																					
Equipment		1	85	109	122	61	1	12	24	24	12	24	24	24	24	24	24	36	24	36	24
Replacement								85	109	122	61	1	97	133	146	73	25	121	157	170	147
Maintenance and Operations			9	20	32	38	38	39	41	43	44	46	48	50	52	54	56	60	62	66	68
TOTAL COSTS	334	455	508	668	710	655	535	632	670	685	715	669	694	784	747	676	630	742	768	797	735
Number of Students (in thousands)		7	16	26	31	29	30	32	34	35	37	39	41	43	45	47	50	52	52	55	57

a. The assumptions underlying the cost data presented are detailed below:

Production facility. This only includes the costs of the four television studios, as other production and administrative operations presently utilize excess space within the Audio Visual Department of SEP. There are four studios, constructed over a two-year period, at a cost of $32,000 per studio, and they are assumed to have a twenty-year life.

Production equipment. This includes the costs of studio equipment and videotapes. Studio equipment cost $204,000, was purchased in the two years prior to initial operation, and is assumed to have a ten-year life. The present stock of 1,500 hour length video tapes, costing $240 per tape, was purchased over the first six years of the project. It is assumed that tapes are used once only, 10% of the programming is taped (as was the case in 1972), and that after 12 years; when the present stock is exhausted, new tapes will be purchased as needed.

Production operations. This includes the costs of production administration, maintenance, and teleteachers. These costs are assumed to remain constant, in real terms, at their respective 1972 values of $220,000, $120,000, and $104,000. In the first three years of the project these costs are assumed to be proportional to the number of grades covered.

Transmission operations. Since transmission time is donated, this figure reflects an estimate of the costs of broadcasting 1,080 hours annually on a system of the same size and power as Channel 5. Lower costs in early years reflect the reduced hours of broadcast resulting from fewer grades covered.

Reception equipment. The price of a television receiver is assumed to be $280, which is somewhat high so as to include the cost of antennas, where needed. The number of receivers needed is assumed proportional to the number of students enrolled, with the average class size estimated at 23 students.

Reception equipment replacement. This assumes a five-year life for television receivers.

Reception maintenance and operations. The cost of maintaining and operating the reception equipment each year is assumed to be 10% of the total costs of reception equipment in operation in any year.

Number of students. Prior to 1973 the actual number of students in the system is utilized. It is hypothesized that after that time enrollment grows at a rate of 5% annually.

respective lifetimes and the costs of personnel, equipment maintenance and videotapes as recurrent costs, we arrive at a total cost of production equal to $472 per hour assuming the future is not discounted, $490 per hour with a 7.5% rate of discount, and $513 at a 15% interest rate.

Transmission costs are also assumed to vary directly with the number of hours of programming broadcast. Actually, transmission costs should vary with the social rate of discount chosen; however, in this instance we are basing our calculation on the imputed operating costs of Channel 5 and do not have sufficient information to break down costs into capital and recurrent. We therefore use the $52,000 annual operating cost figure, which yields a cost per broadcast hour of $48.

Reception costs are assumed to vary directly with number of students in the system. In actuality this should only be true of reception equipment and maintenance, while operational costs should vary directly with the number of hours of receiver operation (which is usually proportional to hours broadcast). Again, unfortunately, we do not have sufficiently detailed information to accomplish this breakdown and therefore all reception costs are assumed variable with N. Treating the television receiver as a capital expenditure whose cost is annualized over a five-year lifetime and maintenance and operational costs as recurrent costs, we obtain, assuming an average class size of twenty-three students, the total costs of reception to be $3.65 per student when the future is not discounted, $4.23 per student at a 7.5% discount rate, and $4.85 at a 15% rate.

Below we may summarize the total cost function and the average cost information for the year 1972 as follows:

	Total Cost Equation	AC_N	AC_N/V_N	Cost per Student Hour
$r = 0\%$	$TC = 3.65N + 520h$	23.02	6.31	.064
$r = 7.5\%$	$TC = 4.23N + 538h$	24.27	5.74	.067
$r = 15\%$	$TC = 4.85N + 561h$	25.74	5.31	.072

The cost information above assumes an enrollment of 29,000 students, with each student viewing approximately 360 hours of instructional television lessons during the year (based on 1,080 hours distributed among three grades). It should be noted that not discounting the future may cause one to understate system cost by almost 12% ($23.02 vs. $25.74). The relatively low value of the ratio of average cost per student (AC_N) to variable cost per student (V_N) indicates that some economies of scale have already been achieved, although costs per student could be still lower if enrollments expand.

ACij's

As discussed in Chapter II, we can utilize the information presented in the year by year cost table above to derive summary measures of the average costs per student of the project, which takes into account changing utilization over time. Specifically, we can compute AC_{ij}, that is, the average cost per student from year i to year j were:

$$AC_{ij} = \frac{\sum\limits_{k=i}^{j} C_k/(1+r)^{k-i}}{\sum\limits_{k=i}^{j} N_k/(1+r)^{k-i}}$$

The formula above provides a measure of average costs that discounts the future for both costs and student utilization. This provides a more interesting and useful measure than the average cost figure derived in the previous section, since the latter only takes into account utilization at one point in time. The AC_{ij} measure also allows the project planner to determine the length of time the project needs to continue to permit unit costs to fall to a reasonable level. It also permits one to look at project costs from different points in time over the life of the project.

Tables XI.3, XI.4, and XI.5 present the AC_{ij}'s for selected years of the instructional television component of Telesecundaria at social rates of discount of zero, 7.5%, and 15% respectively. They serve to illustrate several points. First, costs decrease quite rapidly as we project the continuance of Telesecundaria for more than a few years. For example, if Telesecundaria were to be discontinued next year, the average cost per student over the lifetime of project ($AC_{1966,1976}$) would be only $30 (at a 7.5% interest rate). Assuming a twenty-year lifetime, the average cost ($AC_{1966,1986}$) would be considerably less, $23.

Second, we see that in general, the project cost picture changes as we examine it from different times and with different assumptions as to its duration. As we assume a longer project lifetime, average costs usually decline, due primarily to enrollment increasing faster than total costs (as is true in most instructional technology projects). We also see that, in general, the further into the project we are, the less expensive it is to continue, due primarily to many initial project development expenses becoming sunk costs and due also to enrollment expansion.

Finally, we observe that the choice of a discount rate is quite important; as the opportunity costs of resources become greater, so do the real costs of

TABLE XI.3

Average Costs of the ITV Components of Telesecundaria
From Year i to Year j (interest rate = 0%)

Year i	Year j 1968	1970	1972	1974	1976	1978	1980	1982	1984	1986
1966	185	55	35	30	27	25	24	22	21	20
1969		33	25	24	23	21	21	20	19	18
1971			20	20	20	20	19	18	18	17
1972			18	20	20	19	19	18	17	17
1973				21	21	20	19	18	17	17
1974				21	20	19	19	18	17	16
1975					20	19	19	17	17	16
1976					20	19	19	17	17	16
1977						18	18	17	16	16
1978						18	18	16	16	15
1980							17	15	15	15
1984									15	14

TABLE XI.4

Average Costs of the ITV Components of Telesecundaria
From Year i to Year j (interest rate = 7.5%)

Year i	Year j 1968	1970	1972	1974	1976	1978	1980	1982	1984	1986
1966	198	59	39	33	30	28	27	25	24	23
1969		33	26	24	23	22	22	21	20	19
1971			20	20	20	20	20	19	18	18
1972			18	20	20	20	19	18	18	17
1973				21	21	20	19	18	18	17
1974				21	21	20	19	18	18	17
1975					20	19	19	18	17	17
1976					20	19	19	17	17	16
1977						18	18	17	16	16
1978						18	18	17	16	16
1980							17	15	15	15
1984									15	14

TABLE XI.5
Average Costs of the ITV Components of Telesecundaria
From Year i to Year j (interest rate = 15%)

Year i \ Year j	1968	1970	1972	1974	1976	1978	1980	1982	1984	1986
1966	210	64	43	37	34	32	30	29	28	28
1969		33	26	25	24	23	23	22	21	21
1971			20	20	20	20	20	19	19	19
1972			18	20	20	20	19	19	18	18
1973				21	21	20	20	19	18	18
1974				21	21	20	19	19	18	18
1975					20	19	19	18	18	17
1976					20	19	19	18	17	17
1977						18	18	17	16	16
1978						18	18	17	16	16
1980							17	15	15	15
1984									15	14

the project. Neglecting the discount rate (that is, choosing a zero discount rate), as many cost studies unfortunately do, serves to understate project cost substantially, even more so than the average cost figure derived in the previous section for 1972, since utilization was not discounted in this latter figure. For example, if we look at the average cost per student from 1966 to 1986 (that is, assuming a twenty-year lifetime for Telesecundaria), not taking the value of resources over time into account (that is, using a zero discount rate) can result in understating costs by almost 30% if the appropriate rate is 15% (that is, $20 per student vs. $28 per student).

DISCUSSION

Given the relatively low utilization of Telesecundaria, it is a surprisingly inexpensive system. As can be seen by a close look at Chapter III, Telesecundaria is less costly than many of the other ITV systems. It is perhaps closest in form to that in El Salvador (the "secondary school only" alternative), whose average cost per student was similar for 1972, even though the El Salvador system was serving 65% more students than Telesecundaria; further, costs per student hour were considerably lower for Telesecundaria, $.067 versus $.143 (at a 7.5% interest rate) for El Salvador. The cost comparison between the two systems would favor Telesecundaria even more if, similar to the El Salvador system, it were operating in urban areas with an average class size of forty-five, as opposed to functioning in rural areas with an average class size of only twenty-three students. (The AC_{ij}'s for Telesecundaria are higher than those for El Salvador, due to the substantially higher utilization projected for the latter system—see Chapter VIII.)

One of the primary reasons for the low overall cost of Telesecundaria is its low production cost. As we have seen in an earlier subsection, even utilizing a 15% discount rate, production costs per hour of programming are only $513. Schramm (1973) reports typical production cost estimates for similar ITV projects in other countries range from $1,200 to $2,000 per hour, and indicates that Mexico's Telesecundaria is one of the least expensive systems of its kind in the world. Of course, variations in production costs are not necessarily indications of relative efficiency, and more probably reflect differences in program quality and perhaps therefore instructional effectiveness (although this latter linkage is far from clear, see Schramm, 1972, and Chu and Schramm, 1967, for summaries of the existing evidence). Telesecundaria has been often criticized for inferior program quality and perhaps rightly so; given its live presentation format and tight production schedule, little opportunity exists for program improvement. It seems possible that program quality could be improved at little or no cost through greater use of available videotaping facilities and a proposal for such use is presented in Klees (1975, Appendix B).

3. COST COMPARISON WITH THE TRADITIONAL SYSTEM

Telesecundaria is one of the most interesting ITV systems in operation in the world today since it appears to be one of the few that has been shown to be cost-effective vis-à-vis the traditional direct teaching system. We have already seen in Section 1 that Telesecundaria appears to be at least as effective as the traditional direct teaching system; below we compare Telesecundaria costs with those that would be necessary for the traditional system to extend its operation to the areas in which the Telesecundaria is presently operating. Actual costs of Mexico's direct teaching system are not discussed in this section (the interested reader is referred to Klees, 1975, and Mayo, McAnany, and Klees, 1975, for this information) since they do not form a relevant basis of comparison; presently the traditional system operates mainly in urban areas with class sizes twice those of Telesecundaria, better and more expensive classroom facilities and substantially higher administrative overhead.

Table XI.6 presents the costs, on a per student basis, of the total Telesecundaria system, including traditional components and ITV components, along with the costs per student necessary for the traditional system to accomplish the same task. We observe that to use the traditional direct teaching system to bring secondary schooling to rural areas would be much more expensive than using Telesecundaria; costs would be over 65% higher—$248 per

TABLE XI.6
Annual Cost Per Student of Telesecundaria Versus Direct Teaching[a]

	Direct Teaching	Telesecundaria
Traditional Components[b]		
Administration	$ 6	$ 6
Classroom teachers[c]	203	88
Facilities — fully equipped classroom	11	11
Student costs — books, uniforms, etc.[d]	28	20
Subtotal	$248	$125
ITV Components[e]		
Production	$ 0	$ 18
Transmission	0	2
Reception	0	4
Subtotal	$ 0	$ 24
TOTAL	$248	$149

a. More detailed information concerning the basis of these cost calculations may be found in Klees (1975; Table III.1, Table III.5, and Appendix A) and in Mayo, McAnany, and Klees (1975; Table II.3, Table II.7, and Appendix B).

b. Administrative and classroom facility costs for both systems are equal to those given for the Telesecundaria system in the two sources above.

c. As stated in the above sources, traditional system secondary school teachers earn $4,680 per year while Telesecundaria teachers are drawn from the ranks of primary school teachers and earn only $2,016 per year. Cost per student estimates assume an average class size of 23.

d. Students and their families pay the costs of books, supplies, and uniforms. Uniforms cost $4 per student in either system. Books for the Telesecundaria system are $8 less per student than those used for the traditional system; the latter uses general textbooks, while the former uses books especially prepared for and keyed to the instructional television lessons.

e. These costs are taken from Section 2, assuming 29,000 students in the system as in 1972 and a 7.5% social rate of discount.

student for the traditional system versus $149 per student for Telesecundaria. Costs per student for Telesecundaria could even be lower, thus increasing its relative cost advantage, if more than 29,000 students were in the system, since fixed (with respect to students) costs of ITV production and transmission would be spread over a larger enrollment. For example, with 500,000 students using Telesecundaria, the cost per student would be about $130 (for a more detailed look at expansion alternatives and costs, see Section 4).

As is apparent from Table XI.6, the chief reason that Telesecundaria has a significant cost advantage over the direct teaching system is due to its use of lower salary teachers (in addition, Telesecundaria uses lower cost textbooks). Indeed, this is the raison d'être for Telesecundaria. The salary of secondary school teachers was (at the time of the study) almost two and a half times that of the primary school teachers hired for Telesecundaria classrooms. This cost differential more than offsets the additional costs of the ITV component of Telesecundaria.

It is not clear how long such a large cost difference will exist between the salaries of primary and secondary school teachers. In most developed countries there is no longer a difference in salaries between the two, which probably reflects the equal amounts of education required for both these teacher groups. However, in most developing countries, a substantial discrepancy in both salary and training is quite common, although the gap may be narrowing somewhat. It is quite interesting to note that subsequent to the collection of the above data in 1972, the Telesecundaria teachers went on strike, partly as a consequence of seeing that the research showed Telesecundaria to be cost-effective when compared with the traditional system, and won a salary increase. Nonetheless, secondary school teacher salaries have also increased, and the degree to which there are possibilities for a lower cost technology based instructional system will depend on the absolute (not relative) difference between the salaries of these two teacher groups; it appears likely that such a substantial salary gap will exist in most developing countries, including Mexico, for some time into the future.

It should be noted that there may be political problems associated with the type of capital-labor substitution which Telesecundaria engages in; in particular, there may be strong resistance from secondary school teacher associations or unions to the use of other, lower-paid teachers in secondary schools. In Mexico this was not a significant obstacle, due to a shortage of secondary school teachers available and willing to work in rural communities; in fact, the circumstances were even more fortunate as there was also a surplus of qualified primary school teachers. Although this combination may not be common to most countries, there is often a problem in developing countries in attracting sufficient teachers to rural areas. Thus, it is possible that many countries could take advantage of a substitution such as that utilized by Telesecundaria, to increase educational opportunities in rural areas, without a great deal of resistance. The political problems would, of course, become much more serious if the intention were to utilize such a system in urban areas, where existing secondary school teachers' positions would be threatened.

4. EXPANSION ALTERNATIVES

Telesecundaria's future is still in question; there have been discussions in recent years as to possible ways in which the system may be expanded. Below we will examine some expansion alternatives, both within the eight state region where Telesecundaria presently operates, with regard to potential nation-wide coverage. We will only consider expansion in terms of a Telesecundaria as a formal secondary school system; there has been interest in utilizing Telesecundaria for nonformal adult education, but an analysis of that option is beyond the scope of this report. Furthermore, we will not consider expansion through increasing class size, although the marginal costs for so doing in rural areas appears low ($26 per student per year, from Table XI.6). System expansion through increasing class size, although theoretically viable, is probably difficult to accomplish because of low population densities in rural areas. The analysis below is again based on that reported in Klees (1975) and Mayo, McAnany, and Klees (1975), and the interested reader is referred to those sources for more details.

If Telesecundaria were to expand its enrollment within the existing eight state region and restrict itself to rural areas, as at present, the annual marginal cost per student of expansion would be $129, as can be seen from Table XI.6 in Section 3 (the costs of the traditional system components of Telesecundari plus reception costs, all of which are assumed to vary directly with the number of students). However, if Telesecundaria were to expand into urban areas in direct conjunction with, or as a replacement for, the traditional direct teaching system, its costs could be substantially different from those discussed above.

Table XI.7 represents a rough approximation of the comparative costs of the Telesecundaria, if it were to operate in urban areas, with those of the traditional system. The higher administrative and classroom facility costs assumed in this case, compared to those presented in Table XI.6, reflect the historical operating costs of the traditional direct teaching system in Mexico's secondary schools. The difference in classroom teacher costs is a result of an average class size of 50 in urban areas, as opposed to 23 in rural areas. The lower costs of production and transmission are a result of assuming a much larger system enrollment of 580,000 students, equal to that in 1972 for the total direct teaching system within the eight state region that receives the signal of Channel 5. In sum, if Telesecundaria were to expand into urban areas and replace the traditional system there, costs would be almost 30% lower than they are presently for the direct teaching system; this would yield a savings of $33.1 million per year. Of course, the social welfare and political problems posed by attempting to displace current secondary school teachers are large; nonetheless the magnitude of the potential benefits should

TABLE XI.7
Annual Cost Per Student of Telesecundaria Versus
Direct Teaching in an Urban Environment[a]

	Direct Teaching	Telesecundaria
Traditional Components[b]		
Administration	$ 50	$ 50
Classroom teachers[c]	94	40
Facilities – fully equipped classroom	28	28
Students costs – books, uniforms, etc.	28	20
Subtotal	$200	$138
ITV Components[d]		
Production	$ 0	$ 1
Transmission	0	0
Reception	0	4
Subtotal	$ 0	$ 5
TOTAL	$200	$143

a. More detailed information concerning the basis of these cost calculations may be found in Klees (1975, Appendices A and B).

b. Administrative costs and classroom facility costs are higher than those assumed in Table XI.6 which reflected Telesecundaria's historical experience; the costs figures utilized above are the actual historical costs of the traditional direct teaching system in Mexico, which has a much higher administrative overhead and employs much more expensive classroom facilities than does the rural-based Telesecundaria system.

c. Classroom teachers for both systems are less expensive per student than was the case in Table XI.6, since in urban areas the average class size is 50 students.

d. These costs are taken from Section 2, assuming a 7.5% social rate, and an enrollment of 580,000 students, which was that of the traditional system in the eight state region in 1972. Transmission costs per student are virtually zero with such a high utilization.

serve to indicate the possible advantages of such a system to other countries without an existing well developed urban secondary school system.

If Telesecundaria coverage were to be expanded nationwide, a different broadcast transmission system would have to be utilized. Mayo, McAnany, and Klees (1975) estimate that it would be possible to lease broadcast time from the only network with nationwide coverage, Channel 2, at a rate of $1,944 per hour, which would represent an annual cost of $2,100,000. Despite this substantial cost increment, with 1,000,000 students in the system (which was the enrollment of the traditional secondary school system in Mexico in 1972), the average annual cost per student of Telesecundaria in urban areas would rise to only $145 per student; such a nationwide substitution of Telesecundaria for the traditional system would yield a total savings of $55 million annually.

Again, an expansion of Telesecundaria that fosters direct competition with the traditional system will probably engender hard political opposition, and thus any expansion may necessarily be confined to extension of the secondary school system to rural areas. Nevertheless, it must be recognized that despite potential political and social problems, a replacement of the traditional system by Telesecundaria is not a patently absurd alternative, especially if done over an extended period of time so as not to threaten the positions of existing secondary school teachers. It should be remembered and emphasized that an educational system faces a limited budget; the millions of dollars that could be saved through utilization of Telesecundaria could potentially be used to offer increased educational opportunities elsewhere, for example, for a massive expansion of educational opportunities for rural youth.

5. SYSTEM FINANCING

When examining the costs of the system it is important not only to analyze the total costs of the system but also to look at who is paying these costs. Since most educational systems involve substantial governmental expenditures, an analysis of governmental tax incidence (that is, who pays the taxes, usually framed in terms of a comparison of the tax burden on families at different income levels) should be an integral part of such a financial analysis. Unfortunately, such a study of tax incidence has significant theoretical and practical difficulties and is beyond the scope of this report; nonetheless there is some easily available information on financing that is quite interesting from an equity point of view.

Table XI.8 indicates the costs, on a per student basis, by funding source, that have been operative for Telesecundaria and the traditional secondary school system. The local community pays a significantly higher percentage of schooling costs with the Telesecundaria system than with the direct teaching system—24% versus 16%—due to the former's reliance on the community to provide classroom facilites, reception equipment and maintenance of both. Although the difference in terms of absolute amount is not especially large, there is indeed a question of fairness to be raised. Why must Telesecundaria students, who come from rural families with low incomes, be forced to spend more, both in absolute and relative terms, for their education than students in the traditional system who come from wealthier families? It would seem much more equitable, given the relatively lower cost of the Telesecundaria system, for the government at least to fund classroom facilities and equipment, as it does in the traditional system, especially if Mexico is serious about its stated commitment to rural education. Indeed, the lack of expansion to

TABLE XI.8

Sources of Funding for Telesecundaria Versus Direct Teaching

Source of Funding	Direct Teaching[a]		Telesecundaria[b]	
	Cost/Student/Year	%	Cost/Student/Year	%
Government	$168	81	$112	75
Locality-student, families' and parents' organizations	32	18	35	24
Private industry – Channel 5	– –	–	2	1
Totals	$200	80	$149	100

a. These costs reflect the historical costs of operating the traditional direct teaching system (see Mayo, McAnany, and Klees, 1975, for details). Students and their families pay $28 for books and uniforms, plus a $4 annual fee that the Secretariat of Public Education collects and puts towards system operation costs.

b. For Telesecundaria, Channel 5 contributes the transmission facilities, while students and their families are required to pay the costs of books and uniforms, $20 per student per year, the cost of constructing and maintaining classroom facilities, $11 per student per year, and the costs of reception equipment and maintenance, $4 per student per year. The $4 annual fee is waived by SEP for Telesecundaria students.

rural communities that have asked for teleschools to be established in their locale, due to the government's not allocating funds to pay for a classroom teacher (which would be the only major additional cost of the system to them, as presently financed), raises doubts as to the extent of their real commitment to rural education.

6. CONCLUSIONS

Telesecundaria emerges as one of the more fascinating experiments with instructional technology in that it is one of the few such projects that have been designed in such a way as to be cost-effective in terms of the criteria above. It is interesting, and perhaps significant, to note that Telesecundaria, unlike other similar projects, was initiated entirely by the country utilizing it, without outside financing or technical assistance. It is possible that the particular manner in which educational aid is usually given to developing countries for such projects may militate against a cost-effective design (see Chapter VI for related discussions).

There are, of course, qualifications on the research results reported here. For example, the subject matter test given to students in both systems, although based directly on the curriculum content, did not show large gains for either group. Although the judgment as to what constitutes a large gain in cognitive knowledge is a subjective one, both Klees (1975) and Mayo, McAnany, and Klees (1975) caution that the test results should be interpreted as saying only that the two systems seem to be doing similarly—not that either system is doing a good instructional job. Nonetheless, given the information available (it must be remembered that adequate research is costly and engaging in additional research on this question may not be cost-beneficial), Telesecundaria is a more cost-effective secondary school system than the traditional one, and alternative expansion possibilities should be given serious consideration.

Nevertheless, we must again point out that what is cost-effective may not be cost-beneficial (see Klees, 1975, Chapter 9 for an extensive discussion of this point relative to Telesecundaria); in particular, a system which encourages the migration of the most bright and able rural youth to the overcrowded Mexican urban areas, that have significant unemployment problems already, may not be in the best interests of the individual students or of the country as a whole. Although this does not reflect on the cost effectiveness of Telesecundaria as opposed to the traditional system, it does highlight a problem common to most developing countries faced with a growing social demand for education, especially in the oft-neglected rural regions. A commitment to rural development cannot be met by a wholesale transfer of an urban oriented curriculum to a rural educational system, but must involve resources invested to create rewarding employment opportunities within rural areas and the development of an education system designed to deal specifically with rural problems. Systems such as Telesecundaria may have great potential, but careful attention needs to be given to the goals towards which this potential will be directed.

PART FOUR

SUMMARY AND CONCLUSIONS

Chapter XII

SUMMARY AND CONCLUSIONS

In this chapter we briefly summarize the results of our empirical cost analyses. The five ITV and two IR projects discussed in the case studies, as well as the two additional IR projects discussed in Chapter III, are drawn upon.

Tables XII.1 and XII.2 summarize the annualized cost information, at a social rate of discount of 7.5%, for the four instructional radio projects and five instructional television projects, respectively. The four radio projects differ widely in size and scope, as is indicated by the wide variations in N, h, and average cost per student (AC_N) exhibited on Table XII.1. The two Mexican radio projects at present have a rather high average cost per student, which reflects their relatively low utilization; the high value of the ratio of average costs to variable costs (AC_N/V_N) for these two projects indicates that substantial economies of scale, and consequent reductions in average costs, could be achieved with the expansion of system enrollment. The relatively high variable cost per student (V_N) for the Nicaraguan project reflects the assumption of extensive school supervision and the utilization of a relatively expensive battery-powered radio receiver, as well as the inclusion of teacher training and printed support materials costs.

The five television projects examined also exhibit a wide range of scope, size and application. The high cost per student of the Stanford Instructional Television system is indicative of the greater ITV expense often incurred in a university setting, especially one that utilizes a distance-learning mode of operation. The reader should note that the costs of the Stanford system may still be considered quite reasonable, since they cover the *total* costs of instruction—classroom teachers are not used to supplement the video lessons. The high ratios of average costs to variable costs (AC_N/V_N) for all but one of the projects indicate that average system costs can be reduced substantially in most of these systems if their enrollment expands.

TABLE XII.1
Cost Summary of Four Instructional Radio Projects[a]

Project	Year of Information Source	N	h	F	V_N	V_h	AC_N	AC_N/V_N	Cost Per Student Hour
Nicaragua[b]	1975	250,000	450	73,400	3.06	282	3.86	1.3	.051
Mexico-Radioprimaria	1972	2,800	280	0	.15	130	13.12	77.2	.054
Mexico-Tarahumara	1972	1,081	640	33,424	.40	18	42.20	105.5	.264
Thailand[c]	1967	800,000	165	100,400	.22	--	.35	1.6	.014

a. Values in this table were computed with a social rate of discount of 7.5%; all values are in 1972 U.S. dollars. The symbols are defined as follows: N = number of students using project (in the given year, unless otherwise noted); h = the number of hours of programming broadcast per year; F = annualized fixed costs; V_N = annualized variable cost per student; V_h = annualized variable cost per hour broadcast; AC_N = average annual cost per student for the given values of N and h; and the student hour cost is the annual cost per student-hour of viewing for the given values of N and h.

b. The values of N and h chosen for the IR project in Nicaragua reflect potential utilization of the system as discussed in the case study in Chapter V.

c. The cost function for instructional radio in Thailand was derived solely as a function of V_N; therefore V_h is not given in the table (costs that are variable per broadcast hour are thus included in the project's fixed cost figure).

The variations in the variable cost per student for the four nonuniversity ITV systems strongly reflect differences in class size, which can greatly affect per student costs (as discussed in Chapter I); the low value of V_N for the Hagerstown project is also a consequence of the much longer than usual lifetimes obtained for reception equipment. It is also interesting to compare the AC_{ij} column, which gives the average costs per student over twenty years of system utilization, with the AC_N column, which gives average costs per student at one point in time. In most cases these two summary cost measures turn out to be quite close; the discrepancy between the two figures, however, is quite pronounced for the El Salvador system due to the substantially increased ITV utilization projected for future years. As discussed in Chapter I, we believe the AC_{ij} figure represents a better summary cost measure than the average cost per student for a given year (AC_N), since the former achieves a perspective of costs and utilization over time that the latter lacks. As we have just seen, however, empirically the two measures may be quite close, except when current costs and/or utilization vary considerably over a project's lifetime.

In summary, a number of general conclusions emerge from our analysis:

1. It is realistic to expect the costs of instructional radio to range from $.01 to $.04 or $.05 per student per hour, about one fifth as much as instructional television. The high end of this range can be reached with very small numbers of students (several thousand); the low end might require several hundred thousand.

2. It is realistic to expect the costs of instructional television to range from $.05 to $.15 per student per hour, or about three to five times as much as instructional radio, depending most importantly on the number of students in the system. The low end of this range can usually be reached only if close to a million students are using the system in a reasonably compact geographical area.

3. Cost estimates respond sensitively to the social rate of discount; going from a zero to a 15% social rate of discount can increase annualized cost estimates by 15% to 40%.

4. High present costs combined with future utilization of technology projects may result in a requirement that projects last ten to twenty years to allow unit costs to fall to a reasonable level. This is vividly illustrated through examination of "average costs from i to j," our AC_{ij}'s (see the appropriate tables in the ITV case studies reported in Part Three). Once into a project, future AC_{ij} values are much lower than prior to its initiation, as one would expect.

TABLE XII.2
Cost Summary of Five Instructional Television Projects[a]

Project	Year of Information Source	N	h	F	V_N	V_h	AC_N	$AC^d_{1,j}$	AC_N/V_N	Cost Per Student Hour
El Salvador[b]	1972									
(a) Total Costs		48,000	540	1,116,000	1.10	--	24.35	14.97	22.1	.143
(b) GOES Costs		48,000	540	799,000	1.10	--	17.75	11.25	16.1	.104
Stanford	1974	4,942	6,290	196,900	9.20	87	159.20	165.00	17.3	6.20
Hagerstown	1973	22,000	1,440	234,500	.90	652	54.23	53.40	60.3	.46
Korea[c]	1975	1,000,000	560	214,000	1.81	2,128	3.22	--	1.8	.045
Mexico	1972	29,000	1,080	0	4.23	538	24.27	23.00	5.7	.067

a. Values in this table were computed with a social rate of discount of 7.5%; all values are in 1972 U.S. dollars. The symbols are defined as follows: N = number of students using project (in the given year, unless otherwise noted); h = the number of hours of programming broadcast per year; F = annualized fixed costs; V_N = annualized variable cost per student; V_h = annualized variable cost per hour broadcast; AC_N = average annual cost per student for the given values of N and h; $AC_{1,j}$ = the average annual cost per student from year 1 to year j, where j is that year in which the project has been broadcasting to students for 20 years—for El Salvador we report $AC_{1,23}$, for Stanford $AC_{1,20}$, for Hagerstown $AC_{1,20}$, and for Mexico $AC_{1,21}$; and the student hour cost is the annual cost per student hour of viewing for the given values of N and h.

b. The cost function for instructional television in El Salvador was derived solely as a function of V_N; therefore V_h is not given in the table (costs that are variable per hour broadcast are thus included in the project's fixed cost figure); "GOES costs" refer to costs incurred by the government of El Salvador, net of international aid.

c. The N and h for Korea reflect planned utilization of the system as discussed in Chapter X.

d. The data for this column are taken from the case studies presented in Part Three (sufficient data were not available to allow calculations of AC_{ij}'s for the Korean instructional television project).

Cost analyses, of the sort presented here, are necessary ingredients in project evaluation. However, as our treatment should have shown, such analyses may be complicated. Many explicit and implicit assumptions go into a cost analysis, and the results of such studies must be viewed as only approximate. Nonetheless, despite inevitable shortcomings in methodology and data, approximate cost analyses can be done, and done in the timely and relatively straightforward way that can provide useful input to decisions. It has been our objective in this book to assist others, including noneconomists, in undertaking such cost analyses of educational projects.

APPENDIX

EXCHANGE RATES AND GNP DEFLATORS

Exchange Rates Utilized in this Study:

Nicaragua:	7 Cordoba	=	1 U.S. dollar
Mexico:	12.5 Pesos	=	1 U.S. dollar
Thailand:	15 Baht	=	1 U.S. dollar
El Salvador:	2.5 Colones	=	1 U.S. dollar
Korea:	490 Won	=	1 U.S. dollar

GNP Deflators Utilized to Convert to 1972 U.S. Dollars:

Year	Index	Year	Index
1958	100.00	1968	122.30
1960	103.29	1969	128.20
1961	104.62	1970	135.23
1962	105.78	1971	141.61
1963	107.17	1972	145.88
1964	108.85	1973	154.31
1965	110.86	1974	170.18
1966	113.95	1975	182.74
1967	117.59		

REFERENCES

Amid, T. Aerostats broadcasting in Iran, *Asian Broadcasting Union: Technical Review,* 1975, 41, 14-18.

ASCEND. *Advanced System for Communications and Education in National Development.* Stanford University: School of Engineering, 1967.

Ayrom, M. T. "Autonomous electrical power sources for isolated telecommunications stations." National Iranian Radio and Television, Stanford University, June 1975. (Mimeo.)

Baker, F. B. "Computer-based instructional management systems: A first look." *Review of Educational Research,* 1971, 41, 51-70.

Balassa, B. "Estimating the shadow price of foreign exchange in project appraisal." *Oxford Economic Papers,* 1974, (July), 26, 147-168.

Baldwin, L. V., Davis, P., and Maxwell, L. M. "Innovative off-campus educational programs of Colorado State University." Special report to the President's Science Advisory Committee Panel on Educational Research and Development, April 1972.

Ball, J. and Jamison, D. "Computer-assisted instruction for dispersed populations: System cost models." *Instructional Science,* 1973, 1, 469-501.

Baumol, W. "Macroeconomics of unbalanced growth: The anatomy of urban crises." *American Economic Review,* 1967, 57, 415-426.

Bostick, R. *Differentiated Teaching Teams and Their Effect on Recurrent Teacher Expenditures: The Korean Primary-Middle School Reform.* Unpublished master's thesis, George Washington University, 1975.

Bourret, P. "Television in rural areas: A low-cost alternative." In R. Arnove (ed.), *Educational Television: A Policy Guide and Critique for Developing Countries.* Stanford University, School of Education, 1973.

Bowles, S. *Planning Educational Systems for Economic Growth.* Cambridge, Mass.: Harvard University Press, 1969.

Bowman, M. J. "The costing of human resource development." In E.A.G. Robinson and J. E. Vaizey (eds.), *The Economics of Education.* New York: St. Martin's Press, 1966. Pp. 421-450.

Broadbent, D., Brooke, D. A., Stone, W., and Parrish, W. *Report of the Commission of Inquiry into Television in the Territory of Papua and New Guinea.* Port Moresby, New Guinea, 1966.

Butman, R. C. *Satellite Television for India: Techno-economic Factors.* Cambridge, Mass.: MIT, 1972.

——— , Rathjens, G. W., and Warren, C. *Techno-economic Considerations in Public Service Broadcast Communications for Developing Countries.* Academy for Educational Development, Report Number Nine, 1973.

Carnoy, M. "The economic costs and returns to educational television." *Economic Development and Cultural Change,* 1975, 23(2), 207-248.

——— and Levin, H. M. "Evaluation of educational media: Some issues." *Instructional Science,* 1975, 4, 385-406.

Carpenter, H. A. "Teaching science by radio." *Junior-Senior High School Clearinghouse,* March 1934.

Carter, J. "Using wind as energy." California Living. *San Francisco Chronicle,* June 15, 1975.

Chu, G. C. and Schramm, W. *Learning from Television: What the Research Says.* Washington, D.C.: National Association of Educational Broadcasters, 1967.

Coleman, J. S. and Karweit, N. L. *Multi-level Information Systems in Education* (Report 19287-RC). Santa Monica, Calif.: The Rand Corporation, 1968.

College of Engineering, University of Maryland. *A Proposal for the University of Maryland.* Instructional Television Network, February 1972.

Consumer Reports. "FM/AM radios." *Consumer Reports,* July 1975, 436-349.

Cook, D. C. and Nemzek, C. L. "The effectiveness of teaching by radio." *Journal of Educational Research,* 1939, 33, 105-109.

Cook, J. O. "Research in audio-visual communication." In J. Ball and F. C. Byrees (eds.), *Research, Principles, and Practices in Visual Communication.* East Lansing: Michigan State University, National Project in Agricultural Communications, 1960.

Coombs, P. H. *The World Educational Crisis: A Systems Analysis.* New York and London: Oxford University Press, 1968.

——— and Hallak, J. *Managing Educational Costs.* New York and London: Oxford University Press, 1972.

Dasgupta, P., Sen, A., and Marglin, S. *Guidelines for Project Evaluation.* UNIDO Project Formulation and Evaluation Series, No. 2. New York: United Nations, 1972.

Davis, R. C. *Planning Human Resource Development.* Chicago: Rand McNally, 1966.

Dodds, T. *Multi-media Approaches to Rural Education.* Cambridge, England: International Extension College, 1972.

Dordick, H. "The Bavarian tellekolleg: A case study." Unpublished paper, (n.d.).

Dubin, R. and Hedley, R. A. *The Medium May Be Related to the Message: College Instruction by TV.* Eugene: University of Oregon Press, 1969.

Dunn, D., Lusignan, B., and Parker, E. *Teleconferencing: Cost Optimization of Satellite and Ground Systems for Continuing Professional Education and Medical Services.* Stanford University: Institute for Public Policy Anslysis, 1972.

Edding, F. "Expenditure on education: Statistics and comments." In E.A.G. Robinson and J. E. Vaizey (eds.), *The Economics of Education.* New York: St. Martin's Press, 1966. Pp. 24-70.

Educational Policy Research Center. *Instructional Television: A Comparative Study of Satellites and Other Delivery Systems.* Syracuse, N.Y.: Syracuse Research Corporation, 1976.

Evans, S. and Klees, S. "ETV program production in the Ivory Coast." Washington, D.C.: Academy for Educational Development, 1977.

Fisher, G. *Cost Considerations in Systems Analysis.* Santa Monica, Calif.: The Rand Corporation, 1971.

Forsythe, R. O. *Instructional Radio: A Position Paper.* Unpublished paper. Stanford University, 1970. (ERIC Document Reproduction Service No. ED 044 933)

General Learning Corporation. *Cost Study of Educational Media Systems and Their Equipment Components.* Vols. I and II. Washington, D.C.: ERIC Clearinghouse, Document ED 024 286, 1968.

Goreux, L. M. and Manne, A. S. (eds.) *Multi-level Planning: Case Studies in Mexico.* New York: American Elsevier, 1973.

Greenhill, L. P. "Penn State experiments with two-way audio systems for CCTV." *NAEB Journal,* 1964, 23, 73-78.

Hallak, J. *The Analysis of Educational Costs and Expenditures.* Paris: UNESCO International Institute for Educational Planning, 1969.

Haller, E. J. "Cost analysis for educational program evaluation." In W. J. Popham (ed.), *Evaluation in Education.* Berkeley, Calif.: McCutchan Publishing Co., 1974.

Harrison, M. "Measures of the effect of radio programs in rural schools." *Education on the Air.* Columbus: Ohio State University, 1932.

Hayman, R. W. and Levin, H. "Economic analysis and historical summary of educational technology costs." To appear as Appendix C of A. Melmed (Rapporteur), *Productivity and Efficiency in Education.* Washington, D.C.: Federal Council on Science and Technology, 1973.

Henderson, J. M. and Quandt, R. E. *Microeconomic Theory.* New York: McGraw-Hill, 1958.

Heron, W. T. and Ziebarth, E. W. "A preliminary experimental comparison of radio and classroom lectures." *Speech Monographs,* 1946, 13, 54-57.

Hornik, R., Ingle, H., Mayo, J., McAnany, E., and Schramm, W. *Television and Educational Reform in El Salvador: Final Report.* Stanford, Calif.: Institute for Communication Research, Research Report, No. 14, 1973.

Jamison, D. *Alternative Strategies for Primary Education in Indonesia: A Cost-effectiveness Analysis.* Research paper 46, Graduate School of Business, Stanford University, 1971.

––– "An early assessment of costs." In B. Searle, J. Friend, and P. Suppes. Application of radio to teaching elementary mathematics in a developing country (2nd annual report). Stanford, Calif.: Stanford University, Institute for Mathematical Studies in the Social Sciences, 1974.

––– *Cost Factors in Planning Educational Technology Systems.* Paris: UNESCO International Institute for Educational Planning, 1977a.

––– *Radio Education and Student Repetition in Nicaragua.* Washington, D.C.: The World Bank, 1977b.

––– , Jamison, M., and Hewlett, S. "Satellite radio: Better than ETV." *Astronautics and Aeronautics,* 1967, 7, 92-96.

Jamison, D. and Klees, S. "The cost of instructional radio and television for developing countries." *Instructional Science,* 1975, 4, 333-384.

Jamison, D. and Lumsden, K. G. "Television and efficiency in higher education." *Management Science,* 1975, 21, 920-930.

Jamison, D., Suppes, P., and Wells, S. "The effectiveness of alternative instructional media: A survey." *Review of Educational Research.* 1974, 44, 1-67.

Jamison, M. *Low Cost Educational Systems for Developing Regions: An Application of Systems Analysis to Educational Planning.* Unpublished doctoral dissertation, University of California, Los Angeles, 1966.

––– and Bett, S. *Satellite Educational System Costs.* Washington, D.C.: Office of Telecommunications Policy, 1973.

Janky, J. M., Potter, J. G., and Lusignan, B. B. *System Alternatives for the Public Service Satellite Consortium,* (n.d.).

KEDI (Korea Educational Development Institute). *Annual Report 1972-74.* Seoul, Korea: KEDI, 1974.

Kemeny, J. G., Schleifer, A., Jr., Snell, J. L., and Thompson, G. L. *Finite Mathematics with Business Applications.* Englewood Cliffs, N.J.: Prentice-Hall, 1962.

Klees, S. "Education in Mexico: The primary and second school system." Unpublished paper, Stanford University, 1972.

––– *Instructional Technology and Its Relationship to Quality and Equality in Educa-*

tion in a Developing Nation: A Case Study of Instructional Television in Mexico. (Unpublished doctoral dissertation, Stanford University, 1974.) Princeton, N.J.: Educational Testing Service, 1975.

––– and Wells, S. "Cost-effectiveness and cost-benefit analysis for educational planning and evaluation: Methodology and application to instructional technology." Washington, D.C.: U.S. Agency for International Development, 1977a.

Klees, S. and Wells, S. "Economic analysis and education: Critical issues in applications to instructional technology evaluation." Paper prepared for presentation at the Economic Analysis of Educational Media Conference, Washington, D.C., March 2-4, 1977b.

––– "Satellites for development: Cost considerations and the ATS-6 experience." Washington, D.C.: U.S. Agency for International Development, 1977c.

––– "Cost-effectiveness and cost-benefit analysis for educational planning and evaluation: Methodology and application to instructional technology." Washington, D.C.: U.S. Agency for International Development, 1977a.

––– "Economic analysis and education: Critical issues in applications to instructional technology evaluation." Paper prepared for presentation at the Economic Analysis of Educational Media Conference, Washington, D.C., March 2-4, 1977b.

––– "Satellites for development: Cost considerations and the ATS-6 experience." Washington, D.C.: U.S. Agency for International Development, 1977c.

Krival, A. *Project Report: Radio/Correspondence Education Project No. 615-11-650-129, USAID/UWEX.* University of Wisconsin, 1970.

Laidlaw, B. and Layard, R. "Traditional versus Open University teaching methods: A cost comparison." *Higher Learning,* 1974, 3, 439-467.

Layard, R. "The cost-effectiveness of the new media in higher education." In K. Lumsden (ed.), *Efficiency in Universities: The La Paz Papers.* Amsterdam: Elsevier, 1973.

Lee, C. J. "The life cycle cost analysis of the transmission system for the educational reform in Korea." Unpublished typescript, Seoul, Korea: KEDI, 1975.

Lefranc, R. "Educational television in Niger." In W. Schramm, et al. (eds.), *New Educational Media in Action: Case Studies for Planners.* Vol. II. Paris: UNESCO International Institute for Educational Planning, 1967.

Levin, H. M. "Cost-effectiveness analysis in evaluation research." In M. Guttenberg (ed.), *Handbook of Evaluation Research.* Beverly Hills, Calif.: Sage Publications, Inc., 1974.

Los Angeles City School Districts, Division of Extension and Higher Education. "An evaluation of closed-circuit instructional television in Los Angeles City College and Los Angeles Valley College, 1959. (Mimeo.)

Lumley, F. H. "Rates of speech in radio speaking." *Quarterly Journal of Speech,* June 1933.

Lumsden, K. "The Open University: A survey and economic analysis." Unpublished paper, Stanford University.

––– and Ritchie, Ç. "The Open University: A survey and economic analysis." *Instructional Science,* 1975, 4.

Lyle, J. "Colombia's national programme for primary level television instruction." In W. Schramm, et al. (eds.), *New Educational Media in Action: Case Studies for Planners.* Vol. II. Paris: UNESCO International Institute for Educational Planning, 1967.

Madden, J. V. "Experimental study of student achievement in relation to class size." *School Science and Mathematics,* 1968, 68, 619-622.

Martin-Vegue, C. A., Morris, A. J., Rosenberg, J. M., and Talmadge, G. E. "Technical and economic factors in university instructional television systems." *Proceedings of the IEEE,* 1971, 59, 946-953.

Martin-Vegue, C. A., Morris, A. J., and Talmadge, G. E. "University instructional tele-vision networks." *Journal of Educational Technology Systems*, 1972, 1, 35-55.

Masoner, P. H. *Report of Preliminary Planning Project for an Analytical Case Study of the Korean Educational Development Institute*. April 1975.

Mayo, J., Hornik, R., and McAnany, E. *Educational Reform with Television: The El Salvador Experience*. Stanford, Calif.: Stanford University Press, 1976.

Mayo, J., McAnany, E., and Klees, S. "The Mexican Telesecundaria: A cost-effectiveness analysis." *Instructional Science*, 1975, 4, 193-326.

Mielke, K. W. "Asking the right ETV research questions." *Educational Broadcasting Review*, December 1968, 2(6), 54-62.

Miles, J. R. "Radio and elementary science teaching." *Journal of Applied Psychology*, 1940, 24, 714-720.

Morgan, R. and Chadwick, C. B. (eds.), *Systems Analysis for Educational Change: The Republic of Korea*. Tallahassee, Florida: Florida State University, 1971.

National Instructional Television Center. *Guidebook: Television Instruction*. Blooming-ton, Indiana: National Instructional Television, 1974.

New ERA (New Educational Reform Associates). *Radio Listening Patterns in Nepal, 1974*. Katmandu, Nepal: New ERA, 1974.

NHK Radio-Television Cultural Research Institute. *The Listening Effects of Radio English Classroom, April 1954-March 1955*. Tokyo: NHK, 1955.

——— *The Effects of Educational Radio Music Classroom, April-December 1956*. Tokyo: NHK, 1956.

Pettitt, J. M. and Grace, E. J. "The Stanford instructional television network." *IEEE Spectrum*, 1970, 7, 73-80.

Polcyn, K. et al. *Broadcast Satellites and Other Educational Technology: Possible Key Policy Decision Points 1972-1976*. Washington, D.C.: Academy for Educational Development, 1972. (Draft)

Rao, B. S. and Manjunath, A. S. "Primary power sources for community television re-ceivers." In B. S. Rao et al. (eds.), *Satellite Instructional Television Systems: A Compendium of Monographs*. Papers presented at the UN Panel Meetings at Ahmeda-bad, India, December 1972.

Rathjens, G. "Communications for education in developing countries." In R. Butman, G. Rathjens, and C. J. Warren (eds.), *Technical-Economic Considerations in Public Service Broadcast Communications for Developing Countries*. Washington, D.C.: Academy for Educational Development, 1973.

——— Butman, R., and Vaidya, R. *Radio Broadcasting and Telecommunications in Nepal*. A paper prepared for USAID, 1975.

Schmelkes de Sotelo, S. "Estudio de evaluación aproximativa de las escuelas radió-fonicas de la Tarahumara" (Mexico). *Revista del Centro de Estudio Educativos*, 1972, 2. (Reprints unpaginated.)

——— "The radio schools of the Tarahumara, Mexico: An evaluation." Stanford Uni-versity: Institute for Communication Research, 1973.

Schramm, W. "What the research says." In W. Schramm (ed.), *Quality in Instructional Television*. Honolulu, Hawaii: University Press of Hawaii, 1972. Pp. 44-79.

——— *Big Media, Little Media*. Stanford University: Institute for Communication Re-search, 1973.

——— , Coombs, P. H., Kahnert, F., and Lyle, J. *New Educational Media in Action: Case Studies for Planners*. (Vols. I, II, and III). Paris: UNESCO International Institute for Educational Planning, 1967.

——— *The New Media: Memo to Educational Planners*. Paris: UNESCO International Institute for Educational Planning, 1967.

Schultz, T. W. *Investment in Human Capital–the Role of Education and Research.* New York: Free Press, 1971.

Searle, B., Friend, J., and Suppes, P. *Application of Radio to Teaching Elementary Mathematics in a Developing Country.* Stanford, Calif.: Institute for Mathematical Studies in the Social Sciences, 1975.

Searle, B., Matthews, P., Suppes, P., and Friend, J. *A Formal Evaluation of the Radio Mathematics Instructional Program: Nicaragua, Grade 1, 1976.* Stanford, Calif.: Stanford University, Institute for Mathematical Studies in the Social Sciences, 1977.

Smith, D. C. and Janky, J. M. "Direct broadcast satellites." In P. Spain (ed.), *A Direct Broadcast Satellite for Africa?* Institute for Communication Research, Stanford University, 1972.

Société Centrale des Inventions Pratiques and J. Gallard. *Etude d'Alimentation Autonome Pour Televiseurs Tropicalises Realisée a L'attention de la Compagnie Africaine de Television,* 1972.

Société d'Informatique, de Conseils et de Recherche Opérationnelle (S.I.N.C.R.O.). *Manuel du Programme d'Education Télévisuelle: l'Analyse Financiere.* (Vol. III) Paris: 1972.

Southwestern Signal Corps Training Center in Camp San Luis Obispo, California. *Instructur-student Contact in Teaching by Television.* Training evaluation and research programs, Part IV. Training Research Programs, 1953.

Sovereign, M. G. *Costs of Educational Media Systems.* ERIC Clearinghouse on Educational Media and Technology, Stanford University, 1969. (This is a summary of General Learning Corporation, 1968.)

Spain, P. (ed.) *A Direct Broadcast Satellite System for Education and Development in Africa?* Stanford University: Institute for Communication Research, 1972.

––– "A report on the system of reaioprimaria in the state of San Luis Potosi, Mexico." Stanford University: Institute for Communication Research, 1973.

Speagle, R. E. *Educational Reform and Instructional Television in El Salvador: Costs, Benefits, and Payoffs.* Washington, D.C.: Academy for Educational Development, 1972.

Squire, L. and van der Tak, H. G. *Economic Analysis of Projects.* Washington, D.C.: The International Bank for Reconstruction and Development, 1975.

Stickell, D. W. *A Critical Review of the Methodology and Results of Research Comparing Televised and Face-to-Face Instruction.* Unpublished doctoral dissertation, Pennsylvania State University, 1963.

Stuit, D. B. et al. *An Experiment in Teaching. Iowa Closed-Circuit Television Teaching Experiment: Summary Report.* Iowa City: State University of Iowa, 1956.

Thomas, J. A. *The Productive School–A Systems Analysis Approach to Educational Administration.* New York: John Wiley & Sons, 1971.

UNESCO. *The Economics of New Educational Media.* Paris: UNESCO Press, 1977.

––– *Working Group on Information Exchange on Technical and Economic Studies Related to Educational Technology: Final Report.* Paris: UNESCO, January 1975.

U.S. Subcommittee on Economy in Government. *Economic Analysis of Public Investment Decisions: Interest Rate Policy and Discounting Analysis.* Washington, D.C.: U.S. Government Printing Office, 1968.

Vaizey, J. and Chesswas, J. D. *The Costing of Educational Plans.* Paris: UNESCO International Institute for Educational Planning, 1967.

Vaizey, J., Norris, and Sheehan, J. *The Political Economy of Education.* London: Gerald Duckworth and Company, 1972.

Wade, S. "Hagerstown: A pioneer in closed-circuit television." In IIEP, *New Educational Media in Action: Case Studies for Planners.* Paris: UNESCO, IIEP. 1967.

Wagner, L. "Television video-tape systems for off-campus education: A cost analysis of SURGE." *Instructional Science*, 1975, 4.

——— "The economics of the Open University." *Higher Education*, 1972, 1, 159-183.

Walsh, V. C. *Introduction to Contemporary Microeconomics*. New York: McGraw-Hill, 1970.

Washington County Board of Education. *Circuit Television Report*. Hagerstown, Maryland: Washington County Board of Education, 1963.

——— *Data Concerning the Cost of Television Services*. Hagerstown, Maryland: Washington County Board of Education, 1973.

Washington County Instructional Television Evaluation Committee. *The Report, of the Washington County Instructional Television Evaluation Committee*. Washington County, Maryland: County Commissioners, 1973.

Wells, S. *Technology, Efficiency, and Educational Production*. (Unpublished doctoral dissertation, Stanford University, 1974.) Princeton, N.J.: Educational Testing Service, 1975.

Wells, S. *Instructional Technology in Developing Countries: Decision-making Processes in Education*. New York: Praeger Publishers, 1976a.

——— "Evaluation criteria and the effectiveness of instructional technology in higher education." *Higher Education*, 1976b.

——— and Klees, S. "Cost analysis for educational decision-making: The radio mathematics project in Nicaragua." In B. Searle, J. Friend, and P. Suppes, *The Radio Mathematics Project, Nicaragua, 1976*. Stanford, Calif.: Stanford University, Institute for Mathematical Studies in the Social Sciences, 1978.

——— "A cost analysis of the Hagerstown ITV system." *Journal of Educational Technology Systems*, 1976.

Wiles, M. K. *The Evaluation of School News Broadcasts*. Unpublished doctoral dissertation, Ohio State University, 1940.

Wilson, J. Q. "On Pettigrew and Armor: An afterword." *The Public Interest*, 1973, 30, 132-134.

Wilson, T. J., Spaulding, W. E., and Smith, D. C., Jr. "Books and economic development." In *Human Resources; Training of Scientific and Technical Personnel*. (Vol. XI) United States Papers for the United Nations Conference on the Application of Science and Technology for the Benefit of the Less Developed Areas. Washington, D.C.: U.S. Government Printing Office, no date (about 1963).

Woelfel, N. E. and Tyler, I. K. (eds.), *Radio and the School: A Guidebook for Teachers and Administrators*. Yonkers-on-Hudson, N.Y.: World Book Co., 1945.

Wolgamuth, D. *A Comparative Study of Three Techniques of Student Feedback in Television Teaching: The Effectiveness of an Electrical Feedback System*. NDEA Title VII Project No. 453. Washington, D.C.: U.S. Office of Education, 1961.

Woodhall, M. and Blaug, M. "Productivity trends in British secondary education 1950-1963." *Sociology of Education*, Winter 1968.

ABOUT THE AUTHORS

DEAN T. JAMISON is a member of the Development Economics Department of the World Bank where he undertakes research on the role of education and communication in development. He holds degrees in philosophy and engineering from Stanford University, and he completed his Ph.D. in economics at Harvard in 1970. After leaving Harvard, he returned for four years to Stanford, where he taught economics, decision theory, and education. Then, prior to joining the World Bank, he spent several years as chairman of the Economics and Educational Planning Group at the Educational Testing Service.

STEVEN J. KLEES received his doctorate in economics and business, with a specialization in the economics of education, from Stanford University, and is subsequently teaching at Cornell University and Stanford University. He has worked extensively with educational television and radio projects in the Ivory Coast, Mexico, and the United States. He has numerous publications in the economics of education field.

STUART J. WELLS is an assistant professor of management at San Jose State University. He received his doctorate in economics and business from Stanford University. His main research focus has been on the economics of education and communication and he has several publications in this field including a book titled *Instructional Technology in Developing Countries: Decision-Making Processes in Education.*